Experiencing Mozart

Published by Rowman & Littlefield
A wholly owned subsidiary of The Rowman & Littlefield Publishing Group, Inc.
4501 Forbes Boulevard, Suite 200, Lanham, Maryland 20706
www.rowman.com

Unit A, Whitacre Mews, 26-34 Stannary Street, London SE11 4AB

British Library Cataloguing in Publication Information Available

Library of Congress Cataloging-in-Publication Data
The hardback edition of this book was previously catalogued by the Library of Congress as follows:

Schroeder, David P., 1946–
Experiencing Mozart : a listener's companion / David Schroeder.
pages cm. — (Listener's companion)
Includes bibliographical references and index.
1. Mozart, Wolfgang Amadeus, 1756–1791—Criticism and interpretation. I. Title.
ML410.M9S377 2013
780.92—dc23   2013006793

ISBN 978-0-8108-8428-1 (cloth : alk. paper)
ISBN 978-1-4422-4919-6 (pbk : alk. paper)
ISBN 978-0-8108-8429-8 (ebook)

Printed in the United States of America

To Emily, Daniel, and Linda—with love.

CONTENTS

SERIES EDITOR'S FOREWORD

The goal of the *Listener's Companion* series is to give readers a deeper understanding of pivotal musical genres and the creative work of its iconic practitioners. This is accomplished in an inclusive manner that does not necessitate extensive music training or elitist shoulder rubbing. Authors of the series dramatize specific listening experiences so the music under consideration can be seen within its various historical contexts, allowing the author to explore the compositional and societal parameters of that music. By positioning readers in imagined listening environments that inform and explain this music's genesis and performance, authors can teach readers—who are also listeners—how to enjoy and appreciate much more deeply the genius behind the art. Contributors to the series, often drawing on their own expertise as performers and scholars, supply readers a broad understanding of major musical genres and the achievements of composers and artists within those genres as a *lived* listening experience.

It is then no surprise that one of the first editions of the series should explore the music of Wolfgang Amadè Mozart. To understand his music is to unlock the basic tenets of compositional technique during the late eighteenth-century period in the history of Western music. As both an admirer and correspondent of Joseph Haydn, Mozart closely studied the best of what he could hear in his enlightened Austria, and then amplified the possibilities of the most popular genres of the time, which encompassed piano sonatas, opera, concertos, and multimovement symphonies.

To that end, Mozart serves not only as a working genius in his own right but as an exemplar of the evolution of the working musician, a development that paralleled shifts in the social and economic character of music-going audiences of Europe, development which his music gallantly responds to as both promise and plight. His piano concertos and symphonies number among his most developed and, one might argue, riskiest compositional abstractions while sundry works for solo piano, art song, or even opera constitute compositional efforts that reflected a need to pay the bills by appealing to popular tastes. This blend of—and sometimes conflict between—soaring genius and working musician is what makes Mozart such an exemplary figure in the *Listener's Companion* series, expressing so elegantly the *contexts*—financial, social, historical, as well as musical—in which music is created and then performed.

Many eminent authors could have written this book. For Scarecrow Press, we consider David Schroeder singularly qualified, indeed a "catch": he is professor emeritus and university research professor at Dalhousie University, and his knowledge of the classical tradition is unimpeachable as the author of many fine works from his *Haydn and the Enlightenment: The Late Symphonies and Their Audience* (1990) to *Mozart in Revolt: Strategies of Resistance, Mischief and Deception* (1999) to his remarkable *Our Schubert: His Enduring Legacy* (2009). All reflect the decades-long work of a scholar with a rich understanding of Mozart's craft and his era. Schroeder expertly walks the reader through Mozart's musical life, including his years under the watchful eye of Leopold, his friendship with Haydn, his maneuverings through the politics of Austrian royalty, his serious and comedic operas, as well as the creative genius Mozart poured into virtuosic works for solo and orchestral instrumentation. With a knowledge of Mozart's contributions to his own era as well as his contemporary legacy—in modern performances and recordings, in soundtracks and movies—Schroeder is more than the learned Mozart expert and classical music enthusiast: he is a scholar who grasps how much more we have to learn about Mozart because, in so many ways that we realize and don't, Mozart is all around us. We have but to listen—and know how to listen.

Gregg Akkerman
Series Editor

INTRODUCTION

Why should we care about Mozart? He lived two and a half centuries ago, and since then we have gone from the Industrial Revolution to the Spice Girls, with world wars and Elvis in between—how can someone who lived in the eighteenth century have anything to say of relevance to us? The purpose of this book is to show how that can be so, not casting Mozart as a museum piece from a bygone century but as someone who cared about many of the issues that remain as pressing to us now as they were to his audiences then, as someone who speaks to us with a perceptiveness that has not dulled in the least over time. The name Mozart conjures up different images to different people, not least of all because he was one of the most extraordinary geniuses who ever lived, and the possibility of someone possessing such abilities remains fascinating and even intimidating. My objective is not to dwell on Mozart the genius but instead as best as possible to reveal what he has to say to all of us, regardless of background. During his time he directed much of his work to those from fairly privileged backgrounds, but Mozart himself did not come from that social class. In fact, the deeper we probe into his music, the more we see that he often criticized the privileged and ruling classes subtly but firmly. Part of what keeps him so relevant is the fact that he frequently addresses political, religious, social, and ethical issues—not only in his operas but sometimes in instrumental music as well. When his works focus on such matters as misogyny, misuse of power, inequality, difficult choices, and injustice, we quickly see how close to our own concerns his approaches can be.

This book is a listener's guide, not a biography or even a "life and works" study, but that does not mean I will avoid aspects of Mozart's life. In some cases information about his life is necessary in order to make sense of his works. One possible way of writing a listener's companion would be to cram in as many works as possible, saying a few salient things about each one, although I doubt readers would find that type of approach especially useful, since in the end it results in something far too superficial. Instead, I have opted to focus on a fairly small number of works, in the case of instrumental compositions typically no more than about three per chapter, and of operas sometimes only a single opera per chapter. I have gone about it this way in hopes that a fairly in-depth probing of a few works will give strong clues as to how similar kinds of pieces can be understood. That works only up to a point, however, since with a composer of Mozart's stature virtually all of his works are unique, and my discussions generally emphasize that uniqueness, meaning that some of the ideas applied to one work will not be transferable to another. But in spite of that, the nature of the discussion should prompt ways of careful listening to other works, sometimes almost assembling a type of toolkit to make that possible.

I have avoided as much as possible the type of dry terminology that music professionals use when writing for each other, since for the most part that kind of language simply turns off those not familiar with it. Of much greater importance here is the attempt to convey the excitement that I feel about the works I discuss, and I want to set up as few roadblocks as possible to readers wishing to share that enjoyment. Occasionally technical terms cannot be avoided, and when I do use them, I add a basic definition immediately, hopefully without disrupting the flow of the description too much. I have also included a short glossary of terms at the end of the book with slightly fuller definitions of these terms.

One of the issues that inevitably arise in a book about an eighteenth-century composer is whether I as the author have a sufficiently full grasp of the century that I am writing about. Without that grasp enormous mistakes can be made, although with a listener's guide not all that much space can be taken to demonstrate the appropriate level of awareness. On this matter I have already had a kick at the can, with a book I wrote about Mozart over a decade ago, in which I focused mainly on his letters to his father and others, and the perils of reading these letters without a clear understanding of what letter-writing meant in the eighteenth century. I have also written a book about Mozart's dear friend Joseph Haydn which shows Haydn not as an isolationist but as someone fully engaged with the thinking of the Enlightenment, knowledge he acquired in numerous ways. Mozart belonged to a different generation than Haydn, being younger by twenty-four years, and he moved in different directions based on the uniqueness of his experiences and ways of thinking. Having had a go at these composers in the context of the eighteenth century, I have now shifted the focus to the present, and I attempt to answer the question of why we should care deeply about Mozart now.

A number of technical issues come up in a book such as this, some of which may seem baffling in the extreme to the uninitiated. One of these concerns the numbers used to identify Mozart's works. If we take the symphonies, for example, of which he wrote about forty, we discover that two entirely different sets of numbers exist: the last three symphonies, for example, are sometimes counted as nos. 39, 40, and 41, but also as K543, K550, and K551. The first set of numbers, given by the publisher Breitkopf & Härtel (BH) for its edition of the symphonies, goes up to 41, in chronological order based on what was known at the time. Subsequent research has shown this numbering to be flawed, with 29, 30, and 28, for example, in the wrong order, and even worse, with no. 37 not by Mozart at all. Despite the flaws, these numbers remain, and many prefer to use them instead of the other set. The other set has become something of a nightmare, since the more accuracy scholars have achieved in getting the chronological order right, the more useless these numbers have become. The letter "K" stands for Ludwig von Köchel (KV in German—Köchel Verzeichnis, or index), who produced a massive thematic catalogue of Mozart's works just after the middle of the nineteenth century, with chronological numbering of all the works that goes up to K626 (the Requiem).

This seemed a great step forward, but it was soon discovered he did not always get things right either, so revisions of the catalogue started to appear, with the one generally used now being the sixth edition (although a new one is currently in the works), edited by Alfred Einstein in 1964 (not to be confused with his physicist cousin Albert). Many of the original Köchel numbers survived, but others did not, which has led to two sets of K numbers for many works, for example the "Paris"

Symphony (31) from 1778 as K297 and K⁶300a. The attempts to refine the new numbers have gotten completely out of hand, with no. 25, K183, becoming 173dB. This may be of use to scholars, but not to Mozart lovers who could not care less about the minutia of chronology, and simply want a straightforward way of identifying works. Alas, I will not be entirely consistent throughout the book, sometimes using K numbers when these are best known, as for piano concertos or quartets, and sometimes BH numbers, as with their common usage for symphonies.

I cite Mozart's letters from time to time in the book, and while a virtually complete edition of them exists in the original German, *Mozart: Briefe und Aufzeichnungen* (MBA), unfortunately nothing as complete can be found in English translation. The British writer Emily Anderson provided a translation of many of the letters in 1938, and while it has stood up remarkably well, her sense of propriety prevented her from getting the right tone in some of the off-color letters, of which there are many. Other translations have appeared recently, although again not complete, and this leaves something of a dilemma for anyone writing in English about Mozart now. I have dealt with this in three ways: 1) over the years I have made many of my own translations, and I will identify these as MBA (as translated from the German source); 2) one of the best new translations, *Mozart: A Life in Letters*, edited by Cliff Eisen and translated by Stewart Spencer, I use as much as possible (MLL); 3) if neither Spencer nor I have done it, I use Emily Anderson's *The Letters of Mozart and His Family*, 3rd ed. (LMF). I provide page citations for the letters in the case of my own translations from the original German source (MBA) as well as the other letter sources, but otherwise in the book I do not use citations or footnotes. All sources of information used can be found in the bibliography.

Getting access to scores and recordings of Mozart's music can be fairly painless. The best edition of the scores, the *Neue Mozart-Ausgabe* (the New Mozart Edition), fortunately is readily available on the website of the Mozarteum, the epicenter for Mozart research in Salzburg, at http://dme.mozarteum.at. Not only can the complete edition be accessed by anyone online, but so can the complete letters in German. Sound recordings present a somewhat different issue, since quality varies, and the listener can be confronted by a bewildering array of choices of modern performances or those that purport to be authentic—using historical instruments. I can only suggest that you listen to as many different recordings as possible and consider how one differs from another. The same is true of performances of operas on DVDs, and with these the ones from the most famous opera houses will not necessarily be the best. Much of the music will be available on the Internet as downloads, either for MP3 or other formats, and those with user credentials from many university libraries and some public libraries will likely have access to the extensive *Classical Music Library* database, and possibly *Opera on Video* as well. In the Selected Listening section at the end of the book I have provided a list of CDs and DVDs that should be helpful.

One of the most enjoyable parts of writing this book has been setting up the "you were there" sections that appear in each chapter, part of the standard format for the entire series, in which you the reader are transported to actual performances. Writing about an eighteenth-century composer has allowed some extra room for creativity with this, since I could chose performances from either the present or Mozart's own time. The ones from the present, including concerts at Lincoln Center or operas shown as films either in a theater or on television, could be treated in fairly straightforward ways, but with those from the eighteenth century, I readily admit to indulging in a certain amount of fiction. I have based these on documentation from the time, such as letters or other contemporary descriptions, but that has not prevented me from going beyond the documents into accounts that become much more novel-like, hopefully capturing something of the lively spirit of the time. I have clearly taken liberties with some of the people who play their parts in these sections, allowing them (including Mozart himself) to say things or behave in ways that cannot be verified. I hope these will be taken in the spirit of good fun in which they are intended.

TIMELINE

1756 Born 27 January in Salzburg to Maria Anna and Leopold Mozart. Baptized as Joannes Chrysostomus Wolfgangus Theophilius Mozart (uses Wolfgang Amadé [or Amadè] Mozart throughout his life).

1761 First appearance as a performer, in Salzburg.

1762 First trips to display the performing prodigies, with Leopold, to Munich and Vienna.

1763 Start of 3½-year performance tour to Munich, Augsburg, Frankfurt-am-Main, Paris, London, The Hague, Amsterdam, and Brussels. Composes first violin sonatas.

1764 Composes first symphony.

1765 Composes first liturgical work.

1767 Performs in Vienna. Composes first oratorio and divertimentos.

1768 While in Vienna his first opera is performed.

1769 Appointed by Archbishop Schrattenbach as an unpaid third concertmaster at the Salzburg court. Travels to Italy for first time.

1770 Performs in Verona, Milan, Bologna, Florence, Rome, and Naples. Meets Padre Giovanni Battista Martini, who facilitates his appointment to the Philharmonic Society of Bologna. Awarded the Order of the Golden Spur by the Pope.

1771 Returns to Salzburg and sets out on second trip to Italy.

1772 Archbishop Schrattenbach dies and is succeeded by Hieronymus Colloredo. Leaves for third trip to Italy. Composes first string quartets.

1773 Composes the motet "Exsultate, jubilate," first piano concerto, and first violin concerto.

1774 Is mostly at home in Salzburg.

1775 Becomes second concertmaster.

1776 Spends the year in Salzburg. Composes the "Haffner" Serenade.

1777 Composes Piano Concerto K271. Leaves on sixteen-month trip with mother to Munich, Augsburg, and Mannheim to find employment.

1778 Continues trip, traveling to Paris from Mannheim. In Paris his mother dies and he lives at the apartment of Louise d'Epinay.

1779 Reluctantly returns to Salzburg and is appointed court organist at a salary of 450 gulden per year.

1780 Leaves for Munich to work on *Idomeneo*.

1781 *Idomeneo* premiered on 29 January. Goes to Vienna in June and is dismissed from his position in Salzburg. His father wants him to return to Salzburg. Stays in Vienna as a freelance musician. Receives commission for *The Abduction from the Seraglio* for Joseph II's National Singspiel.

1782 *The Abduction* premiered on 16 July at the Burgtheater. Marries Constanze Weber. Also composes and performs piano concertos K414, 413 (1782–1783), and 415 (1782–1783). Composes string quartet K387.

1783 Visits Salzburg for last time. Composes piano sonatas K330–32 (1781–1783), string quartets K421 and 428.

1784 Composes and performs piano concertos K449–51, 453, 456, 459; also composes Quintet for Piano and Winds, K452; keyboard sonatas K333 and 457; and string quartet K458.

1785 Leopold Mozart visits Vienna. Composes and performs piano concertos K466, 467, and 482. Also composes Serenade for

Winds in B flat, K361 (possibly 1783–1784); and string quartets K464 and 465.

1786 *The Marriage of Figaro* premiered on 1 May at the Burgtheater. Also composes piano concertos K488, 491, and 503; and the "Prague" Symphony, no. 38 (K504).

1787 Visits Prague twice, for performances of *Figaro* and premiere of *Don Giovanni* (commissioned during first visit). Leopold dies in May in Salzburg. Also composes string quintets K515 and 516; and "Eine kleine Nachtmusik." Appointed to the position of chamber musician to the court on 7 December, with no defined duties.

1788 *Don Giovanni's* Vienna premiere was on 7 May. Also composes three symphonies, nos. 39, 40, and 41 (K543, 550, and 551—the "Jupiter").

1789 Travels to Dresden, Leipzig, Potsdam, Berlin, and Prague. Composes keyboard sonatas K570 and 576; Clarinet Quintet, K581; and most of *Così fan tutte*.

1790 *Così* premieres on 26 January at the Burgtheater. Travels to Frankfurt for celebrations for the coronation of Joseph's successor, Leopold II.

1791 *La clemenza di Tito* premieres on 6 September in Prague and *The Magic Flute* at the suburban Theater auf der Wieder in Vienna on 30 September. Also composes the Clarinet Concerto, K622; and Requiem, K626. Dies on 6 December.

I

MARCHING BANDS, CHURCH MUSIC, AND ESCAPE FROM SALZBURG

We may think of Salzburg, with its baroque architecture nestled on the Salzach River between the slopes of the Mönchsberg and Kapuzinerberg, as a charming and beautiful city (a UNESCO World Heritage Site since 1997), but Mozart, born there in 1756, came to detest it intensely, and he finally made his permanent escape in 1781. He had more than one reason for feeling that way about it, and not only because of his disagreeable employer, Count Hieronymus Colloredo, the archbishop of Salzburg, who ruled over this bishopric starting in 1772, succeeding the kinder and gentler Sigismund von Schrattenbach. In attempting to reform Salzburg both economically and religiously, Colloredo managed to offend many, not least of all Mozart and his father, Leopold, to the point that even Leopold hoped to find employment elsewhere. Our view of this may be skewed, taken from the vantage point of the Mozarts, and we do need to admit that they could have been as difficult as employees as the archbishop was as their employer, but he clearly held the upper hand. Beauty, of course, can be deceiving, since Salzburg also had a reputation for intolerance; only twenty-five years before Mozart's birth the archbishop of the time, Count Leopold Anton von Firmian, signed the Edict of Expulsion which forced all non-Roman Catholics to repudiate their religions (mostly Protestantism) or be driven out of the district, which in fact happened. The complete lack of ethnic diversity and stuffiness of a city under the control of an administration that made no separation between church and state perplexed

Mozart in the extreme, and he called its inhabitants loathsome idiots, incapable of comprehending his music: "Whenever I play or if any of my works are performed [in Salzburg], it's just as if the audience was made up entirely of tables and chairs." (MLL, 413)

During the twenty-five years that he called Salzburg home, thanks in large part to his father's maneuverings, he managed to spend close to half of his time elsewhere. Leopold had come to Salzburg from Augsburg as a young man to study at the university, and he seems not to have fit into his adopted home especially well. When he discovered that his toddler son had unbelievable musical talent, he resolved that the world had to be exposed to this talent, so he took him on frequent trips to put him on display. He did this with his daughter as well, Maria Anna (always called Nannerl), five years older than Wolfgang, who had every bit as much talent. In many of the leading courts of Europe the two children played piano duets and duos for violin and piano, or solo pieces and improvisations, astonishing audiences who could not believe what they heard. These trips took them not only to Vienna and southern Germany but just about as far afield as one could imagine going in the eighteenth century, to England in the north and Italy in the south (some of these trips are itemized in the timeline). While traveling they not only provided entertainment, but they also met leading musicians and conservatory professors, who occasionally subjected young Mozart to highly rigorous musical tests, which he always passed with flying colors. As Mozart got older, composing also became an integral part of these trips, as he wrote some of his best early works while on the road, including operas starting at the age of twelve for Vienna and Italy.

At the heart of Mozart's early life stood his father, a highly intelligent, talented, and complex man, whom Mozart loved dearly as a child but had much more trouble dealing with as a young adult. Mozart received from him what we would consider "home schooling," with Leopold providing every aspect of the boy's education, including music, mathematics, literature, languages, philosophy, and religion, in fact everything and more than a school could have provided. Most parents like to believe they have exceptional children, but it did not take Leopold long to realize what nature had given to him and his wife Maria Anna Walburga, and he determined that the education of this child could not be left to the vagaries of a school curriculum. He willingly provided this education with great love and tenderness, and of course he had an apt pupil, who could usually figure things out before being told, with an insatiable appetite for more study. The manuscript scores of Mozart's earliest compositions, starting at the age of about five or six, always reveal the strong hand of Leopold, guiding and correcting the young prodigy in developing and refining his craft. For Leopold's generation, composition had little or nothing to do with genius or self-expression, but it was a craft which needed to be honed in a fairly workman-like way. Leopold envisaged that his son could perhaps someday become the equal of some of the finest composers of the time, such as Gluck (whom he did not like), J. C. Bach (whom they had met and got on famously with in London), and perhaps even Joseph Haydn, the illustrious brother of the Salzburg composer Michael Haydn, undoubtedly the greatest living composer.

We should not imagine that Leopold necessarily carried out all of these duties from pure selfless devotion to his son. By the time of Mozart's birth, he was something of an international celebrity himself, having published A Treatise on the Fundamental Principles of Violin Playing in the year of Mozart's birth, not simply a how-to book on violin playing, but a treatise on moral education as well, which quickly went into a number of translations. Because of this and other factors, he had contacts in many parts of Europe, which could be used to facilitate their performance schedules while traveling. His brilliant children reflected on him as well, and while there may have been some grumbling about the pushy father running a kind of circus act with his children, even at times appearing to risk their health, for the most part he emerged with the reputation of a person who had the ability to teach this wunderkind. He obviously hoped for financial gain from these trips, but that proved a little more precarious, especially when aristocrats gave gifts of items such as gold watches or snuffboxes instead of money, objects that often could not be pawned.

The older Mozart grew, the more complex and difficult his relationship with his father became, and at a certain point it all but collapsed completely. As Mozart wrote more and more extraordinary works, including fairly early ones such as the Piano Concerto, K271, to be discussed in chapter 5, the more he realized that composition could take him beyond the level of craftsmanship, into what the Romantics starting late in the eigheenth century recognized as art. In order to pursue this, he could not tie himself indefinitely to a patronage position (employment in an aristocratic or sovereign court), especially one like Salzburg's, with its (in his opinion) limited cultural life, about which he complained bitterly. At times Leopold aspired to something better as well, but he could not see beyond the possibility of court patronage positions; freelancing simply did not exist in his realm of experience. A great deal of tension arose in an already troubled relationship when Mozart insisted on leaving the service of the archbishop in 1781, since Leopold regarded this as a grievous mistake that would lead to financial ruin. The possibilities that a great capital such as Vienna had to offer, with its appetite for opera and every imaginable type of instrumental music, meant nothing to Leopold, who simply could not understand why his son had to rid himself of the shackles of Salzburg. To make matters worse, Mozart had recently returned from almost a year and a half on the road, ostensibly to find a better position which could have perhaps included Leopold as well, but which turned out to be a time of relative indolence for Mozart, who enjoyed a good time without his father breathing down his neck. The trip had cost a fortune, with nothing to show for it, and Leopold had to pay back his financial backers in Salzburg; he believed Mozart's first responsibility lay in doing any work that would be dependable to pay off this debt, and working for the archbishop would be more of a sure thing than taking the chance on freelancing in Vienna.

That trip, starting late in 1777 and ending early in 1779, drove another wedge between them, aside from the fact that Leopold's wife, who accompanied Mozart on it, died in Paris, and Leopold believed Mozart deserved some blame for this. Once again Leopold's own personal ambitions came to the fore, and since he had to stay in Salzburg, he used this as an opportunity to carry on a lengthy correspondence with his son that could form the basis for an epistolary biography of his son that he intended to publish someday. If he could pull this off, it would be even more of a sensation than his violin treatise, since it would be a moral manual of instruction that a father offers to his son, a well-established genre in the mold of his writing hero, Christian Fürchtegott Gellert, arguably the most popular writer in German-speaking countries at the time. Not simply an instructional work, it would have had great reader appeal by being about the most popular young musician in the world. It did not take Mozart long in this correspondence to figure out what his father was up to, since much of the advice being offered either did not pertain to his actual situation or seemed intended for someone much younger than himself. Since both sides of the correspondence would need to be present to make it legitimate, he went out of his way to reply (or not reply) in ways that would undermine what Leopold hoped to achieve. Leopold too saw through his son's attempts to subvert it, and near the end of the correspondence his exasperation reached such a fevered pitch that if letters could scream, his were screaming. When Mozart finally dragged himself reluctantly back to Salzburg, months later than Leopold expected, the relationship had been damaged beyond repair, and needless to say the correspondence was unpublishable. Luckily for us it makes absolutely fascinating reading, but it should not be taken as the factual basis for biography, since Mozart often did not tell the truth, learning to do that skillfully from his exposure in Paris to letters by the likes of Voltaire.

Mozart's early compositions can be divided roughly into two groups: those written in Salzburg for performance there or to cut his teeth on as compositional exercises, and those written while traveling, in some cases on commission. Since Salzburg had a limited operatic life, something Mozart deeply resented, he wrote about half of his early operas for performances elsewhere, generally either Vienna or the home of opera, Italy. Opera would become the most recognized part of Mozart's legacy, and while these early operas show some signs of what would come later, they have not survived as part of the repertory; if they had not been written by Mozart, we would probably not be interested in them at all. While traveling in the late 1770s, he had some ideas about what he could do with opera, but little of this materialized (despite what he was telling Leopold). Writing an opera requires enormous time and effort, and no composer in the eighteenth century, including a teenager, would take this on without a commission and a real prospect for performance; for the mature Mozart that finally came from Munich, the nearest major court to Salzburg, with the commission for *Idomeneo* in 1780.

While at home in Salzburg, his output can once again more or less be divided in half, between many different types of composition that he wrote to get experience, including the standard types such as symphonies, chamber music, concertos, and sonatas, and works that were in demand in Salzburg itself, as small as that list of genres may be. Considering who the patron was, the head of the church as well as the state, one genre trumped all others: sacred music, which could include not only masses but smaller works as well, such as litanies, vespers, and a host of others where the content would provide the name, such as Veni Sancte Spiritus, Regina coeli, Te Deum laudamus, Dixit et Magnificat, Venite populi, and many others. By no means did he write all of his liturgical works for Salzburg; he wrote them for other German cities as well and also Italy, especially Bologna, where he met and learned from the outstanding music professor Padre Martini, and Milan, for which he wrote one of his best-known sacred works, "Exsultate, jubilate."

Aside from the archbishop and the needs of the church, he managed to drum up some other compositional commissions in Salzburg as well, revealing an early resourcefulness and perhaps penchant for freelancing. These came not from heads of state or the church but from fairly ordinary people—at least ones who could afford the modest fee—and all of the Salzburg composers got their share of these, of course Michael Haydn and Joseph Hafeneder, but even Leopold Mozart as well. The types of light music that resulted from this, almost always intended for outdoor performances, included serenades, cassations (a term possibly derived from "Gasse," which means street or alley, and strolling these often old, narrow streets), and divertimentos. While they could be used for different types of soirées, two events proved the most likely for the commissions to be forthcoming, and these were carnival—just before the beginning of Lent, with lots of tomfoolery and silly carnival plays that required incidental music—and university or gymnasium graduation celebrations at the end of the academic year.

SERENADES

It's a warm summer evening in August of 1776, and having just graduated from the University of Salzburg, a Benedictine institution, you are looking forward to the informal evening celebrations after the fairly pompous ceremony earlier in the day when you had to endure tedious speeches before receiving your parchment. After hearing your fill about how privileged you were to have this degree and how you would make the world a better place, you were ready to let off some steam, which a long-standing tradition for the evening of graduation day made possible. Now a type of mock ceremony could take place, with lots of wine and beer flowing, which even some of the professors enjoyed. It took place in one of the outdoor quads of the university, where facetious speeches could be made, jokes could be told, and irreverence that the chancellor and priests might very well find offensive could take over. To set the right tone for the event, a pseudo-formal march first took place, with the professors who wished to attend in the lead, followed by the graduates still in caps and gowns, starting at University Hall and winding through narrow passageways to the quad. The march, of course, required music, as did the event at the quad, which would include dancing and then background music when the serious drinking began.

The music for the march presented a tricky but not insurmountable problem, which was that the musicians would have to be part of the march itself, since no one could possibly hear them if they were already set up at the quad. Not only that, but another part of the tradition required those among the graduates able to play an instrument to be part of the marching band, joining the other musicians in leading this motley procession. As fate would have it, you played the cello, a necessary instrument for the mostly string band, but you could not think how on earth you would march performing an instrument that has to be played sitting down. Two centuries later Woody Allen would come up with one possible solution for this, and he shows us how it works in his movie *Take the Money and Run*, in which Allen happens to be the only cellist in his high school's marching band. He plays sitting down, and every ten paces he dashes ahead with cello in one hand and chair in the other, plays until the rest of the band catches up, and then runs ahead again to repeat the maneuver over and over. Apparently he did not think of putting the chair and cello pin on wheels, or doing what bands in the eighteenth century did to solve the problem. At the time no one seemed too concerned if the instrument playing the bottom line was actually a cello, and even the musical scores more often than not specified "basso," as if to say any low instrument would do as well as another, and the trick involved using straps to bind the instrument to the front of the body, allowing it to be played while marching. Something larger than a cello generally worked best, an instrument halfway between a cello and a double bass, for which the finger board would be above the shoulder and could be coordinated with the bow slightly below the waist. It took a little getting used to, but after a few tries on the small double bass you borrowed for the occasion (called a violone), you found it worked reasonably well, provided you didn't trip on large cobblestones in the lanes.

For this occasion in 1776, your good friend Willi von Andretter had the perfect solution for getting the Finalmusik, as it was called: for his brother Johann's graduation three years earlier, their father had been persuaded to commission Mozart to write it, and he did, coming up with a delightful serenade (K185). Having heard these types of pieces by the other composers in town, Willi insisted that the serenade should be by Mozart, since only he seemed capable of capturing the facetious atmosphere of the occasion, and so he once again persuaded his father to approach Mozart with a new commission. They had not taken into account the difference between Mozart at the age of seventeen and a young man of twenty, who, despite spending the whole year in Salzburg, was up to his ears with other compositions, including concertos and church music, and also had to spend more time with the orchestra, having been promoted to second concertmaster. He simply did not have the time to write something new, but he said he had a perfectly suitable work he had written earlier in the year, called the Serenata Notturna (Evening serenade), or simply the Serenade in D (K239), which had been performed only once previously at a private carnival party, and would therefore not be known to anyone likely to attend. The work had everything they needed (although not the usual eight movements), including a march at the beginning, a minuet in the middle, and a rondo finale with lots of musical joking; it did seem ideal, and the Andretters happily accepted it in lieu of a newly composed work.

On this evening in August the marchers gathered in front of University Hall, with the musicians as the lead group, and, not being able to strap the bass to your body by yourself, you got Willi to help, putting one strap just above the instrument's bridge around your waist, and another strap tied to the pin around your legs. The first attempt to secure it in the right position failed miserably, since you still wore your academic gown, made with cotton that had a slightly slippery sheen, and the bass kept sliding down. Also, since the gown came about halfway between your knees and ankles, the lower strap slipped lower every time you took a step because it had to be loose enough to allow your legs to move. You and Willi solved that one by pushing the gown up to your hips, and instead of one lower strap, you used two—one for each leg; you looked ridiculous with the gown spilling over the lower straps, but it worked.

The other matter, already dealt with, was how to secure the music in front of you so you could read it while walking, a special problem for a bass player, whose instrument does not project out in front, as many other instruments do. These instruments can have a nifty little music stand, usually in the shape of a lyre, affixed to their end. We have all seen these on clarinets or trumpets in marching bands, and even on flutes that extend out sideways, forcing the player to develop good peripheral vision. Violins and violists can manage more or less in the same way, with a little lyre stand attached to the end of the scroll, but a bass, which the player hugs close to the body, has no such option. You tried various things, including attaching a yardstick to your mortarboard cap, with a lyre hanging upside down from the end of the stick, but the mere weight of it made it gradually slip off your head, even with a ribbon to hold the cap in place. In the end it seemed most convenient to memorize the part, which, for the tutti (or ensemble) group, seemed not all that arduous, and after the march, a music stand could be used for the minuet and rondo. With the ensemble in place, consisting of four soloists (two violins, one viola, and one violone), a small string orchestra, and a timpani (but no other wind or brass instruments), the procession could begin. You thought you had problems fastening the bass to your body, but you were glad not to be the timpani player, who had to attach two relatively large drums to himself, one in D and the other in A.

The march began, and fortunately your part had lots of rests, which allowed you to concentrate on not stumbling, and you could always watch the solo violins for the cue to re-enter since they typically had flourishes at those points. Mozart may have written this work earlier in the year, but it could not have been better suited to the occasion. In some ways it sounded a little like a concerto grosso from earlier in the century, with the group of solo instruments who had their solos while you had rests, and four professionals had been hired for the solo parts. Mozart marked the march "maestoso," but the nature of the writing seemed anything but magisterial, especially in the second of the two repeated sections, where the soloists drop out for two bars while the ensemble (along with the timpani giving a cheeky little rhythmic figure) very quietly plays pizzicato in the appropriate response to what the soloists have just played. In the four bars preceding this, the soloists, in contrast to the expectations of a march, put the accent on the second beat instead of the first for the first two bars, and then used offbeats for the next two, making it tricky for the marchers to keep in step. With all of that repeated one more time, the march no longer seemed like much of a march at all, and by the time you arrived at the quad, it looked as though your band had had an early start on the new wine of the season (which happens to be much stronger than aged wine).

After some outrageously funny short speeches from students pretending to be administrators and priests, with the usual scatological jokes such as squatting when telling of great deeds that would be accomplished by this class, your band played the minuet, which some people tried to dance to but discovered quickly they could not, since it lacked the right phrasing patterns, and the scotch snap figures (quick notes followed by longer notes in succession) did not lend themselves to graceful dancing. In the minuet's trio (for soloists only), as in the march, Mozart occasionally placed the accent on the weak beats—also not conducive to dancing. The dancers quickly gave up, and simply enjoyed the cleverness of the music. We fully expect some musical monkey business in the rondo final, and Mozart does not disappoint, interjecting into this cheerfully lighthearted dance-like movement an adagio section that comes as a complete surprise, but still using the dance-like motif, as if to make this sudden apparent seriousness seem a little foolish—perhaps not unlike the pompousness of the earlier part of the day, which can now be turned into nose-thumbing. After these ten bars of adagio the fun returns, with more musical jokes such as the pizzicato reply to the main theme near the end, followed by turning the soloists into the accompaniment. By the time the music ended the mood could not have been merrier, and a good part of the mirth of the evening could be attributed to the tone set by Mozart's serenade.

CHURCH MUSIC: SALZBURG

The contractual terms of composers in the employment of the archbishop specified they should write masses as well as other liturgical music for the Salzburg Cathedral in the center of town, but the peculiar system involving the various music directors did not guarantee that performances would take place. The different composers took turns directing services, and Leopold Mozart as a mere assistant kapellmeister did not have great authority in these matters. When his turn came, he tried to promote the masses or mass movements of his young son, who wrote his first full mass at the age of twelve (for Vienna), but Leopold had made himself a difficult colleague, and his wishes were often blocked by others. When Mozart did start to write masses for services in Salzburg, at the end of the 1760s and then during the 1770s, he was the least prolific of the Salzburg composers, and some have questioned how seriously he applied himself to these duties; even the archbishop complained about his lack of productivity. Compared to those around him, the quality of Mozart's church music cannot be doubted, but when traveling, especially in Italy, he often wrote exceptional works. When he left Salzburg for good his production of church music trailed off to a mere trickle, in part because of the impossibility of getting it performed in Vienna after the liturgical reforms by Joseph II, but after Joseph's death in 1790 and his appointment to the position of assistant to the director of music at St. Stephen's Cathedral, he once again showed serious signs of re-establishing himself as a composer of church music.

Of the various things he composed for Salzburg, church music may have been associated with an element of drudgery because of the demand for this kind of music and the possibility of writing it in an almost formulaic manner, but if he felt that way about it, he generally did not let it show, at least in terms of quality. He may, though, have allowed his distaste to show in other ways, not unlike his subtle mocking in other types of music, for example the Piano Concerto in E flat, K271, from 1777, which I describe in chapter 5 as a possible commentary on some of the more odious aspects of life in Salzburg. In the last mass that he wrote for Salzburg, the Mass in C, K337, written in 1780 after his extended travels in Germany and France, during which time he made no bones about how much he detested his home town, musical features turn up that may very well be mocking the whole religious establishment of Salzburg. This may seem an odd thing to do in a mass, but he could get a kind of satisfaction by planting his insults right under the noses of the archbishop and his entourage in a way that would leave them not quite sure if they were being insulted. In fact, the tricks he interjected here provided ammunition for similar ones he would use in operas later on that could also prick the balloons of social attitudes he wished to attack, in ways that many would not notice.

In this mass he launches his subtle assault in the very short Sanctus (Holy, holy, holy), starting it off with an appropriately pompous vocal treatment, although he backs that up with an accompaniment in the strings that seems entirely too light and even frivolous. By the time he reaches the words "Pleni sunt ca*eli* et <u>ter</u> *ra* <u>glo</u>ria tua" (Heaven and earth are filled with thy glory) only six bars later, he adds rapid changes between piano (p) and forte (<u>f</u>), providing unnecessary accents that render the impact of the text slightly ridiculous. The discussion in chapter 8 of the singing of the final moral in *Don Giovanni* will reveal his doing something similar, there actually putting the accents on the wrong syllables to make a complete nonsense of the text. Here he follows the disjointed text immediately with something much more obviously unexpected, with a shift after a pause from the serious adagio of the Sanctus to a wildly lively allegro non troppo, and the solo soprano sings "Hosanna in excelsis" (Hosanna in the highest), the expected text, in an impish manner that sounds as though it has come from a frolicking scene in a comic opera (he treats the two priests early in Act 2 of *The Magic Flute* in a similar way, as I discuss in chapter 9, mocking their stern words about the treachery of women). The chorus picks up the soprano's theme directly, and seriousness gives way to lampoon for the rest of the section. Even the Benedictus which follows cannot quite get the serious tone back on track. While atypical of his masses, this may have sent a veiled message to the archbishop and Salzburg shortly before Mozart gained his long-desired freedom.

CHURCH MUSIC: ITALY

Late in October of 1772 Mozart returned to Italy for the third time with his father, now with opera very much on his mind, as he spent November and December in Milan rehearsing and giving the first performance of his new serious opera *Lucio Silla*. He had the good fortune to have one of the great castrato sopranos in the cast, Venanzio Rauzzini, singing the role of Celio, and as would be true of all his later operas, he adapted the part to Rauzzini's voice. Most of us will not know that opera, but clearly taken by this singer's voice, Mozart wrote for him what is surely the best known of all his church pieces (the Requiem excepted), the extraordinary "Exsultate, jubilate," first performed at the Theatine Church in Milan on 17 January 1773. The overwhelming exuberance of this motet in three movements has much in common with opera, and its joyous temperament may have something to do with Mozart's own high spirits at the time, in a place he loved, doing musically what he most enjoyed. On the night before the performance he appended a delightfully mixed-up postscript to his sister back in Salzburg (to a longer letter from his father to his mother), a type of writing he enjoyed indulging in when in an especially mischievous and buoyant mood: "I for have the primo a uomo [Rauzzini] motet compose which to tomorrow at Church the Theatine performed be will. Keep well, I you beg. Farewell. Addio. I sorry to any My to our friends, am not have news. greetings all good male and Fare I Mamma's I you a female. well. kiss hand. kiss too thousand times am always faithful at and as your brother Milan." (LMF, 226) She would not have had the slightest difficulty understanding.

While written for performance in a church, this work by the seventeen-year-old Mozart does not sound like anything we would expect to hear in a church, at least not outside of Italy. It eludes normal descriptions, with three arias (the first two connected by recitative) that sound as though they come from an opera, set for two oboes, two horns, strings, organ, and soprano, who gets not only some of the finest melodic lines he ever wrote, but also coloratura-like passages. At the same time each of the arias sounds like a concerto for voice and orchestra because of the cadenzas near the end, allowing the singer to improvise as spectacularly as s/he wishes. Mozart wrote this for a male soprano who possessed an amazingly agile voice, but since castratos disappeared well over a century ago, today it will be sung by a female soprano; even though the lines do not go terribly high, the lightness and agility required make it unsuitable for the lower mezzo soprano voice. Compared to the opera he had just written, *Lucio Silo*, and the ones he would compose in the next two years, *La finta giardiniera* and *Il re pastore*, the writing here if anything seems even more operatic and moving. It's impossible to listen to this work without being drawn into the sheer joy that it exudes.

Each aria, though, possesses a somewhat different atmosphere; all directly relate to the text, especially setting the middle aria apart from the two outer ones. The first allegro aria has a fairly lengthy orchestral introduction (twenty bars) which sets the tone musically for the rejoicing of which the soprano then sings, finding the gentle tone of the "dulcia cantica canendo" (singing sweet songs). The recitative, simple in the extreme with nothing but an organ accompaniment but still operatic, reminds us that darkness and fear have now been banished, and some of that darker tone carries over into the second aria, with its sighing motifs that reflect the text asking for consolation and peace from that which makes the heart sigh. The final aria not only gives this consolation but seems to laugh at the previous clouds, set entirely to a single word: "Alleluja." Not content to give this a conventional setting, Mozart impudently plays with the word, shifting the accents to different syllables as it goes along, not unlike what he would do in 1780 with the Sanctus and Hosanna in the Mass in C noted above, and in operas later in his career to achieve mischievous effects. Here he goes even further, playing with offbeats, suddenly launching into little coloraturas on certain syllables, putting delicious figurations in horn parts when the voice drops out, and even teasing us with unexpected harmonies. If by the end we have not been moved to pure unadulterated bliss, it's hard to imagine what would do it. Not surprisingly the line between sacred and secular music began to blur during the late eighteenth century, with sacred pieces increasingly programmed on secular concerts, and works such as this led the way.

2

THE SHADOW OF HAYDN

Symphonies

In some areas of composition, especially operas and concertos, Mozart had no equal in the eighteenth century, although his contemporaries may not have always taken that view, lacking the test of time that we have the advantage of being able to apply. Unlike some nineteenth-century composers who became more specialized in certain types of composition, Mozart did that less, since in his time a composer's livelihood normally depended on fluency in every genre, whether working for a patron or, near the end of the century, as a freelancer. In the hands of patronage, symphonies served the functions of court, required by the patron for occasions such as weddings, special celebrations (including religious ones), or visits from noble guests, and therefore the tone of these works needed to be uplifting. Later in the century, with the prestige of courts in decline for financial and other reasons, symphonies were more likely to be commissioned by concert societies, usually still very much in the hands of the aristocracy, but now with the possibility of a broader public in attendance. Dozens of composers vied for the dwindling number of court positions and for the commissions from concert societies, and most of their names, including Wagenseil, Monn, Stamitz (Sr. and Jr.), Hofmann, Reutter, Sammartini, Pleyel, Michael Haydn, and even Mozart's own father, have long since been forgotten. We ignore them for good reason: one composer, Joseph Haydn, eclipsed them all, and he, over a span of about four decades, transformed the symphony from the standard celebratory functional piece to something that assured the symphony would thrive for the next two centuries. By the time Mozart wrote his first symphonies that went beyond childhood experiments or displays of youthful cleverness, Haydn had already become a giant in the field, and he would almost always remain a step or two ahead of Mozart as a symphonist.

The age difference between Haydn and Mozart, twenty-four years, meant that Haydn belonged to the same generation as Mozart's father, and it's not exactly clear when Mozart became familiar with the older composer's symphonies. He had opportunities to hear them from a fairly early age; while traveling—especially in Vienna—he may occasionally have been able to see a score of a Haydn symphony, and Haydn's brother Michael also held a position in Salzburg. At least by 1785, if not earlier, the two of them had become friends, either living in Vienna as Mozart did by then or spending the summers there as Haydn did when the Esterháza season had ended, and they moved in the same circles, including attending musical and literary salons, and other private gatherings. They also shared an interest (and briefly membership) in Freemasonry. For his early symphonies, up to and including the first ones he wrote in Vienna in the early 1780s, Mozart followed a path that bore little resemblance to Haydn's, but that changed dramatically after 1785, when Mozart reached his high maturity as a symphonist, and knew Haydn's achievements well. Perhaps because of the age difference they never saw themselves as rivals (at least not with symphonies), but in fact both had the greatest possible respect for each other, which, it appears, blossomed into a warm friendship. Mozart wrote a mere four symphonies after 1785, one in 1786 and three in 1788, but clearly four of the great works of the symphonic repertory; perhaps what strikes us most is how little they have in common with Haydn's. Not only did Mozart, realizing that Haydn cast a very long shadow, avoid getting trapped in that shadow, but by this point he had moved in a direction entirely unlike that of his great contemporary, and what he did with his symphonies reveals the differences starkly.

SONATA FORM

A large part of Haydn's transformation of the symphony involved changing it from a celebratory piece to a type of composition highly charged with drama, especially when writing for his larger public in a way that would engage listeners' interest not unlike a play for the stage, although he started doing this well before his first commissions from international concert societies. Since a symphony does not have words to carry the drama (at least it didn't before Beethoven's Ninth and later some of Mahler's symphonies), it must generate its drama through purely musical means, although it can, as the discussion in the next section will show, use musical references that audiences will recognize as representing something with specific or more generalized associations. The drama, though, does not depend on these kinds of references but can be achieved by the music itself, certainly at a larger formal level, in the way that a play will move through the introduction of characters and issues, a dramatic conflict or interaction, and finally a resolution or at least a dénouement. The musical means for achieving this depend on distinctive themes or motifs, tonality—the movement from the home key (the tonic) through other keys and then back to the home key—contrasts between musical stability and instability, and other possible factors that can include rhythm, meter, orchestration, or range. Symphonies can have three or four movements, although for the last third of the eighteenth century the four-movement symphony predominated, and any one of the movements can participate in the drama, although first movements have a special role here, making them particularly important in the relative weighting of movements. Near the end of his career Haydn started to shift that balance to last movements, something which caught on with Beethoven and later nineteenth-century composers, but this happened less in the eighteenth century.

The means for generating drama in first movements came by way of a procedure called sonata form (not to be confused with the label "sonata" by itself), in some ways an unfortunate term since the word "form" suggests something much more fixed than the actual process that takes place. In a fairly loose way something fixed does exist, although it's a mistake to think of this as the important part. Composers may deviate from it drastically, but when they do, we generally know what they're deviating from, and it adds to the drama to know that they're distorting what we expect. Since Haydn more than anyone brought this dramatic approach to sonata form into being, we need to give him credit, not for inventing the form itself, but certainly for taking it to a new level of dramatic vitality. Sonata form continued to be a major force in music during the nineteenth century, although at times it almost appears unrecognizable, as with some of Beethoven's late works (the Piano Sonata, Op. 101, for example), and it even made its way into the twentieth century, showing a great deal of resilience and longevity. For this and other reasons, we consistently underestimate the extraordinary effect that Haydn had on music for a good two centuries, and some twentieth-century composers, for example Prokofiev, readily acknowledged the debt they owed him.

Because sonata form is not a form, I'm a little reluctant to try to define it at all, but of course we have to start somewhere. As with drama for the stage, we can broadly define it as being in three parts: the exposition as the introduction of characters and issues, the development as the working out section with the greatest conflict, and the recapitulation as the attempt to find resolution. Sonata form almost always happens in first movements, but it can turn up in other movements as well, especially finales; in first movements it can have its own introduction, usually a slow one preceding the fast tempo of the movement, and it can end with a coda, in some cases fairly extended. But before concluding that the form has three parts, it can be thought of as having a two-part division as well, with a first part ending with the exposition that gets repeated, and a second part including the development and recap together. With the exposition repeated, it gives something balanced in length to the second part, and that balance may be crucial, even in the works of Beethoven. In the first movement of the *Eroica* Symphony, for example, Beethoven makes an essential division right in the middle of the development, and that division needs to be heard as the middle of the entire movement, which it will not be if the exposition has not been repeated. The two-part division in the eighteenth century also has tonal implications, since the first part involves progression from the tonic key to another key, while the second part brings things from other keys back to the home key. We need not get hung up on the three-part/two-part business; for dramatic purposes it's important to think of it as three parts.

Within the three sections, we can expect that there will be a key change from the tonic to the dominant (or relative major for a work in a minor key) in the exposition, ending not simply touching on the dominant but actually in it. The arrival of the dominant usually defines a division in the exposition of the second group from the first, although even here that arrival may be obscured, with tonal ambiguity taking over to prevent a clear arrival. Themes may correspond with these divisions, but the listener should not be looking for a new theme to mark the arrival of the second group, since there can be new themes before that, or the movement may have no more than one theme, making it monothematic. Often there will be a new theme corresponding with the arrival of the dominant key, but since that doesn't always happen, the change of key needs to be taken as the more important defining characteristic of division. Some older textbooks and dictionaries used to call the opening theme a masculine theme, and the second theme (assuming there were two) as feminine because of its more melodic characteristic, but thankfully that kind of sexist language, which often had nothing to do with the actual nature of the themes, has long since vanished. In some expositions a third theme comes up as a closing theme, but in fact there can be any number of themes in an exposition, from one in some of Haydn's symphonies to as many as eight in Mozart's Piano Sonata in F, K332, to be discussed in chapter 6. The themes can behave like the characters of a play, with distinctly different features that set them apart and help to generate the conflict; additional tension may arise from tonal stability or instability in which the themes appear, or in the transitional material between them.

The tension intensifies in the development, through tonal instability that can start on the dominant or a more remote key and progress in some cases through surprising keys before returning to the dominant to set up the arrival of the recap in the tonic, by way of counterpoint that allows themes or motifs to interact with each other—sometimes like characters in discussions or arguments, and any other procedures that the composer wishes to use to build tension. Some resolution may come in this section as well, and the development can be an alternating exchange of tension and resolution, either building one way or the other. With often fairly rapid digression to foreign keys, the composer may trick us into thinking that the recap has come, giving the original theme of the movement in the wrong key, creating a false recapitulation, which can go on for some time or be cut short, with lots more ambiguity to come. In order to reach the end of the development, there needs to be sufficient reinforcement of the dominant key as preparation for the arrival of the home key. Some developments, contrary to the above description, have very little tension or working out at all, making the term "development" fairly inappropriate.

During the eighteenth century, composers would usually begin the recap in the tonic key, but it did not take long for Beethoven, Schubert, and others to play around with that, letting the original theme return in the wrong key, temporarily tricking the listener into thinking it's a false recap. Musical form depends on memory, the return of something heard earlier, but the recap normally offers anything but a straightforward repetition of the exposition in the home key. Material can be added or taken away, and some things will have to be changed, such as the transitional modulation from tonic to dominant from the exposition, since the recap no longer has that modulation, more or less staying in the home key. Depending on the work, the recap can be fairly simple, or it can be extraordinarily complex, as often happens in Haydn's later symphonies, to be described below, in relation to what Haydn hoped to accomplish and make evident to his audiences. Mozart's dissimilar approach here points not just to musical procedures, but also to the very different meaning he apparently wished his late symphonies to convey. All recaps in the eighteenth century have in common the basic fact of ending in the home key.

HAYDN'S SYMPHONIES

Unlike some of his colleagues in Vienna such as Hofmann and Dittersdorf, whose symphonies were performed at concerts organized for the Burgtheater or elsewhere, Haydn found employment with Count Morzin and, after 1761, with the Esterházy family, and therefore wrote all of his early symphonies for court purposes. Despite these limitations—his contract of 1761 with the Esterházys made all of his works the property of his patron—he quickly came to see much more potential for the symphony than simply providing music for celebrations. By the late 1760s some of those possibilities became amply evident, occasionally serving dramatic religious purposes, for example in Symphony No. 26 in

D minor, the "Lamentatione," which quotes in the first movement a well-known plainchant and tells the passion story, complete with an evangelist, Christ, and voice of the people, in effect presenting a little vocal cantata in instrumental music. He then makes certain that the appropriate spirit of reverence carries through to the second movement, again quoting a familiar lamentation of Jeremiah which becomes the basis for the movement. This symphony and some others from 1768 to 1772 used minor keys to find a more vivid dramatic character, but since his patron objected to this, he spent the next decade writing symphonies in major keys. That does not mean that he went back to writing cheerful works that mean nothing; a number of these major-key symphonies originated as incidental music for plays, or programmatic pieces related to works of literature.

Haydn negotiated a new contract in 1779 with Prince Nicolaus Esterházy which gave him much more freedom to have his music performed elsewhere, something Nicolaus could accept since Haydn had become a jewel in his crown, and the performance of this music abroad would bring additional prestige to the court. As the audience base expanded, not only did the symphonies become more dramatic, but they began to serve a social function as well, in line with the enlightened thinking Haydn became exposed to through friendships in Vienna, attendance of literary salons, and his interest in Freemasonry. In part through Mozart's instigation, he joined the lodge Zur wahren Eintracht (True Concord), although he had the chance to attending no meetings aside from his initiation, since Joseph II dissolved this and most other lodges in 1785, and this lodge functioned more as an academy of arts and sciences than a normal lodge. As such, it served the educational function of Freemasonry, spreading the word about the enlightened aspirations of its members, and Haydn, it appears, concluded that he could join this effort with his symphonies. When interviewed by biographers near the end of his life, he did not hesitate to explain what he hoped to achieve along these lines, pointing out that "he oftentimes had portrayed moral characters in his symphonies." Here he uses the language of the moral weeklies so common throughout Europe at the time, for example in *The Tatler* and *The Spectator* of Addison and Steele in England. Taking this a step further, he went on to say that in one of his symphonies "the dominant idea is of God speaking with an abandoned sinner, pleading with him to reform. But, the sinner in his thoughtlessness pays no heed to the admonition." Probably he did not mean that the symphony represented this scenario literally, but that this could be taken as a type of programmatic image of how a symphony might achieve its extramusical function.

Symphonies, he believed, should serve the goals of the Enlightenment, which involved secular notions of morality, tolerance, altruism, and higher levels of refinement. Going far beyond the earlier celebratory notion of the symphony, he told one of his biographers late in life that "I also believe I have done my duty and have been of use to the world through my works." One of his first best chances to show what this meant came right after his initiation as a Freemason, with a commission from a Masonic concert society in Paris, the Concert de la Loge Olympique, for six new symphonies. In one of these, Symphony No. 83 ("La Poule"), possibly the first of the set, he set things up in a way in the first movement that showed in musical terms one of the most basic human aspirations of the Enlightenment—that opposing forces can coexist, living together in a state of tolerance.

This wish on Haydn's part to be certain that listeners could hear what he intended became even more pronounced in his final twelve symphonies, written during his two trips to London for audiences that simply could not get enough of him. The most extreme case of this happens in one of the last, No. 103 ("The Drum-roll"), which, like all but one of the English symphonies, begins with a slow introduction, prepared in this case by a drum-roll at the very beginning. This unusually long introduction does something fairly typical of the introductions of these late symphonic first movements: it starts with a passage that has an association with death, this time using the first four notes of the familiar *Dies irae* plainchant, the song of the dead from traditional Roman Catholic liturgy. With the arrival of the second group of the exposition, coming after a less than straightforward modulation to the dominant key, he introduces a puzzling two-bar passage that gives the identical thematic outline as the opening of the slow introduction, but now with a lively dance rhythm, which he identifies a few bars later as belonging to the distinctive dance character of the closing theme. Just like the persistence of the death-associated material from introductions, he often gives dance themes in the fast section of the exposition, providing an extreme contrast by way of a life-affirming character, since these dances often come from wedding music or folk dances used at spring growth festivals.

Here in the space of two bars he combines these two opposite forces in the most ingenious way, not placing them side by side but integrating them into one tightly compressed theme. This happens at the beginning of the second group, usually a fairly audible point in the movement, but it seems fairly safe to say that this will drift right over the heads of most listeners, and it puzzles us why he would place this most important integrating passage of the movement in a way that few will hear it. After the working out of the development, that puzzlement ends in the recap, with the most pronounced stoppage of any of his symphonies, this time actually bringing the drum-roll back, adagio as it had been at the beginning, and with a fermata to make it even longer. If this musical equivalent of a kick in the shins does not get our attention, nothing will, although Haydn takes no chances, repeating the first two phrases of the introduction, still adagio. He now has us exactly where he wants us, listening in stunned amazement, and immediately after these two adagio introduction phrases, he goes back to the fast tempo with the two crucial bars from the exposition, now making absolutely certain we will hear them. He has taken us by the hand, giving us a lesson in listening, and that lesson tells us to be aware of an extraordinary fusion of opposites, very much a coexistence, since both forces, of life versus death if you like, remain fully evident, perhaps giving the ultimate lesson about coexistence. With these late symphonies Haydn set the standard for symphonic achievement, showing at the highest possible level how an instrumental work can go far beyond itself to address social and spiritual issues, and he created the raison d'être for the symphony for the next two centuries. Beethoven claimed he came to Vienna to get the spirit of Mozart from Haydn, but in fact he got the spirit of Haydn, entirely evident in his *Eroica* Symphony and the ones to follow. Without Haydn's innovations, it would be impossible to imagine the symphonic achievements of Schumann, Brahms, Mahler, Shostakovich, and a host of others.

MOZART AND THE GENERATION GAP

Unlike Haydn, who composed his first symphony at the age of twenty-five, Mozart was a mere eight years old, and his early symphonies show the brilliance of the most extraordinarily talented musical child the world has ever seen. For symphonies to endure they must be much more than that, and were it not for his last six symphonies, we would probably not be listening to Mozart's symphonies today. The exact number of symphonies he wrote remains something of a mystery, since some attributed to him could be by (or mostly by) his father or some other unidentified composer, but he did write about thirty before reaching the age at which Haydn wrote his first. By that comparison Haydn seems like a late bloomer, but of course no one stands up well when compared to the young Mozart. Of those roughly thirty, a few continue to be performed, but mostly because they are by Mozart and not because of their great merit; symphonies appeared not to be his highest priority, as he preferred to lavish his attention on other types of composition. The first two that he wrote while in Vienna, the "Haffner" and the "Linz," still do not point in the direction of a great symphonist, as he wrote both of them for specific events and places with other more pressing matters on his mind, dashing them off quickly, and even feeling somewhat annoyed at the intrusion on his precious time. These clearly deserve to be in the repertory, and we can marvel at what Mozart could achieve on a tight schedule.

That leaves only four more symphonies to round out his entire life's output, but those four are so exceptional and rightly belonging to the repertory that we can count him among the great writers of symphonies. If we imagine though that he simply looked over his shoulder to see what Haydn was doing and followed that course, we could not be more wrong. We must remember that Mozart, twenty-four years younger than Haydn, belonged to a different generation; Haydn in fact had much more in common generationally with Leopold Mozart than with Wolfgang. Of course Mozart picked up some techniques and procedures from Haydn, and after Mozart's last symphonies Haydn probably did from Mozart as well, but going beyond technical procedures or matters of craft into what the role of a symphony should be vis-à-vis the audience and the composer's artistic, social, and religious outlook, these two giants of the late eighteenth century could not be more different.

This can be nicely illustrated through their attitudes to certain writers, and especially the writer that Haydn considered his hero: Christian Fürchtegott Gellert. Leopold also had the highest possible admiration for Gellert, the leading moral writer in Germany in the middle of the century, and possibly the most popular German writer at that time through his novels, plays, poems, essays, letters, sketches of moral characters, and much more. Leopold thought so highly of him that he attempted to strike up a correspondence with him, and even became a type of agent for the sale of Gellert's books in Salzburg. Much of Leopold's public profile as a writer, including his treatise on violin playing and his letters with his son that he hoped one day to publish as a type of moral epistolary biography, was shaped by the thinking of Gellert, with the latter even modeled after a prototype of letters from a father to his son by Gellert. When Gellert died in 1769, the almost fourteen-year-old Mozart, who had grown up inundated by Gellert's ideas because of his father's mania for him, wrote a letter to his sister with a comment that seems to reveal what he thought: "I have nothing new except that Herr gelehrt, the poet from Leipzig, died, and since his death has composed no more poetry." (MBA i 309) In addition to expressing his relief not to have any more of this tedious poetry foisted on him, he even made a sarcastic pun on Gellert's name (gelehrt = learned).

The generational difference between Mozart and Haydn had much to do with morality, which for Haydn's generation stood as the cornerstone of the Enlightenment, and it prompted Haydn to attempt to infuse it into his symphonies. Morality should not be construed in any narrow religious sense, involving only behavior and views of God, as it extended well beyond that, certainly to notions of refinement that could be acquired through reading and music, as well as a sense of order in the universe—a type of master plan which could be grasped through a logical and orderly unfolding, ultimately revealing God's plan for humankind. Haydn emulated this in his symphonies not only by the refinement that could be grasped through the music but also through the musical logic in the working out of symphonic ideas, showing forces in conflict and bringing them to a type of reconciliation that points to the higher aspirations of humanity. This type of logic, also evident in the best of German philosophy, most closely associated with Kant and Hegel, in fact seemed to have something distinctively German about it, and perhaps not surprisingly the great practitioners of pure reason were also leading proponents of moral philosophy. The earlier eighteenth-century versions of this type of thought had been thoroughly impressed on Haydn by the thinkers he encountered at salons and through Free-masonry (Ignaz von Born, Joseph von Sonnenfels, Baron van Swieten, and many others), and he even had the works of the Earl of Shaftes-bury, Adam Smith, Edmund Burke, and Alexander Pope (in German translation) in his personal library. I have written in detail how this thinking permeated his symphonies in my book *Haydn and the Enlight-enment*.

Mozart belonged to a new generation which no longer shared these passé notions of the Enlightenment and morality, and the thrust of the new thinking emanated not from Germany but from France, with the intellectuals collectively known as the *philosophes*. Mozart came direct-ly into contact with this thought during his half-year in Paris in 1778, in part through his friendship with one of the leading lights of the group, Louise d'Épinay. Leopold had a contact in Paris, Baron Grimm, a solid German moralist, who edited the influential *Correspondance littéraire*, and Grimm shared this with his partner d'Epinay, a close friend of Voltaire, Diderot, d'Holbach, and all the other *philosophes* (although not on good terms with Rousseau). When Mozart's mother died, he moved into d'Epinay's apartment, and while he had many quarrels with Grimm, he got on famously with her; she no doubt brought him up to speed on French thinking, and how that affected correspondence, among other things. In fact, the extensive exchange of letters between Mozart and his father at this time reflects the differences, with Leopold writing in the older German moral style of Gellert, and Mozart adopt-ing the approach of Voltaire and the French, writing in much more deceptive and even dissimulating ways, telling his father what he would want to hear even if it bore scant resemblance to the truth. From Voltaire's thought he also learned of a much more pessimistic world-view than that held by the Germans, that catastrophic random acts of nature such as the great earthquake of Lisbon did not fit into any plan of the universe that could be reconciled with a loving God, that the prevailing view of God seemed to be of one filled with anger, and that the best of all possible worlds often turned out to be illusory. Happy to find something substantial to replace his father's religious and moral views, about which he had misgivings, Mozart cultivated the new way of thinking and infused it into his works, something we see most strikingly in all of his late operas but also in instrumental works such as symphonies.

MOZART'S LAST THREE SYMPHONIES

There has been much speculation about how the final three symphonies came into being, but few facts have emerged. Because no concert venue for them can be positively identified, some have assumed Mozart wrote them for his own satisfaction, as art for art's sake, satisfying a personal urge or inspiration. Writing them with no commission or immediate prospect of performance seems unlikely in the extreme; just because a commission cannot be identified does not preclude its existence, and as the operas will reveal abundantly, having a commission did not in any way prevent Mozart from satisfying his personal inclinations. Haydn had recently been commissioned to write symphonies for performance in London, and while the proposed trip fell through in 1782, he did write three symphonies for that purpose; Mozart may have had a similar commission or believed if he wrote a set of three he would have good prospects there, both for performance and publication. Some also believe that he never had an opportunity to hear these symphonies performed live, although with the demand for symphonies in Vienna and elsewhere, and the regular inclusion of his works in public and private concerts, that too seems unlikely. By 1788 his successful run as a composer of piano concertos for Vienna had all but ended, and the symphony, also immensely popular with Viennese audiences, may have seemed a reasonable way to go. Opera could be risky, despite the recent successes of *The Marriage of Figaro* and *Don Giovanni*, and something solid for the more dependable concert schedule could get him back into circulation in Vienna. As puzzling as the origins of these symphonies may be, the nature of these works presents an even greater challenge.

Symphony No. 39

The first of the three, No. 39 in E flat, shows how radically Mozart had deviated from the Haydn model well established with his Paris symphonies from the mid-1780s. Mozart starts this one with a slow introduction, as he had the Prague Symphony a couple of years earlier, and with trumpets, drums, solid chords, and dotted rhythms starting at a forte level, it generates something of a military atmosphere, a tone that the solo flute very much modifies when it makes its more melodic entry. Dramatic potential appears to have been established with these two contrasting forces, but with the arrival of the allegro exposition, after an introduction almost twice the length of Haydn's at this time, nothing of that drama carries over to the new easy-going theme. Whereas Haydn would give us the characters of the play with his themes in the exposition, Mozart does nothing of the sort, picking up a theme in the new key area every bit as easy-going as the one heard earlier, and no more tonal digression than he required to get from the tonic key to the dominant. With Haydn we would expect a complex exchange in the development section among the dramatic forces presented in the exposition, but since Mozart has not given drama, we will not be surprised that the development also has very little. In fact, his development is so short—less than one-third the length of the exposition—that it ends barely after it begins, with little thematic interplay and only a short conversation between violins and cellos, on the same rhythmic passage from the exposition.

Since no problem has been put forward that needs to be resolved in the recap, as Haydn would have done, Mozart gives a recap almost the clone of the exposition, making the slight adjustments necessary to keep it in the tonic key, and adding a very short coda simply to wrap the movement up. If we imagine that this makes Mozart's movement in some way inferior to Haydn's more dramatic use of sonata form in first movements, we have missed the point; Mozart has intended to give something very different, foreign to the logical procedures of Haydn and his generation, engaging the ear not with conflict but instead with sensuality of sound, with thematic richness and above all orchestration. Throughout the nineteenth century in Germany the symphony would continue on the path of Haydn, and not until the end of that century would the lushness of sound as an end in itself come to the fore, as it did in France, especially in the hands of one of the greatest of all orchestrators, Maurice Ravel, and also Claude Debussy. They had little use for the way Beethoven would direct his audiences, but they adored Mozart and happily acknowledged the debt they owed him. In the first movement of this symphony, Mozart seemed to be almost a century ahead of his time.

This is not to say that drama will be absent from this and the other two symphonies, any more than in Ravel's music, for example in the disintegration of the waltz in his *La Valse*. Mozart seemed to wish to defy expectation, presenting a relatively undramatic first movement, but then realizes it in movements where we least expect it, such as the slow movement. Haydn's slow movements often have a vocal character, behaving in some ways like arias, with a strong melodic line that could be passed among the solo winds or first violin, and some even had an aria form (ABA). In this symphony Mozart opts for something more rondo-like (ABACA), and again he focuses on orchestration at the beginning, making the entire first section sound something like a string quartet, despite the exchanges between cellos and basses in the bottom parts. When the winds enter alone, they herald the beginning of the episode, which in contrast to the gentle meandering of the earlier theme becomes much more aggressive and tense, with some tonal digression and syncopation in the inner strings. We expect the episode of a rondo to contrast the first theme, but to do it this stridently, breaking the peaceful atmosphere of the beginning, comes as a surprise, and it almost borders on terror when the episodic material returns the second time, now with more tonal ambiguity and intensity in the syncopations, seeming to lead to a point of no return, delaying the return of material from the opening section. Listeners familiar with some of Schubert's slow movements, such as the ones from the Quintet in C, the Piano Trio in E flat, or the "Great" Symphony in C, will recognize a possible model, although for Schubert, after the destruction of nostalgia there could be no return to the beauty that once existed. Mozart's short final section may at first seem something of a ruse, but it quickly does take on elements of the more destructive episodic material, with repeated notes and chromatic descending passages. The drama absent from the first movement has now hit with full force in the slow movement, turning our expectation completely on its head and forcing contemplation of something that may have been too good to believe. With the sonata-form finale he returns to brilliance of sound with a lively and engaging theme that permeates the entire movement, and again sparkling orchestration in the way he uses the winds. Oboes usually provided a mainstay in symphonic writing, but Mozart shuns them in this work, finding a new type of richness with the exchanges of flutes, clarinets, bassoons, and horns.

Symphony No. 40

If we hope to find continuity of style or procedures from No. 39 to No. 40, Mozart refuses to give it, making No. 40 as strikingly dissimilar from the one before it as can be. Now he abandons the slow introduction, starting the first movement as though in the middle of things, and also puts it in a minor key, G minor, raising expectations about how a movement in a minor key should behave, with a different level of gravity or emotional intensity than would be likely with a major key. But as we will see from his operas, especially *The Marriage of Figaro*—written two years before this symphony—Mozart can put the most serious arias in major keys and give a minor key any tone or atmosphere that he may wish. The minor theme that begins No. 40 has an almost chameleon-like character, relatively cheerful with its dance rhythm and symmetrical phrasing, simple harmony, and jaunty little accompaniment in the violas. A new theme leads off the second group in the relative major key (B flat), and in contrast to the lightness of the early minor theme, this one has a slightly darker character with its chromatic lines and other kinds of chromatic pulling, but this most untroubled exposition ends with a return to the dance rhythm of the opening theme.

The previous symphony suggested that an easy-going exposition will be followed by a very short and equally relaxed development, but instead, Mozart throws dramatic intensity at us. He at first uses the opening theme, but rather than the previous simple harmony, it now quickly goes off the rails, leading rapidly to tonal points unknown. Anyone who likes to leave the concert whistling the tunes should try these progressions of the main theme in the development, which are so complex they defy even the best musicians to get them right. That tonal complexity gets even more complicated with the dense counterpoint Mozart sets the thematic wandering against, not so much the kind of thematic layering we find in his operatic ensembles (which is the type of counterpoint most often used by Haydn in developments to carry forward the drama), but instead a purer type of counterpoint. This development goes on nearly twice as long as the one from No. 39, and amid the chromatic ambiguity slips almost imperceptibly into the recap. After this upheaval it would be difficult to treat the recap as a clone of the exposition, and Mozart does not, infusing it with tension and nothing relaxed at the end. With this residue of the stressful development, the recap weighs in as a much longer section than the exposition. The source of the tension, unlike Haydn's internal drama emerging from the opposing forces which the themes represent, seems to be imposed from the outside, perhaps, like the earthquake of Lisbon, a destructive force that defies reason or rationale and leaves a mark that cannot be reconciled or removed. The intellectual groundings of the Enlightenment had no capacity to deal with such things, and Mozart's departure from the generation of Haydn and his father places him much closer to our time than theirs.

The edge this symphony has in the first movement continues as the work goes along, with the slow movement finding tension similar to that of the one from No. 39, although now in sonata form instead of a rondo. This movement in E flat major opens with a layering that generates some tension through dissonances that need to resolve, but this always happens in the way that appoggiaturas resolve and make the resolution seem all the more satisfying. Elements of that kind of process continue in the lack of clarity about when the new key arrives and questions about when the second group begins. None of this prepares us for the destructiveness of the development, which continues the type of tension from the development of the first movement, and the recap adds little relief, again remaining off-kilter to the end of the movement. Often the third movement, the Menuetto, can provide relief with a relatively straightforward dance character in 3/4 time, but that does not happen here, as the theme almost immediate shows a preference for 2/4 time, and the metric tension between three and two refuses to go away, except for the more easy-going trio. Then throughout the finale, back in G minor, the tension level remains fairly high, with more of the kind of counterpoint first heard in the development of the first movement, now even turning up in the exposition. Mozart does something fascinating at the beginning of the development: after giving the first phrase of the main theme, he launches into a twelve tone row, entirely audible since the whole orchestra plays it in unison, outmaneuvering Arnold Schoenberg at being a serialist, a century and a quarter before Schoenberg "created" the system. Tone rows (usually) have no tonal orientation, and Mozart uses his at this point to wipe the tonal slate clean, setting things up for the unpredictability of what follows in the development. The coda at the end gives a fittingly rousing conclusion, but this may be something of a ruse, just as the conclusion to *Don*

Giovanni, to be discussed in chapter 8, had been. The grief conjured up throughout a complex and at times irrational work such as this cannot be dismissed by a handful of scales and chords that belt out the perfect cadence and home key.

Symphony No. 41 ("Jupiter")

You are in New York City on one of the hottest days of the year, 21 August 2012, and happily you will beat the heat during the evening because you have a ticket to hear the Mostly Mozart Festival Orchestra at Avery Fisher Hall in Lincoln Center. The program, led by guest conductor Andrew Manze, includes Bach's Orchestral Suite No. 3 in D major, Mendelssohn's Piano Concerto No. 1 with Stephen Hough as the soloist, and Mozart's "Jupiter" Symphony. Partly because of the heat you opt to attend the pre-concert talk at the comfortably cool Kaplan Penthouse in the Rose Building, just behind the Juilliard School of Music, but you also hope to learn why the Mozart symphony has this name. At the lecture you discover that the name "Jupiter" does not actually tell us anything meaningful about this grandest of all Mozart's symphonies, since it was not given by Mozart himself but instead by the impresario Johann Peter Salomon. Many of Haydn's symphonies had names as well, usually given by publishers who thought they might help sales, and they usually signify little more than a quirky preference on the part of the namer, for example, the "Bear" and the "Hen."

The inclination to make sense of symphonies has been with us since Haydn's time, and the lecturer informs the audience that Haydn contributed to that not only with comments but also with the clues he drops in the symphonies themselves, such as with themes that can be identified as having specific associations. Mozart did very little of this in his earlier symphonies, but with No. 41 he seems to have followed Haydn, using themes with associations, particularly in one, which he more or less hangs out as bait for those who wish to dive in and interpret the work's ostensible "meaning." That theme does not come at the beginning of the work, but instead as the first theme of the finale, although enough variants of it turn up in other movements that we feel we know it by the time it comes along in the finale. It consists of four whole notes, given in the first four bars by the first violins, do-re-fa-mi, and then recurs dozens of times in the finale, certainly a simple theme but one with an association. It has been traced, the lecturer notes, to a hymn with the title *"Lucis creator"* (Creator of light), but even more tantalizing is Mozart's use of it in his Missa brevis in F major (K192/ 186f) from 1774, where he set the words "Credo, credo" to it. The lecturer warns you that the awareness of this has led to all sorts of delightful speculation, some of which actually gets things right, although with Mozart, who enjoyed irony, leg pulling, or outright deception, we need to be wary. If this is a credo, the problem of course lies in trying to figure out what that means, since Mozart tends to be much more coy about assigning significance to themes, rhythms, or anything else than Haydn would be. The fact, though, that it turns up in the other movements and then becomes the starting point for the fugal coda of the finale gives some hope to the endeavor. Of course we know none of this until we get to the finale, and connecting it to the rest of the work, where he never states it as overtly as in the finale, depends on some flexibility and resourcefulness in the application of our musical memory.

Despite being none the wiser about the epithet "Jupiter," you walk over to Avery Fisher Hall feeling prepared to sort out some of the complexities of the symphony, and when you hear the forceful figure in full orchestra at the beginning of the first movement, you remember its description as being a *topoi*, or topic, in the grand style. If the movement starts grand, it appears to come down a notch or two with the theme that leads off the second group, now in a much lighter style, although this one temporarily runs aground, cut off by a rest of over a bar which Mozart follows with something seriously disruptive. After much sound and fury, with loud chords and agitated syncopation, that too simply ends, and gives way to an almost folk-like and colloquial closing theme, rounding out the exposition by having veered as far as possible from the grandness of the beginning.

The development begins with a four-note variant of the theme which will dominate the finale, and if we take Mozart's bait, we could be induced to think that he will now show us what's most important. This leads right into the folk-like closing theme, and not just a developing fragment but a full eight-bar phrase of it; he then continues with the extension of that theme, avoiding the grand material altogether and even the lighter second theme. When he finally gets to the opening grand theme, he does so with a false recapitulation—in the wrong key.

With the light treatment of it and tonal meandering, he appears to be toying with it, as though the development is saying we should get past all this grand serious stuff and have some fun. Considering when Mozart wrote this, shortly after *Figaro* and *Don Giovanni*, and only a few years before *The Magic Flute*, there may be something to this. In *The Magic Flute*, we get very contrasting universes set side by side, the serious one of the order led by Sarastro, a Masonic order perhaps, in conflict with the forces led by the Queen of the Night, and a third one of the common folk with no serious aspirations, represented by Papageno. As we shall see in chapter 9, interpretations of that opera which try to make it a celebration of Freemasonry run into all sorts of problems when we note that Mozart gives by far the best music to the Queen and Papageno, not Sarastro or even Tamino!

Connections have certainly been made between this symphony and Freemasonry as well, not least of all with the *Lucis creator* thread, the importance of light in Freemasonry, and the choice of the key for the work—C major, a key often associated with light because it is the same key in which God creates light in Haydn's *Creation*. Perhaps Mozart wishes to throw us off that track, as he appears to do in *The Magic Flute*, holding up the pleasures of the folk-like as the more desirable. The recapitulation, in the end, adds very little to the discussion. If anything, it is remarkably similar to the exposition since there are certainly no dramatic reconciliations or advancements of the musical argument.

If Mozart has presented any sort of creed, he certainly has not hit us over the head with it. That notion continues in the sonata-form slow movement, with its beautifully singable theme (andante cantabile) and lush orchestration, together supplying a glorious sensuality. Third movements (which are usually minuets) in the hands of Haydn could actually steer things in the direction of peasant culture, letting the more rustic ländler, instead of the courtly minuet, set the tone for the movement. But Mozart does nothing of the sort, avoiding the leaps and rhythms of the ländler with smooth and sophisticated lines. In the trio of this movement, though, he does have some fun, starting it with a perfect cadence—what we would expect at the end of the phrase, not the beginning—and in fact he makes the cadence at the end of the phrase weaker than the one at the beginning. Mozart may have well intended this backwards approach in order to turn things upside down by giving a little jab at the courtly minuet. Perhaps it is no surprise that he follows this immediately after the double bar line with very clear variants of the four-note "credo" motif, given three times, each time in an altered variant. After those twelve bars we get the cadence as a beginning instead of an ending, twice in fairly rapid succession, as if to say the backwards, upside-down approach may be more than a mere joke. He could probably depend on much of his audience not getting it, just as they would not get the joke he plays on moralists at the end of *Don Giovanni*.

The finale to this symphony gets most of the attention, and rightly so, with its thematic richness, contrapuntal complexity at various points, brilliance of orchestration, and most of all, a coda that gathers five of the themes from the movement and combines them in some extraordinary fugal writing. That fugal writing (it's not a full fugue), following the sonata-form movement, would have done credit to J. S. Bach, whose music Mozart had studied, thanks to the prompting of Baron van Swieten, who had Bach's works played at his musical salons. Some like to think of this as the crowning glory of Mozart's symphonic output, if not his whole career, but writing this kind of counterpoint was not such a great challenge for someone with his brain. I certainly do not mean to belittle it; of course it's a great achievement, but the unity which it appears to embrace may not be entirely straightforward. Something of that misgiving comes through in the way that the counterpoint ends, on a motif that had not been a part of the counterpoint, one fairly light in character with folk-like dance rhythms, and certainly altogether more jovial than the formal fugal exercise just heard. This happened to be the last thing that Mozart wrote for orchestra, but certainly not by design; his career took him in other directions in the remaining three years of his life, and had he lived to a normal age, he surely would have written more symphonies. He may with these last three symphonies have made statements about himself, about the society he lived in, or he may have simply been writing wonderful music to be enjoyed in its own right. What sets great music such as this apart is that we can listen to it over and over, each time hear something new in it, and not have to settle on any one particular way of thinking about it.

3

THE FRIENDSHIP WITH HAYDN

Chamber Music

While symphonies mainly appealed to a listening audience in public settings, composers during the eighteenth century wrote just as much for people to play for their own enjoyment, with or without an audience. Generally this type of private music would be for relatively small ensembles, one player per part, with two distinctly different categories in Mozart's Austria: "Kenner" (connoisseur), and "Liebhaber" (lover/amateur). We will encounter the Liebhaber in chapter 6, the player of solo keyboard music, which was usually a woman during Mozart's time. The Kenner more often than not was a man who played a string or wind instrument, typically at an advanced level, and would meet with a few musical friends to play chamber music for just about any combination of instruments with roughly equally challenging parts for all. Despite the almost unlimited number of possibilities for combinations, which could put men and women together if that combination included a piano, certain ones emerged as more popular than others and evolved into distinctive genres that appealed to both players and composers. The number of instruments in the ensemble could be as low as two, in fact any two, but the upper limit, going from duos, trios, quartets, quintets, or higher, becomes a little more troublesome to pin down, since if too many instruments participate, the term "chamber" may no longer be appropriate. In the nineteenth century septets, octets, and nonets became more common, but during the eighteenth century most pieces that we now consider to be chamber music had no more than five parts. Mozart, though, liked to write divertimentos and serenades for larger groups of wind players, in one case for as many as thirteen parts, and while this may push the boundary, I will include at least one such piece in this chapter. In fact, for the eighteenth century, the term "chamber music" included almost every kind of instrumental music, including symphonies.

In symphonies different combinations of instruments can be used to produce the exact type of sound the composer wishes, but with chamber music, let us say a trio for piano, violin, and cello, with the entire work written for that combination, a very different type of dynamic takes hold, whereby the composer tries to get as much as possible from that mixture of these three timbres. That particular ensemble sets up a contrasting blend of piano with two strings, and the combinations can also be for three (or more) similar instruments, or ones with even greater contrasts, such as piano, clarinet, and viola, all of which Mozart tried. The ensembles can be more off the wall as well, creating some fairly strange combinations, such as two clarinets and three basset horns (Adagio, K411), or two basset horns and bassoon (Adagio, K410). Most of us will likely never hear these works, but we can get some idea of how they may sound from the very first music we hear in *Citizen Kane*, scored by Bernard Herrmann for three muted horns and three bassoons. I used to wonder who would have thought of such a combination to create the eerie atmosphere at the beginning of this film but Herrmann, until I remembered that Mozart may have. For combinations as strange as this Mozart wrote very few works, preferring in his wind ensembles mixtures of oboes, clarinets, horns, and bassoons, occasionally also flutes, basset horns, or English horns.

By far the most likely combination of instruments that Mozart wrote chamber music for is two violins, viola, and cello, with just over two dozen of these—the string quartet. With chamber music even more than the symphony, and especially the string quartet, Haydn comes into the picture, since in this case we can say fairly safely that he actually invented the genre, and every other composer that wrote these owed him a debt. If that composer was not only a contemporary but a friend, as with Mozart, the debt takes on a very different urgency than it would later for Beethoven, Schubert, or, much later, Shostakovich and Bartók. As the inventor, Haydn took it through its growing pains over a number of decades, although it seems unlikely that the way he described the origin to one of his biographers just a few years before he died—roughly half a century after the fact—depicts the way it actually happened. According to the biographer, Haydn reported that

> The following, purely coincidental circumstance led him to try his hand at the composition of quartets. A Baron Fürnberg had an estate in Weinzierl, several stages from Vienna; and from time to time he invited his parish priest, his estates' manager, Haydn and Albrechtsberger (a brother of the well-known contrapuntist, who played the violoncello) in order to have a little music. Fürnberg asked Haydn to write something that could be played by these four friends of the Art. Haydn, who was then eighteen years old, accepted the proposal, and so originated his first Quartet . . . which, immediately upon its appearance, received such uncommon applause as to encourage him to continue in the *genre*.

It's a delightful story—the string quartet invented by a teenager writing for a party of friends who happened to play these instruments—and Haydn may have bent things a little to make himself sound a bit more like a prodigy, since by this point everyone compared him with Mozart. He neglected to point out that during the first two decades that he wrote quartets, he never specified the cello as the low instrument, simply instead putting in "basso," which could refer to any bass instrument and linked the quartet with the older trio sonata, with its basso continuo. In the earliest ones, that appeared to be the style, since the bass line lacked individuality, serving a harmonic function, as did the second violin and viola as well.

The growing pains for the quartet involved the transformation from a solo line with accompaniment to an integrated texture with potential equality for each part, something we can give Haydn the credit for accomplishing. Once he found his feet as a writer of quartets, Haydn became fairly prolific at it, although not quite as fertile as was thought at one time. As an undergraduate my music curriculum included a delightful quartet in F, Haydn's Op. 3, no. 5, taught to us as an especially fine example of his early style, but when a decade later this set of six quartets was shown not to be by Haydn but instead by Romanus Hofstetter, it quickly became a fairly mediocre work. It's remarkable how author identification changes our perception of quality. With those six gone others dropped out as well, for a variety of reasons such as oboe and horn parts turning up, so the actual number stands at less than the eighty-three originally thought to exist, but still Haydn's achievement can only be described as staggering. As Haydn's new quartets came out, Mozart snapped them up as enthusiastically as the players they were written for, and he took very special notice of the Op. 33 set of six, issued in 1781. Publishers often brought quartets out in sets of six, certainly with most of Haydn's, and then for Mozart's Op. 10 set as well as Beethoven's Op. 18.

HAYDN'S "NEW WAY"

When Haydn released his Op. 33 quartets to subscribers, he did so with a notation that he wrote them in "a new and special way." Some have put this down to nothing but salesmanship, considering how advanced the previous set from nine years ago, Op. 20, had been; of course he would not say he wrote them in the same old way, even if he had. In fact, he did not, since they reveal some striking new approaches, ones that went a long way in defining the quartet as a genre for the next century and a half. Well acquainted with the salon scene in Vienna and the important role of literature in these larger or smaller gatherings, he seemed to realize that music could function in a similar way, and that nothing could do this better than the string quartet. Certain types of literature, and especially the new genre that was all the rage, the novel, had a very intimate nature, both in content and the appeal to an audience. Some of the earliest novels were epistolary, as exchanges of letters among a fairly small number of characters, and those characters interacted with each other in intensely conversational ways. Seldom at the time would someone read a novel alone, but more often than not reading would be done in small groups—with family members, among friends, or at salons—again underlining the interactive conversational feature. Aside from these aspects of novels and their reading environment, people practiced proper etiquette of conversation at these small gatherings, even with guidebooks on how to do it, such as Adolf Knigge's *Über den Umgang mit Menschen* (On dealings with people), a copy of which Haydn owned.

What Haydn accomplished with his new quartets, already apparent in previous ones, was a more intensively conversational relationship among the four players, putting them all on equal footing with a sense of unified purpose, in which each player recognizes his individual importance as well as the role he plays in creating the whole. Later in the century quartets became more public types of works, with professional quartets playing them in similar venues as symphonies, but in the 1780s they remained more private than public, and like novels, moral weeklies, and poetry, they appealed to individuals who could enjoy them in their own homes, with families, or in small social gatherings. Haydn's favorite writer, Christian Fürchtegott Gellert, emphasized this attraction of literature over and over, and Haydn thought about some of his works in the same way, writing in response to a fan that "you happily persuade me . . . that I am often the enviable means by which you, and so many families sensible to heartfelt emotion, derive, in their homely circle, their pleasure—their enjoyment." As a regular, along with Mozart, at these types of gatherings in Vienna, Haydn went to them not only for the good Parmesan cheese and strudel.

No type of music suited these gatherings better than the string quartet, something which even theoretical writers on music at the time, such as Heinrich Koch, confirmed, and with Op. 33 we see this blossoming in a new way. Writers in our time have recognized this as well, perhaps none more vividly than Charles Rosen, who put it this way: "The isolated character of the classical phrase and the imitation of speech rhythms in all of Haydn's chamber music only enhance the air of conversation. . . . The eighteenth century was cultivatedly self-conscious about the art of conversation: among its greatest triumphs are the quartets of Haydn." This plays out in the ways that the four parts relate to each other, with writing that does not focus on melody and harmony (although it can at times) but instead allows the four parts to interact with each other in ways that may give any part the potential to carry the melody, may shift subtly within one part from melody to accompaniment, or may be contrapuntal with all four parts treated equally. Occasionally Haydn writes an entire movement as a fugue, as he did twice with finales in Op. 20, but more often than not the counterpoint takes a more modern form, perhaps even related to the kinds of conversational exchanges that go on in operatic ensembles, in which three or four people can all speak at the same time, and because of the musical setting all can be heard individually.

By moving this type of writing toward operatic ensembles, something distinctive to comic opera, quartets in the hands of Haydn often included comic features, which could be recognized as such from corresponding types of comic passages in opera, from tricks that the music could play on our expectations, or from the rustically cheerful atmosphere of folk music. Haydn used all of these, to the annoyance of some of his critics who disapproved of anything comical in serious music, but certainly to the enjoyment of those who played his quartets. Some of this takes the principle of equality even further than the relationship among the four players, as social issues could be introduced—focusing on common people by way of folk music while replacing the courtly minuet movements with scherzos, some of which came closer to the rustic ländler, a dance also in a triple meter but having exaggerated leaps unlike the graceful minuet. Sometimes the comic passages could even be directed at a specific target, as happens in the finale of Op. 33, no. 1, which appears to draw a line between the old and new, placing Haydn definitely on the side of the new. In this movement, after a fairly extended passage that sounds as though it could be by Vivaldi or one of his contemporaries, Haydn introduces a comic passage which seems to thumb its nose at the old style, not necessarily out of disrespect for the old, but more as a way of saying that we have moved on. Many critics at the time believed that Haydn wrote nothing but drivel compared to the great masters of the past, and gestures such as this may have been aimed at least partly at them, for the enjoyment of his supporters.

MOZART'S "HAYDN" QUARTETS

When Artaria published the six quartets Mozart wrote between 1782 and 1785 in Vienna in 1785, they appeared with this dedication to Haydn, written in Italian:

> To my dear friend Haydn,
>
> A father who had decided to send out his sons into the great world, thought it his duty to entrust them to the protection and guidance of

a man who was very celebrated at the time and who, moreover, happened to be his best friend.

In like manner I send my six sons to you, most celebrated and very dear friend. They are, indeed, the fruit of a long and laborious study; but the hope which many friends have given me that this toil will be in some degree rewarded, encourages me and flatters me with the thought that these children may one day prove a source of consolation to me.

During your last stay in the capital you yourself, my very dear friend, expressed to me your approval of these compositions. Your good opinion encourages me to offer them to you and leads me to hope that you will not consider them wholly unworthy of your favour. Please then receive them kindly and be to them a father, guide and friend! From this moment I surrender to you all my rights over them. I entreat you, however, to be indulgent to those faults which may have escaped a father's partial eye, and, in spite of them, to continue your generous friendship towards one who so highly appreciates it. Meanwhile I remain with all my heart, dearest friend, your most sincere friend

W. A. Mozart (LMF 891–92)

This seems a perfectly gracious and generous outpouring from Mozart, but not everyone, including myself in *Mozart in Revolt*, has been prepared to take it at face value, especially when we consider the nature of these quartets in comparison to Haydn's most recent ones. Haydn had a much bigger reputation than Mozart at this time, and the incessant repetition of the word "friend" (nine times) may be Mozart's attempt to portray himself to potential subscribers and the general public as Haydn's equal. Of course they were good friends, but Mozart could not help but be competitive, and maybe even intended to show himself superior to the inventor of the quartet.

It made sense to write this dedication in Italian, the language of high culture in Vienna, but it also gave more opportunity to work in a little irony through the pompousness of the style. In a letter to his father immediately after the death of his mother, Mozart repeated the phrase "God's will" so many times that it rouses suspicion, getting himself and others off the hook for not doing more to save her. In this case the combination of the repetition with the image of Haydn as godfather of the works raises a red flag, invoking Mozart's sorry relationship with his own father, where little remained that could be salvaged. Haydn had no children of his own, and no doubt liked to be considered a father/mentor to Mozart, but as an artful letter writer, Mozart possibly signaled something amiss; Haydn may have been the "father" of the string quartet, but perhaps a father who would be hard pressed even to grasp his son's spectacular accomplishments with this medium. The verification of this must lie in the works themselves, and it's difficult not to recognize that Mozart went far beyond Haydn at this point.

Whether Mozart surpassed Haydn or not, he clearly learned much from studying the older master's quartets, as many of his borrowed ideas make amply evident—one of the most striking being the use of humor. The two of them fairly regularly attended the salons held by their mutual friend Franz Sales von Greiner. Greiner's daughter, Caroline Pichler, an avid writer and observer of Viennese life, while noticing the two of them at these salons, remained completely unimpressed by two of the great geniuses in the city, commenting that they had "an ordinary cast of mind, and made flat jokes." It's staggering to think that she would say nothing more about them, even if they weren't the liveliest conversationalists in this milieu; as for their jokes, one suspects that the brand of humor coming from these two country lads simply didn't appeal to her more gentrified urban taste. In fact, it would be fun to try to imagine the kinds of jokes they did tell, especially to each other, considering that both of them relished lavatory humor (as did Beethoven); we know Mozart's through his letters to his naughty cousin "the Bäsle," some of his friends, and even his mother. Haydn didn't hesitate to put it right into his music, as he did with the great bassoon joke in the slow movement of Symphony No. 93, where the well-prepared, loud, and low solo blat from the bassoon certainly sounds like a fart.

Both of them laced their quartets with humor, although not the type just noted, and while some of the humor seems to cross over, in many respects they made their jokes in cultural idioms foreign to each other. Where similarities exist, Haydn clearly had taken the lead, such as the end of the finale of Op. 33, no. 2, a quartet now known as "The Joke" because of how it stops. Haydn sets us up for it with an adagio passage near the end of this presto finale, slowing things down drastically to get our attention. With the quick return to presto, he repeats the opening motif of the movement four times, each one separated by two bars of rests, following a progression that reaches the concluding cadence on the fourth of these phrases. Musical logic tells us that the work has ended, and that seems to be confirmed by the silence that follows, in fact almost five bars of it. If played in public, the audience would applaud at this point, but Haydn then cheekily throws in a fifth go at the motif, very quietly but still enough to make the applauders feel silly. The joke works, and we can laugh at ourselves for being fooled by it. It may be a fairly saucy form of musical humor, but Mozart liked it and did something very similar in the first of his Haydn quartets, K387, bringing the exposition of the first movement and the recapitulation as well to an end with the appropriate cadence, but then after a short rest adding another two impudent bars of cadence, completely unnecessary, and evoking more of a chuckle than the guffaws at the end of Haydn's quartet.

Of these quartets, the last one, K465, has rightly attracted most of the attention, but the others should not be ignored, especially the first one, with the cadence just noted, and here we find no shortage of humor in just about every movement. In comparison to Haydn's quartets, though, this humor works in very different ways, avoiding the more rustic quips that Haydn likes, and generally aiming for something more sophisticated—something that the likes of Caroline Pichler would appreciate. Some of this involves counterpoint, which Mozart had immersed himself in with his studies in Italy as a youth with the great pedagogue Padre Martini, and more recently in Vienna at the salons of Baron Gottfried van Swieten, a passionate lover of Bach's fugues. Critics who disparaged the direction of new music late in the eighteenth century could always point to counterpoint as the missing link—that the new composers simply dabbled in child's play, unable to develop complex counterpoint. Haydn appeared to concede to some of this thinking, writing fugues in the finales of two of his Op. 20 quartets, but otherwise not including excessively complex counterpoint in his quartets; he opted to challenge notions of the past in other ways, as in the finale of Op. 33, no. 1 just noted. Mozart seemed to take a different view of the matter, certainly mastering the art of fugue writing, especially in some of his keyboard works, but in quartets he went about it in what may seem a surprising way. He avoids fugues here, but occasionally launches into something that sounds like the beginning of a fugue, making it fugue- or fugato-like because of the relative brevity, as happens near the beginning of K387. The opening theme of this quartet lends itself nicely to this kind of handling, and in fact eleven bars in it gets the fugal treatment, though lasting only a few bars. He moves from this to something fairly tongue-in-cheek, a cheerfully impish little theme that may even mock what has just happened, and the movement then seems a play between the learned fugal style and nose-thumbing at it.

That type of exchange becomes even more pronounced in the finale, where a five-note motif, not unlike the prominent four-note one from the beginning of the finale of the Jupiter Symphony, leads off the movement as though it were a fugue, this time with all four voices participating. After sixteen bars it simply stops, and a dance-like theme—possibly a contredanse with its own subversive associations—takes over, first with a simple accompaniment and then with counterpoint that seems more conversational than formal, allowing the parts to chat about things in a lighthearted way, as may happen in the ensemble of a comic opera. After this a new fugue-like section begins, it receives the same type of response that the first contrapuntal section had, and in fact the entire finale becomes an exchange of these two contrasting types, with counterpoint never getting the upper hand. Parallels can be found here to what Haydn had done with his confrontation between old and new in Op. 33, no. 1, but Mozart takes it to a much more sophisticated level, using fugue-like writing as one of the combatants, and providing something dance-like with possible topical associations as the antidote instead of the earthier type of musical jokes used by Haydn. Humor dominates the Minuetto movement as well, which Mozart accomplishes not by replacing the minuet with a scherzo, but by humorously manipulating the minuet itself, already in the third bar starting as alternation of piano and forte that puts the music in 2/4 time instead of the expected 3/4. Even the andante cantabile third movement plays with a certain amount of contrast between serious and comic, as the gently singable theme occasionally gives way to some fairly impish passages.

Over the few years that Mozart wrote these quartets, humor gradually became less a factor; K421 still has touches of it, but very little turns up in the later ones. At the same time the type of contrapuntal writing so prominent in K387 also receded, as though he had resolved the issue earlier on, and then moved on to other types of writing. In fact, the later ones sound less and less like Haydn's Op. 33 quartets, Mozart very distinctively putting his stamp on them in ways that set them apart from Haydn's. At the most basic level, Mozart's tend to be significantly longer, with his shortest of the set about the same length as Haydn's longest, and some, such as K421, K464, and K465 almost twice as long as some of Haydn's shorter ones. Length may not seem all that important, but indirectly it is, since the length of any given movement bears directly on the procedures of motivic working and development. If the composer has little to say in this respect, as Haydn does in his scherzos, they will be short, seldom more than half the length of Mozart's minuets (for both composers these can appear as either second or third movements). First movements are more or less comparable in length, but not so other movements; never, as one would expect, does Mozart make his longer with mere filler, but always, as with slow movements, he gives them great substance, often cantabile material that reminds us of characters' arias such as that of the Countess in *The Marriage of Figaro*. Here especially he goes beyond the kind of affective largos and andantes preferred by Haydn into something that not only evokes a particular emotion but draws us into something larger, where the emotions take on a kind of human immediacy. Haydn probably sensed that Mozart had surpassed him, but ever the gracious and modest man, after hearing Mozart's quartets early in 1785, he made his opinion clear to Mozart's father, who happened to be visiting Vienna at that time: "Before God, and as an honest man I tell you that your son is the greatest composer known to me either in person or by name. He has taste, and, what is more, the most profound knowledge of composition."

By the time Mozart reached the last of these six quartets, K465, he inhabited a musical planet entirely unlike any of his contemporaries, including Haydn. Most strikingly, he started this quartet with a slow introduction, and not just any adagio introduction. By this time Haydn fairly routinely used them for his symphonies, in half of the six Paris symphonies and later all but one of the twelve English symphonies, but he assiduously avoided them in quartets, only once starting a quartet with a slow introduction (Op. 71, no. 2, from the mid-1790s). Mozart, then, had waded into uncharted waters starting a quartet this way in 1785, and the stunning character of this introduction pushed this work more into the public domain, with fascination for not only the players but also a listening audience. For this work in C major, often a festive or celebratory key at the time, Mozart begins with the cello by itself, repeating C on eighth notes—so far so good. The viola comes in next, on an A flat, followed by the second violin on E flat, throwing the tonality of C out the window as the chord seems to be A flat. When the first violin enters on an A natural, all orientation vanishes; by now the viola has started to move, preventing the clash of A against A flat, but still, we have no idea where this may be heading, and along with the frequent short chromatic passages in all the parts, Mozart generates the effect that contributes to the nickname of this quartet: "Dissonance." Twenty-two bars later it settles on the right cadence for C major, but almost everything before that, with apparent independence of will in all the separate parts, chromatic passages, and appoggiaturas, no stability emerges, to the point that we seem to have a representation of chaos. Not coincidentally, when Haydn represented chaos at the beginning of *The Creation* over a decade later, he started with harmonic dissonance very similar to what Mozart uses here.

When Haydn started symphonies with slow introductions, especially in the English symphonies, he often linked them to the fast material that follows, either motivically or harmonically, integrating the intros into the dramatic fabric of the first movement (and occasionally the entire work) in a way that allows the listener to hear the contrast as a confrontation of opposing forces; as the movement develops it addresses this conflict, sometimes with resolution, but more often showing the possibility of coexistence. When Mozart begins the allegro part of this movement, no hint of the introduction clouds the sunny atmosphere of the new theme, although as the movement unfolds, both in the exposition and development, a type of contrapuntal writing develops that does seem related to the introduction, with repeated eighth notes in the cello against counterpoint in the other voices with touches of chromaticism. Later in the recapitulation, and especially in the coda, this type of writing takes over, seeming to create a kind of drama in which the cheerful allegro appears to be susceptible to the chaos from the beginning, unable to free itself from the darker forces. The human drama that unfolds continues in the andante cantabile second movement, which more than any in these quartets resembles an aria by the Countess in *Figaro*, specifically "Porgi amor," using similar phrasing gestures and syncopation. The regret the Countess sings of could be the appropriate response here as well to what has happened in the first movement. Mozart appears to have steered this quartet toward opera, which he soon returned to with *Figaro* in 1786, making it much more than an entertainment for connoisseurs.

QUINTETS AND MORE

With the string quartet a thoroughly established genre by the early 1780s, adding another instrument to the mix made something very different than a quartet plus one, or simply thickening the texture. Unlike Haydn, Mozart liked combinations of five instruments, and while he may have surpassed Haydn with string quartets in 1785, his foray into string quintets, with all but a single early one coming after this time, unfurled a chamber music league of his own. If another stringed instrument were to be added, different choices existed: it could be another viola, another cello, or maybe even a double bass. A generation later Schubert would add an additional cello to his one string quintet, perhaps surprisingly because of his favored viola; Mozart wrote six string quintets altogether, five between 1787 and 1791, and all of them use two violas. His interest in quintets went beyond strings with other combinations, bringing winds in as well, with one for horn and strings, another for clarinet and strings, and perhaps the most unusual combination excluding strings altogether, for piano, oboe, clarinet, horn, and bassoon. The differences between quartets and quintets extended to the issue of publishing as well, since a ready market existed for quartets, while quintets tended to be for players at a higher skill level. Only a professional of the highest order, such as Mozart's friend Anton Stadler, could play the clarinet quintet, and the great difficulty of the piano part in the quintet for piano and winds meant only Mozart or someone comparable to him could play it.

Even more basic differences existed, related to the way that Mozart treated the interaction of the parts. His first string quintet, from 1773, does not show his potential with this combination, but when he took it up again almost a decade and a half later, with two written back to back in 1787, K515 in C major and K516 in G minor, he quickly revealed how unlike a quartet a quintet can be. Written within a month of each other, they seem to form a pair, not unlike the piano concertos K466 (D minor) and K467 (C major), although we should not put too much stock into the differences between major and minor. The two concertos, as chapter 5 will note, could not be more in contrast, but these two quintets do not in any way stand as polar opposites. Some writers have tried to make them out to be that, with one even convinced that the G minor quintet is a tragic work, reflecting the profound disappointments in

Mozart's life at this time—having been abandoned by the concert-going public—but that seems unlikely in the extreme, both from the nature of the music and the unfolding of his career. Mozart knew Vienna well enough to understand how fickle its audiences could be. If they no longer had the attention span for his concertos, he could move on to something else, as he did with opera, and if the Viennese proved too dense to grasp them, audiences elsewhere would understand, as they did in Prague. Trying to draw parallels between life and works in this sort of way can be risky at the best of times, although by no means impossible, but if it's done, as it certainly can be with Schubert, the works themselves have to sustain the argument, which K516 does not.

A more probable way of looking at these quintets concerns the focus on sound itself, as other writers have suggested, not unlike my description in the previous chapter on symphonies. This is not to say these quintets lack the ability to stir the listeners' emotions, especially the slow movements, but their balance of serious and lighter qualities, including K516, makes them anything but tragic. On paper it may seem that the differences from quartets are not all that great, but the addition of a second viola—which can take a leading role, as it often does, especially in slow movements—gives an entirely unique quality to the sound. These works more often than not would be played for a listening audience, not unlike symphonies, and they engage that audience not so much through the drama created by tension in harmony and interaction of themes, but more through the delights of the sound itself, finding striking combinations among the strings. Also, the nature of the counterpoint most frequently used here, unlike the learned techniques of fugue or fugato belonging to J. S. Bach's era, points more toward the modern approach of interaction of the voices generated by motivic writing.

That focus on sound becomes even more pronounced in the quintets that include other instruments, such as a single horn or clarinet. In this case he wrote them for friends who played those wind instruments at a virtuoso level, again making them works intended for public performance by professionals. He also wrote concertos for the horn player Joseph Leutgeb and clarinetist Anton Stadler, and the quintets, K407 and K622, should not be thought of as mini concertos, placing the instrument as a soloist with a small string ensemble. Mozart took the opportunity with these once again to play with the possibilities of unique combinations of sound, and while the wind or string instruments may from time to time be isolated as soloists, the greater emphasis is on the way the sounds of all five of them come together. Featuring the horn at this time had special challenges since, unlike the modern horn, the one in Mozart's time lacked keys, meaning pitch changes had to be achieved within the limitations of the overtone series, by the player manipulating the embouchure to find the different pitches. Doing this in ways other than the usual role of relatively straightforward harmonic backup, as happens in symphonies, required players of unusual ability, such as Leutgeb, but even so, it constrained what Mozart could write, and the horn quintet and concertos do not reach the same level of works written for most other instruments.

By the time Mozart wrote works that feature the clarinet, a keying system had been developed which gave the instrument considerable versatility, and with the Clarinet Concerto, K622, we find one of the great achievements of his career, to be discussed in chapter 5. Writing a quintet for piano and four wind instruments raised even more interesting possibilities for sound, and Mozart exploited this to the fullest with K452 by writing in such a way that each instrument gets a part distinctive to it, whether in ensemble, featured singly, or in smaller groups. The oboe and clarinet share melodic and thematic passages, the horn has more distinctive inner voice characteristics, the bassoon brings up the lowest line with harmonic writing, and the piano can do just about anything, but it especially adds rapid figuration impossible on any of the other instruments. Even topics could be introduced, especially if the instrument itself had topical associations, such as the horn with hunting, or the bassoon with buffa passages.

SERENADE FOR WINDS

It's late September 1984, and you're at the Oxford Theater on Quinpool Street, the only old-style single auditorium movie house left in Halifax, Nova Scotia; you've come to see a new film about Mozart by Milos Forman, a director you know well from his work both in the former Czechoslovakia and in the U.S. This film, *Amadeus*, based on the play of the same name by Peter Shaffer, also has Shaffer as the screenwriter, and since you know some of his other plays, such as *Equus* and *The*

Royal Hunt of the Sun, you arrive at the Oxford not expecting a biopic (more description of this comes in chapter 10). The first sixteen minutes of the film confirm your assumption, since almost everything here features not Mozart but Antonio Salieri (played by F. Murray Abraham), the one-time powerful court composer of the Habsburg Empire and now in old age confined to an insane asylum. Here he speaks to a priest and narrates the story of his pact with God to give him the means to be a great composer; God, in his opinion, prevents this by placing the godless genius Mozart in his way. He tells the priest how he first encountered Mozart (Tom Hulce) at the Vienna residence of the archbishop of Salzburg. While hiding in a side room, he sees a young woman and man playing scatological and sexual games on the floor, but has no idea who they are. Suddenly the young man hears music and exclaims they have started his music without him; Salieri watches in astonishment as the person playing these debauched games rushes out and takes over conducting the adagio of his Serenade in B flat for 13 wind instruments, K361.

Mozart gets a disgusted look from the archbishop, and with a fleeting glance you can see that the ensemble he conducts consists of two oboes, two clarinets, two basset horns, four horns, two bassoons, and a double bass (the score indicates this can replace a contrabassoon, which can be hard to find). This combination of instruments produces a stunning sound; if works can be written for strings by themselves, why not winds, and Mozart did this more than once. Shaffer has a limited regard for historical accuracy, and this 1781 event turns out to be one of many oversights, since Mozart did not write this serenade until 1783 or a year later; no one but a musicologist will be troubled by this. Whether we should think of works such as this serenade as chamber music also need not concern us. Mozart certainly took his emphasis on sound itself as far as it would go with this unusual but stunningly beautiful combination of winds.

After the performance of the adagio, Salieri goes up to the music stand to look at the score, and his remarks (even more extensive in the play) give you a very nice sense of what Mozart achieved with the combinations of sounds and the ways that specific instruments could be featured. At first Salieri's musings seem to be a voice-over of his thoughts, but they shift in a flash ahead to the asylum as he converses with the priest:

On the page it looked, nothing—the beginning simple, almost comic, just a pulse—bassoons, basset horns, like a rusty squeeze box. And then, suddenly, high above it, an oboe, a single note hanging there, unwavering, until a clarinet took it over, sweeping it into a phrase of such delight. This was no composition by a performing monkey; this was a music I had never heard, filled with such longing, such unfulfillable longing. It seemed to me that I was hearing the voice of God. [Mozart steps in front of him and grabs the music.] But why, why would God choose an obscene child to be his instrument?

You can identify with this description, referring to a phrase that delights instead of something heavily laden with emotions tugging at the heartstrings. You will hear many other performances of Mozart's music in this film, occasionally with very perceptive comments by the star of the film—letting Salieri do the work of a pre- (or post-) concert commentator. (Or that of a writer of a companion to Mozart's works!) The pleasure that exudes from these remarks finds the right spirit for the enjoyment of this music.

4

IN THE REALM OF JOSEPH II

The Abduction from the Seraglio

After sixteen months on the road looking for better employment than the pedestrian position waiting for him in Salzburg, Mozart returned home in January 1779 with no prospects, with hardly any new compositions, and to a furious father. He knew his best chance to escape the drudgery of Salzburg, without ending up as a court organist somewhere else or in some other menial musical job that would leave him with less respect than a lackey, lay in opera, but for that he needed a commission. While traveling through Augsburg, Munich, Mannheim, and Paris he thought much about opera, and from time to time even convinced his father in his letters that he had one in the works, although when nearing home he had to invent excuses for not being able to produce the manuscript—such as claiming it ended up in the wrong truck en route to Russia. We can safely assume such works were phantoms intended to get his father off his back. At one point Mozart told his father he had to break off writing to him because he was up to his ears setting an adaptation of Voltaire's *Sémiramis*, but no evidence exists that he ever actually started it.

In the case of another work by Voltaire, *Zaïre*, Mozart did set to work on an adaptation in 1780 while biding his time in Salzburg, completing two of the three acts. The story, like many popular ones at the time set in a Turkish harem, had potential, despite losing much of its bite in Johann Andreas Schachtner's version. It pits Muslims against

Christians, something that strikes a resonant chord today, and gives no moral preference for either side, showing both capable of brutality and compassion. Mozart's father, cut from the older, conservative German cloth, hated everything about Voltaire, gloating at his death that the dog Voltaire had kicked the bucket, but Mozart did not share Leopold's bias; the subject of the unfinished opera which has come to be known as *Zaide* no doubt attracted him because of its principles of human equality. Mozart attempted this one without a commission, naively hoping it could be staged in Salzburg or Vienna, and the half-baked enterprise revealed something of the desperation he felt about changing his fortune and place of residence.

On his way back to Salzburg he had just been in Munich, a great musical center since the court in Mannheim, with its magnificent orchestra, had moved to Munich, presided over by Count Joseph Anton Seeau, whom Mozart had met in Mannheim along with musicians and other members of the court, and Seeau gave Mozart his big break. The commission for a serious opera arrived in 1780, and while he could start working on it in Salzburg, by November he had to move to Munich for a number of reasons involving production, but mainly to work with the singers and write specifically for their voices. The theatrically inexperienced librettist for *Idomeneo*, Giambattista Varesco, happened to be the archbishop's chaplain in Salzburg, and since Mozart needed revisions from him on a regular basis, he arranged that Leopold should be the intermediary for getting from Varesco what he required. Happily the full correspondence between father and son on the composition of *Idomeneo* has survived, giving us fascinating insights into the compositional process and demands placed by Mozart on a librettist. This correspondence, though, like any between Mozart and his father, needs to be read as strategic rather than factual, as I have described in my book *Mozart in Revolt*. Mozart had to get from the exchange what he needed while at the same time avoiding the inevitable interference from Leopold, and this he accomplished by saying things about the opera he had no intention of actually doing. After the horrible rift between the two of them a couple of years earlier, it seemed to work, and father and sister packed their bags for the trip to the premiere of *Idomeneo* in Munich late in January of 1781.

Before the sojourn to Paris in 1777–1779 Mozart had already written nine operas, starting at the tender age of eleven, but none of these youthful works put him on the operatic map as *Idomeneo* would, now a mature opera with potential for performances elsewhere. Still, that proved not enough to dislodge him from his detested position in Salzburg, and for the time being he had no choice but to return to those tedious duties and do the archbishop's bidding. Fortunately that involved travel to Vienna, where the archbishop kept a second residence, and while there Colloredo had his entourage with him to make the appropriate impression on the court of Joseph II, emperor of the great Habsburg Empire; of course he had to be there for Joseph's accession to the throne early in 1781. Already well known to the Viennese, Mozart arrived on 16 March, but Colloredo treated him as nothing more than a servant, for example forbidding him to play at the salon of Countess Thun for the emperor, where he could have earned half his annual Salzburg salary with one performance. Clearly he could do better as a freelancer, and in opposition to his father's insistence that he stay in Colloredo's service and pay off the debt from the trip two years earlier, Mozart gave the archbishop his resignation. Tired of being obsequious, Mozart appears to have told his employer what he thought of him and his backwater court, and taking this even further with the chief steward, Count Arco, Mozart's freedom came with the famous kick in the arse from Arco early in June.

If things were not already bad enough between Mozart and his father, since Leopold seriously doubted his son could make ends meet in a city with a short attention span, they got much worse when he floated the idea of marrying Constanze Weber, the third of four daughters of Fridolin Weber. Fridolin had recently died, so Frau Weber took the family to Vienna and ran a boarding house, hoping her daughters with singing talent—especially Aloysia, Mozart's former love—would pluck her from financial ruin. Leopold considered them nothing but schemers and immoral theater people, and he had already heard from reliable sources that Mozart was up to no good with Constanze. The marriage took place in mid-1782, a day before Leopold's grudging consent arrived, facilitated by Mozart's dear friend Baroness von Waldstätten. Joseph II had a strong interest in opera, and in 1778, before succeeding his mother Maria Theresa after her death in 1780, he had established his National Theater, in which operas would be commissioned in German instead of the usual Italian. Very few composers of quality actually composed works in German, Ignaz Umlauf being one of the few to benefit from the opportunity, so the newly arrived Mozart, still sporting the success of his *Idomeneo* in Munich, very much flashed on the radar as one to give credibility to Joseph's German enterprise. Through the combined efforts of Joseph's overseer of theatrical affairs, Count Franz Xaver Rosenberg-Orsini, and the librettist Gottlieb Stephanie the Younger, who became director of the National Theater in 1781, Mozart was offered a libretto for a comic opera that would be more than the usual adaptation of a French or Italian opera into German.

The breakthrough had come, and with a commission for all intents and purposes from the emperor himself, Mozart wrote to his father on 1 August 1781 assuring him of his impending financial success in Vienna: "Now, the day before yesterday Stephanie junior gave me a libretto to set. . . . It has a Turkish subject and the work is called: *Belmont und Constanze*, or *Die Verführung aus dem Serail*." (MBA iii 143) Some slips of the pen are more delightful than others, but this one, "Verführung" instead of "Entführung" (seduction instead of abduction), takes the prize. One of the curiosities of Mozart's mature operas, starting with *Idomeneo*, and in many ways following through for the next (and last) decade of his life, concerns the way these works seem to connect to his actual life, no doubt by coincidence, but still worth noting. The subject of *Idomeneo* centers around a father and son, the father having been at war so long he does not recognized his son; caught in a deadly storm at sea he vows to Neptune to sacrifice the first person he will see on land, and, needless to say, that person turns out to be his son. His inability to deal with the situation marginalizes him to the point that the *deus ex machina* forces him to cede power before he's ready to his son. Mozart wrote this opera at the time of the greatest stress in his own relationship with his father, whom he needed to butt out of his affairs. His next opera has Constanze as its leading lady, the name of his future bride, and at least one historical novel on the subject, Stephanie Cowell's *Marrying Mozart*, makes much of this, with Constanze Weber taking the first performance as confirmation that Mozart loves her and she should agree to marry him. A novel can bend these things as the author sees fit, but still, the name Constanze cannot be avoided.

The presentation of a new opera often coincided with an important event at court, and the timing of *The Abduction* seemed right for that to happen. The Grand Duke Paul Petrovich of Russia and his wife, Princess Sophia Dorothea of Wüttemberg, were expected in Vienna in the middle of September, and Stephanie believed showcasing Mozart's opera for this visit would be ideal. That gave Mozart barely a month to write the opera, and Stephanie assumed he could do this, working from the more or less unaltered libretto by the north German writer Christoph Friedrich Bretzner. Mozart normally did not work this way, typically demanding many changes, but in this case he had little choice but to give it a try, in fact completing three of the numbers from Act 1 on the same day he wrote to his father about the commission. By late August Mozart learned that the grand duke would not be coming until November, and this gave him and Stephanie the opportunity to make some changes, increasing the role of the music from Bretzner's original fairly talkative libretto. With further delays, it ended up taking Mozart longer to write this opera than any of his others—before or after—and as annoying as the delays seemed, preventing him from getting his first new work for Vienna into public view quickly, in the end it served him well, since it allowed him to transform what would have been a fairly average work into something exceptional. It grew from an opera with only fifteen musical numbers to one with twenty-one, and with the revisions of the text Mozart could shape the characters and the drama in ways that would not have been otherwise possible, making it not only a charming work suitable for an occasion, but one that has stood the test of time as a masterpiece, still as provocative now as when it premiered.

Operas on Turkish subjects commanded enormous popularity late in the eighteenth century, perhaps odd when we consider the history of fierce wars between the Habsburgs and the Ottoman Empire, and along with opera came fashions, cigarettes, and coffee. While some may have remembered the Turks with bitterness as expansionist invaders, by this point a new dynamic had taken hold, with a greater emphasis on cultural and religious differences. It would be very tempting to draw parallels between that and the early twenty-first century, and to some extent the same biases and misapprehensions hold, as West and East look at each other often with strategic ignorance. In our time we tend to focus on Islamic extremism, since our media gives most coverage to that—the acts of terrorism or brutality directed against other Arabs or the West, while ignoring the peaceful existence of the vast majority, since that elicits nothing newsworthy. Similarly within Islamic states there can be a perception that the West holds a deep hatred toward them, based on the often bizarre behavior and statements of some of our political and religious leaders, among others. During Mozart's time the issues may have been somewhat different and less polarized than now, but on cultural and religious points, some of the same attitudes held, certainly sifting their way into operas and plays. While the best writers such as Voltaire and Pascal strove for a type of "ethical relativity," observing that "what is true on this side of the Pyrenees is false on the other," others cared only about what held true on their side; by Western Christian standards, Muslims behaved like brutes, and Christian acts of brutality toward Islam (such as during the crusades) could conveniently be justified. In operas such as *The Abduction* these issues come into play, and the additional time Mozart and Stephanie had to refine the work no doubt allowed these issues to be placed more in perspective.

The most basic principle for Mozart as a composer of opera lay in his use of music to define drama and strength or significance of character, and that surely applies to this work. Unlike *Idomeneo* or the ones to follow, such as *The Marriage of Figaro, Don Giovanni*, and *The Magic Flute, The Abduction* offers a peculiar challenge in this regard since the character many consider to be the most important in the work, Pasha Selim, lacks music completely: he simply has a speaking role. Unlike the pashas who typically populate Turkish operas, born and bred in the Middle East, this one came from the West, driven out, we learn near the end, by the brutality of Belmonte's own father, and now lives and rules in Turkey in the manner that any pasha would, with a harem and all. He desires Constanze, Belmonte's beloved, and would like, we assume, to add her to the harem as a special wife, prepared to use force— even torture—if she will not come willingly. She refuses to abandon her love for Belmonte, and when he arrives at Selim's house to rescue her along with his servant Pedrillo and Constanze's servant Blonde, but fails miserably in the attempt, Selim finds he has the son of his most hated enemy in his power, and he must decide what to do with him. Things look grim for the hapless Belmonte, but Selim decides to let him go along with the others, invoking praise from all for the great magnanimity and clemency of the one holding power, what most commentators take to be the most important moment of the opera. In any other opera—for example, the Countess's forgiveness of the Count in *Figaro*—a moment of this magnitude would be revealed in some of the most significant music of the opera, but here we have no music at all, only Selim's spoken dialogue. How seriously should we take this act of his?

Spoken roles are rare in the extreme in Mozart's operas, and while we always know which singers Mozart wrote his parts for, we have no idea why Selim ended up with a speaking role. Of course there has been speculation about this: a singer had just been dismissed from the company who would have been the likely one, although being a tenor, Mozart may not have wanted yet another tenor; Bretzner made it a speaking role, and Mozart may have simply accepted that; or Mozart and Stephanie made a conscious decision for this to be a speaking role. If we weigh the options, we can probably dismiss the first two fairly easily. As one of the great musical capitals of the world, Vienna had no shortage of singers, and if one had been dismissed, another could have been found, especially with the additional time available to complete the opera. Mozart may have been young but he did not lack experience, and the thought of him willy-nilly accepting Bretzner's idea for the role flies in the face of everything we know about Mozart's badgering of Varesco for *Idomeneo* (itemized in the correspondence with Leopold) and similarly the demands he placed on Stephanie to get exactly what he wanted for this opera. That leaves the conscious decision, and the possible reason for that will be explored later in this chapter.

Mozart's treatment of the singing roles tells us much about the nature of the drama, the issues that arise, and even about Mozart taking on some of the heavyweights in Vienna on the matter of the direction in which the theater should be moving. The most notable of these heavyweights, Joseph von Sonnenfels, an influential minister in Maria Theresa's government and later chief theatrical censor in Vienna, had gone to absurd lengths as a literary reformer to rid the Austrian stage of Hanswurst (Jack sausage), a fixture of low improvised comedy full of scatological language, crude and vulgar jokes, excessive eating and drinking, and worse. Mozart bragged to his father about his hobnobbing with Sonnenfels and others like him, and the sober Leopold would have been delighted to have his son in the uplifting company of a powerful person who would have liked to get rid of comedy altogether. While Leopold enjoyed hearing these kinds of things, and Mozart wrote him often about his progress on Act 1 of *The Abduction*, Mozart noted in one letter that Hanswurst had not yet been eradicated in Austria, and he did not need to say that that was contrary to Sonnenfels's wish. He also did not add that he contributed as much as anyone to that, including in this opera. In the original Bretzner libretto the comic character Osmin had a relatively small role, but with the revisions Osmin became possibly the most important character, not unlike the way Papageno would in *The Magic Flute* a decade later. Not only comic, Osmin can behave badly and get away with it because of his silliness; he can be abusive while we still laugh at him, and even represent a darker radical side of Islam without being taken seriously. He pulls this off by being a reincarnation of Hanswurst in Turkish garb, not a menacing fanatic but actually a character familiar to the Viennese as one of their own, slipped into the work right under Sonnenfels's nose, with a dagger on his belt instead of a phallic sausage.

Osmin's ranting and abusive language in the dialogue make his identity fairly clear, but of much great importance is the music that Mozart gives him, which he describes in considerable detail to his father. The singer for this role, Ludwig Fischer, had a voice so low that the archbishop proclaimed it to be too low for a bass, making him the ideal singer for the role where extreme lowness easily took on a comic edge, and without question the audience loved him. In describing the aria added near the beginning for Osmin, Mozart says his "violent rage oversteps all sense of order, balance, and objectivity," and that the music must even "forget itself." (MBA iii 162) Pedrillo more than anyone recognizes him as Hanswurst; unlike a good Muslim, who would be a teetotaler, he seems susceptible to strong drink, which Pedrillo plies him with to manage the escape from the harem. Unfortunately he underestimates Osmin's large capacity for wine, and the escape fails because Osmin wakes up too quickly from what Pedrillo thought would be a long drunken stupor. The two serious roles, Belmonte and Constanze, set up an interesting gender balance with the music given to them, a balance Mozart also pursues in all of his subsequent operas, in which the women come out on top, and I will explore this in the discussions of specific musical numbers. Even the Janissary (guards of a Turkish sovereign) choruses that praise the pasha have both men and women in them, unlike the male-only Janissaries in other operas with Turkish subjects at this time.

The term for this type of opera, *"Singspiel"* (play with singing), denotes something specific in German—that there will be spoken dialogue, possibly lots of it, replacing the quick or dry (*secco*) recitative found in Italian operas. Some of these works looked more like plays with arias and the odd duet added, although for Mozart the terminology proved not very useful, considering his approach of carrying the drama in the music itself—both arias and ensembles of various sizes. With the amount of dialogue it meant that the singers had to be equally good actors, and this gave the work a touch of realism since characters would converse with each other in normal speech instead of the fairly artificial recitative.

ACT I

It's 19 July 1782, and you have arrived early at the Burgtheater in Vienna to attend the second performance of *The Abduction*. The play-bill posted at the theater for the premiere on the 16th seemed a little strange since it lists no members of the cast, and even Mozart's name you have difficulty finding; in contrast to that the name Bretzner appears in fairly large print just under the title of the work. The premiere would have been impossible to get into, so you have come to this one with the expectation that Mozart himself would still be conducting, which proved true. Another surprise awaits you: almost from the beginning hissing can be heard from the cheap seats in the upper gallery, and it appears that someone hoped Mozart will fail and has planted a cabal to help that along. As the performance continues the enthusiastic bravos and applause easily drown out the hissing, especially after the arias, although the cabal has something to pan during the trio at the end of Act 1. That should have put the audience exactly where Mozart wanted it, but unfortunately Fischer (Osmin) messed up his part, and that tripped up Johann Ernst Dauer (Pedrillo) as well, making it impossible for Joseph Valentin Adamberger (Belmonte) to get things back on track and rescue a musical fiasco. You could see Mozart trying to contain his rage, and you knew there would be hell to pay at the rehearsal before the next performance (for Mozart's version of these events, see his letter to his father dated 20 July 1782).

As the overture begins, you are astonished after the first eight bars of strings by themselves to hear the richness of the orchestration, including piccolo, oboes, clarinets, bassoons, horns, trumpets, timpani, and of course cymbals, triangles, and tambourines to instill the appropriate Turkish atmosphere. You had not heard such lushness of orchestration since visiting Mannheim a few years earlier and hearing its famous orchestra. The overture begins in a bright and sparkling manner, very fast (presto), in the festive key of C major, and then moves to a much more melodic second section starting in C minor, providing an extreme contrast from the opening section with something that tugs on the heartstrings. Before being whisked back into the return of the first section, the clarinets hold a high A for four bars which functions as a type of upper pedal tone as the melodic material carries on below it. Like the opening section, the concluding altered repetition of it does not come to a full close, but ends on the dominant, prompting a return to the tonic in the opening vocal number.

The home key comes, in fact using a melody identical to the one from the middle section of the overture, now major instead of minor, and after a brief introduction, Belmonte sings this melody as a kind of continuation of the overture. The issue of how the overture should connect to the rest of the opera was now very much on the table, having been placed there by both Gluck and Haydn; Mozart would address it in later operas, occasionally planting something thematically crucial there, as he does in *Don Giovanni* and *Così fan tutte*. Here he takes a completely different approach, more or less making the first character who sings a kind of extension of the overture, a returned middle section, and despite the beauty of the music, you get the sense that he may be somewhat marginalizing the character by making him an appendage of the overture. Belmonte, the young nobleman, sings what amounts to a kind of prayer, invoking the god of love to return Constanze to him, not with a full aria to do it, but just a short arietta. This amounts to a cry for help, not a strategy of rescue, and we discover by his first spoken words that he has no clue how he will get into the palace. During the arietta he mopes about the torment he has endured, and while we may take him seriously now, we soon discover that his suffering pales compared to the real agony Constanze has survived. Near the end of this short number Mozart gives Belmonte the same held high note that the clarinets had in the overture, and he functions every bit as much as a pedal tone here, hanging high and dry on this G as the orchestra carries on beneath him with the material of musical interest. In a subtle way Mozart has shown much in this short number of what we need to know and will find confirmed as the opera proceeds about Belmonte—that he lacks resourcefulness and in fact is a bit of a wimp.

After giving short shrift to Belmonte, Mozart gets on with the character he enjoys most, Osmin; his own descriptions to his father on 26 September 1781 of how he changed the work at the beginning to accommodate and develop Osmin are so thorough that we can do no better than to hear this straight from the horse's mouth:

> The opera started with a monologue and so I asked Herr Stephanie to turn it into a little arietta and, instead of having the two of them chatter away together after Osmin's little song to turn it into a duet.—As we've written the part of Osmin for Herr Fischer, who certainly has an outstanding bass voice . . . we must take advantage of him, especially because he has the whole of the local audience on his side. —But in the original libretto this Osmin has only this one little song to sing and nothing else, except for the trio and finale. And so he's now got an aria in the first act and will have another one in the second. (MLL 434–35)

As for the aria in Act 1, "Solche hergelaufne Laffen," Mozart explained exactly how the music should capture the disorder of Osmin's nonsensical ranting:

> I've told Herr Stephanie exactly what I want for this aria:—the bulk of the music was already written before Stephanie knew a word of it. . . . Osmin's rage is made to seem funny by the Turkish music that I've used here. —In developing the aria, I've allowed his beautiful low notes to gleam. . . . *"Drum beym Barte des Propheten"* etc. is still at the same speed, but with the quick notes—and as his rage continues to grow, just when you think the aria is over, the allegro assai—in a completely different metre and different key—is bound to be tremendously effective; just as a person in such a violent rage oversteps all the bounds of order and moderation and overshoots the mark, completely forgetting himself, so the music must forget itself—but because the passions, whether violent or not, must never be expressed to the point of causing disgust, and because music, even in the most terrible situation, must never offend the ear but must give pleasure and, hence, always remain music, I've not chosen a key foreign to F—the key of the aria—but one related to it, not, however, the one closest to it, D minor, but the more remote A minor. (MLL 435)

Osmin gives no real reason for his rage, aside from not liking the way Pedrillo looks, but much of the comedy would evaporate if he actually had a motive. He rants about laziness, ogling, and scheming, and no doubt sees Pedrillo as a troublesome obstacle to his own desire for Blonde.

Pedrillo and Belmonte finally meet, exchange a few details about what has happened to them, and especially Constanze, whom Selim seldom lets out of his sight, forcing Belmonte to question if she still loves him. This prompts a real aria for the lovesick Belmonte, one that Mozart claimed to his father to be his own favorite:

> Now for Belmonte's aria in A major, "*O wie ängstlich, o wie feurig,*" do you know how it's expressed?—Even his beating heart is indicated—by the 2 violins in octaves. . . . You see the trembling—vacillation—you see his breast begin to swell—which I've expressed with a crescendo—you hear the whispering and sighing—which is expressed by the first violins with mutes and a flute playing in unison with them. (MLL 435–36)

Speaking of his trembling, faltering, and throbbing heart, one gets the impression that Mozart does not think of him in heroic terms, and much of the music given to him seems to bear that out, with somewhat silly-sounding clipped passages on the words "klopft mein liebe volles Herz" (beats my loving heart), and then longer coloratura extensions to round out the phrases. Coloratura for a woman may certainly indicate strength of character, but less so for a man; if this really was Mozart's favorite aria, he appears not to have wished to explain why to his father. Mozart went into great detail to his father about Act 1 of the opera, but said practically nothing about the two last acts, and this appears to have been punishment for Leopold trying to give unwanted advice about the libretto.

A chorus of Janissaries sings praises to the pasha, who now makes his entry with Constanze, and with his first words, while suggesting fairness and decency, he leaves a raw edge, reminding her that he could use cruelty and force her to submit to him but instead will give her a chance to come round on her own. This leaves the impression that if she does not give in, he will force her, and although a European, she should never imagine that he will be exclusively hers, but only that she will be a favorite within the harem. Apparently never having explained her reticence to him before, she now does in one of the three glorious arias Mozart gives her, telling of the depth of her love to another in the opening adagio, and in the following allegro lamenting how their separation cut that short. Unlike the puppy-love music Mozart gives Belmonte, her music has real depth, allowing her to approach high notes by building toward them, unlike what happens on his high notes, along with coloratura passages and syncopations that give her emotions urgency. Her passion for someone else seems entirely lost on Selim as he can come up with nothing better than more threats about having her in his power and says that he will give her one more day to rid herself of this baggage. In an aside he does react to her ardor for Belmonte, but only that it has made him want her all the more—certainly not that it has induced any respect for her feelings. When we arrive at the end and must assess his so-called clemency, we need to recall his belligerent attitude at each step along the way.

The act ends with a comical trio which goes awry in the performance you attend, once more with Osmin leading the charge, and again we have a description of this by Mozart:

> Now for the trio, namely, the end of the first act.—Pedrillo has passed off his master as an architect so that he has a chance to meet his Konstanze in the garden. The pasha has taken him into his service;—Osmin, the overseer, knows nothing of this and, being a foul-mouthed boor and the sworn enemy of all strangers, is insolent and refuses to let them into the garden.—The first thing that's indicated is very brief—and because the text gave me an opportunity to do so, I've produced some quite good 3-part writing. But then the major key enters pianissimo—it must go very quickly—and the ending will make a lot of noise—which is exactly what's needed at the end of an act—the more noise the better;—and the shorter the better, so the audience's enthusiasm doesn't have time to cool off and they don't stint on their applause. (MLL 436)

It should have worked this way, but alas it did not at this performance because Fischer bungled his part; with this description Mozart's heads-up on the opera to his father more or less came to an end.

ACT 2

By the end of the first act we have met all the characters, with one exception, Blonde, Constanze's maid, and it's not unusual for Mozart to hold a special character in reserve for introduction at the beginning of the second act. Unlike her European counterparts, she appears not to have a shred of weakness or doubt in her, and she simply sails along being pert and sassy, helping those who need it, or dressing down over-bearing abusers like Osmin, who imagines her to be his love slave. She may have been given to him by Selim, but she has something to say about that, starting at the beginning of Act 2. Before launching into her aria, she puts Osmin's nose out of joint by snapping at him that he has no right to treat her like a slave, expecting her to fear his commands and leap when he says jump; European girls simply cannot be treated that way. Starting the aria with a gently melodic andante grazioso song, she explains the delicate art of tenderness and flattery that he needs to use, not the bluster and threats he's accustomed to, the latter which Mozart accompanies more stridently and aggressively. She too gets some color-atura passages, not on the scale of Constanze's, but enough to capture the combination of strength and civility she hopes to get across to him. Needless to say it goes right over his head, and since the notion of tenderness cuts no ice with him, she uses language he does understand, threatening him with physical violence when he crows about owning her and that he could punish her for being the resisting Englishwoman. This kind of language works, and he likes it, but marvels at the stupidity of European men who allow women to do as they wish; the two of them follow up on this with a lively duet. In his crude way he does not look so very different from Selim.

Blonde has to admit to herself that she has things much better than her mistress, since despite the annoyance of Osmin, she has Pedrillo nearby and can see him occasionally. Constanze's hand had now been forced by Selim, and alone with Blonde, she laments her sad plight, again with entirely convincing music, using chromatic lines to underline the emotions of lament. Blonde tries to cheer her up, but things get much worse when Selim returns, and her day of grace has run out. His threats become more vicious as he wields his power and assures her that no easy death awaits her, but in fact tortures of the most horrible kind imaginable. She answers resolutely that she can endure the most wretched tortures he can devise, and then convinces him with a second aria just after the previous one, "Martern aller Arten" (All kinds of torture), changing from lament to a show of forcefulness. This time a very long orchestral introduction gives us a musical sense of her serious-ness, and when she enters, she does not disappoint, revealing a kind of resolve we cannot imagine in Belmonte, or anyone else for that matter, in by far the longest aria of the work.

The musical treatment for female characters here, already evident in *Idomeneo*, and very much amplified in all of Mozart's operas to come, sets the women apart as the ones with the greatest strength of charac-ter. This takes on a peculiar significance in *The Abduction* since they find themselves in a culture that does not value women; Mozart does not intend their superiority as a comment on Islamic society but instead on that of Europe, from which they hail. In this and the operas to follow it is imperative that we do not simply follow the words of the librettos, which may be ambiguous on this and other points, but listen carefully to the quality and nature of the music that Mozart provides, where strength of character can be defined. Aside from more coloratura, per-haps most notable is the way Constanze arrives at her high notes near the end of the aria, always approaching them from below with a build-ing pattern; while she may hold them for four bars or more, and the orchestra carries on melodically below her, the force of her arrival makes the high notes dynamically charged, and not an upper pedal tone as Belmonte has. Especially her high C near the end, with a rest in the middle of it, instills that sense of building excitement as the orchestra complements the tension with syncopations and rising scale passages.

No other character could hope to compete with what Mozart presents in this aria, so Blonde sings next, the closest equal to Con-stanze, and she now diffuses the tension with a relatively simple song rejoicing in the news just given her by Pedrillo, that Belmonte has arrived and escape will come soon. Despite the simplicity, not only her joy comes through but also her resolve, in stark contrast to Pedrillo's following aria "Frisch zum Kampfe" (On to battle), which should sound warrior-like, but spends far too much time on the comment that only a cowardly dolt loses heart. He should not tremble at the dangerous task ahead, but spends a good part of the aria doing exactly that, to the appropriate trembling music. His first task will be to disable Osmin, and he attempts this with wine, an odd choice for the Muslim watchman, but Osmin seems not averse to the occasional drink, showing himself to be much more the indulgent Austrian Hanswurst type than a Muslim. In a delightful duet Pedrillo gets him drunk enough to fall asleep, with the help of an added sleeping potion, but not enough to turn Osmin's lights out for the whole night.

Belmonte and Constanze finally meet, but instead of a love duet, Belmonte sings an aria about tears of joy flowing, and musically zeros in on his emotions, not hers, which would have been more elevated. Of course we can share his joy, but we do have to wonder if the person now singing about his sighs will be capable of the attempted rescue about to come. He then comments that love will guard them on the escape, but love of the quality of his last aria will probably not do the trick, and someone as love-struck as Belmonte may not be the one to pull this off. Not surprisingly, the half-baked plan fails.

The largest ensemble of the opera comes at the end of Act 2, a quartet for the two sets of lovers, and in what could be dismissed as a bit of comedy, it has a somewhat more serious edge to it, raising a gender issue that will return with full force in Mozart's next three operas. After gushing about being together again, Belmonte raises the issue of whether Constanze has been faithful to him in his absence, and Pedrillo, who hasn't seen much of Blonde, wonders the same. Needless to say, the men ask this question of the women, not the other way round, and this says much about the balance of power between men and women in the eighteenth century, made very clear in much of the literature and dealt with directly in Mozart's next few operas. Women would not ask this of men because the assumption was that men did not have to be faithful but women did, and society did not look down on a man who had been unfaithful, whereas it would ostracize a woman. In *Così fan tutte* we will see the women fighting this gender imbalance, and in *The Marriage of Figaro* exposing the Count for his hypocrisy, but in *The Abduction* something else takes over, not unrelated to the quality distinctions Mozart has drawn between his male and female characters. Here the women rightly take deep offense at the question, considering what they—especially Constanze—have endured to remain faithful, pushed to the brink of torture; someone like Belmonte could never hope to understand what she has withstood. The matter ends without too much ado in this quartet, but it perhaps leaves a lingering bad taste about the insensitivity of the men, one that cannot easily be brushed aside, and confirms what we have known since the beginning of the opera—that the male characters, including Belmonte, because of how Mozart has defined them musically, are either milksops or jerks.

ACT 3

The third act begins with the light footsteps of those setting the escape plot in motion, Pedrillo now firmly in charge, with Belmonte standing by uselessly as Pedrillo condescendingly tells him to sing a song to keep occupied. Since Pedrillo often sings at this late hour the guards will not suspect Belmonte if they come by, and since he seems incapable of helping (or it's beneath his station to do so), he once again becomes marginalized, singing yet another soppy love song, needless to say with coloratura and long pedal tones that remove him from anything of musical interest. When he finally finishes, Pedrillo gets a song too, a romance, or a strophic ballad, intended as the signal for the women that they're ready, and when Belmonte complains about the length of the song, Pedrillo continues since the women have not yet roused themselves, and in any event he wants to finish the ballad about a knight rescuing a captured woman in a Moorish land. The rescue in the ballad finishes successfully, unlike the one about to be attempted. Constanze finally shows herself and the climb down the ladder begins.

Having seriously underestimated Osmin's Hanswurst-like capacity for strong drink, Pedrillo pays the price as the still-inebriated Osmin staggers into the middle of the abduction, and with the help of guards, takes the escapees into custody. It's now his turn to gloat, and he does this with a surprisingly long aria, boasting of his triumph and wishing to see the two men dangling from gallows; Mozart gives him some absurdly low notes to sing—one of which lasts a full nine bars—and even some passages both high and low that nonsensically represent coloratura. Mozart simply could not resist having fun with his favorite character here, certainly not allowing us to take his wild threats seriously as he sings like a soprano on unimaginably low notes. Selim enters to find out what all the fuss is about, and accuses Constanze of treachery when he learns she has used his leniency against him in the abduction plot. She concedes that she should die, but begs for Belmonte to be saved, while Belmonte, the apparently incompetent aristocrat, tries to pull rank (or class), explaining to Selim that he comes from a noble Spanish family which will pay any ransom the pasha demands. Selim cannot believe his good fortune, now having in his power the son of his most hated enemy—the barbarian, as he calls him, who took his beloved and drove him empty-handed from his homeland. He asks Belmonte what his father would do if he were in Selim's place, and Belmonte has to admit that his own fate would be lamentable; Selim leaves with Osmin, telling him of his plans for the torture.

Now knowing their wretched prospects, Belmonte and Constanze sing a duet, a kind of love duet about shared ecstasy not in this world but the next, and Mozart saves some of his best music of the entire opera for this number. Belmonte may not have impressed us all that much prior to this, but now Constanze musically elevates him to her level in the lengthy accompanied recitative and duet, functioning as an aria for two voices completely as one, echoing each other's phrases or singing with complementary counterpoint at times but mostly in harmony a third (or tenth) apart. She has attempted to console him with a romantic vision of death, and he has to agree that his father behaved like a barbarian and he should be punished for those crimes. Selim then surprises us with his act of clemency, taken almost universally as a high point of enlightened thinking. But before getting too carried away, we need to take a closer look at Selim's words: "Your people must indulge in injustices because you seem to take them so much for granted. But you're deceiving yourself. I abhor your father too much to follow in his footsteps. Take your freedom. . . . Tell your father that you were in my power and that I set you free. Tell him it gave me far greater pleasure to reward an injustice with justice than to keep on repaying evil with evil." Much of this sounds enlightened, but the conciliatory words obscure the motive; torture, blood, and gore may have satisfied his revenge for the short term, but by letting the son of his most despised enemy go, he would have him in his power permanently. An enlightened gesture would be given with love and compassion, but we hear nothing of that; instead his words show disdain for a sniveling lad, revulsion for the woman whom he considers a traitor, and abhorrence for the wretch who brought about his demise many years earlier. He can now wave goodbye with his foot still figuratively on their throats.

At this point in the work we must also remember his bloody-mindedness in the past—the threats of torture and worse—and consider that this apparent clemency has been rendered not in music but in a pedestrian speaking voice. Can we imagine Mozart giving this to us in song of the most profound kind? Of course we can, and it appears he chose not to. The music that comes immediately after this not only lacks profundity, but if anything seems to mock Selim's "greatness," setting up the kind of ironic conclusion not uncommon in later works, in this case (and then in *Don Giovanni*) with a vaudeville. Each character sings what amounts to a children's ditty in praise of Selim, answered by the chorus, a commentary by Mozart at the end of the work that Ivan Nagel delightfully describes as a round sung in the spirit and rhythm of a children's counting rhyme. Osmin gets counted out and has to stand in the corner, listening to the mocking refrain. Osmin tries to sing the tune of the others, but he can't do it, quickly reverting to the bluster from Act 1 that Mozart described as overstepping the bounds of order, now stomping off in a rage, and even doing it in the same key he had used earlier. Considering the children's game music, we can hardly take those singing it seriously, but surely Osmin we can, still the delightful churl he had been earlier. The chorus of Janissaries ends the opera, singing the same praises they had in Act 1, but in a way Osmin gets the last word, letting us laugh at him as we have all along, and preventing us with his out-goes-you in the children's game from falling for the ruse of great praise. As you may suspect, the opera scores a resounding and long-lasting success in Vienna.

5

VIRTUOSO PERFORMER

Concertos

Mozart came to Vienna with two aces up his sleeve, and he had no doubt that the two of them combined, based on his international reputation in each, would assure him a successful career in the capital. The first of these cards he had played in 1782 with the composition and performance of *The Abduction from the Seraglio*, but despite the prowess and renown he now enjoyed as an opera composer, he did not complete another one until *The Marriage of Figaro* in 1786. His other ace went back further than writing operas, and that was his extraordinary brilliance as a pianist, known throughout Europe because of his childhood and adolescent tours. The Habsburg Empire teemed with piano virtuosos, but unlike most of these, Mozart as an adult matured beyond anything the world had previously seen, and at that time being a great pianist meant being a composer of concertos as well. During the gap between his successes with opera, he returned to his life as a pianist, presenting fifteen new piano concertos (plus a couple of other movements) to the Viennese public during those four years. The great success of these subscription concerts prompted him to write to his father in 1784 that "the first concert . . . went off very well. The hall was overflowing; and the new concerto I played won extraordinary applause. Everywhere I go I hear praises of that concert." (LMF 872) Mozart still owed his father money from the fiasco of the 1777–1779 trip, and Leopold had never forgiven his son for leaving the safety of employment in

Salzburg, which eventually would have led to the debt being repaid, to pursue a precarious career as a freelance musician in Vienna. He could now gloat about having made the right decision.

As a married man, Mozart had to provide for his family as well as deal with his obligation to Leopold, and this he could do as a pianist and composer, for the moment loved by the public. Like any composer of his time, he took his relationship with his audience very seriously, attempting to strike a balance between what would be appealing and what he could offer beyond the kind of display that would leave listeners oohing and ahhing. Again writing to his father, Mozart explained what he had in mind about this kind of balance, referring to his three newest piano concertos late in 1782:

> These concertos are a happy medium between what is too easy and too difficult; they are very brilliant, pleasing to the ear, and natural, without being vapid. There are passages here and there from which the connoisseurs alone can derive satisfaction; but these passages are written in such a way that the less learned cannot fail to be pleased, though without knowing why. (LMF 833)

Despite the assumption that works had to appeal to the listeners, Mozart still felt compelled to say that they could do this without being vapid; the reason for this lay in the fact that many of his contemporaries wrote nothing but vapid works. Not only does the word vapid not apply to Mozart's concertos, these works engaged the audience then and still do now as dramas not unlike operas and plays at the time, and, as I will attempt to make the case, like the best movies of the present.

Of course Mozart did not invent the genre of the concerto, but in his hands it became something it had never been before, and every serious composer after him had to take note of what he achieved. By no means did that spell the end of vapid concertos that exist only for the aggrandizement of solo performers, who typically also wrote the concertos, but as we look back from our vantage point, we see virtually none of those types still in the repertory. Concertos for keyboard instruments existed before Mozart, mainly for harpsichord and clavichord. The piano (or pianoforte) was a relative newcomer as an instrument, invented only at the beginning of the eighteenth century, and it took some time for it to displace the other keyboard instruments it would eventually supersede. Until at least two-thirds of the way through the century, the harpsichord had a functional place as the provider of the continuo, or a kind of harmonic filler—something it could do with a background or non-invasive role. To make the transition from supporter to leading character required an instrument with more variation of tone and volume, and the piano had that, although not in the way it eventually would in the nineteenth century when it became huge and powerful, a steel-framed Hummer compared to the wooden Morgan of earlier times. Despite the fact that Mozart's piano made relatively little sound (although still more than a harpsichord or clavichord), in the hands of as skilled an orchestrator as himself that proved not to be a problem, since he wrote in such a way that the instrument seldom has to compete with the full orchestra (which itself produced much less sound than the nineteenth-century orchestra).

Before the piano entered the fray, composers loved to write concertos, in massive numbers, for just about every instrument of the orchestra, and especially the violin, flute, or oboe as soloist. In all of these we get what came to be the point of the concerto: the exchanges between the individual voice and the group, allowing the single voice to gain a type of ascendency it could not in the orchestra, even as an obbligato instrument, but almost always with the soloist in a complementary relationship to the ensemble, perhaps rising above it but still following the lead of the group. If the composer wished something in which the soloist provides harmony, as the piano can, that could be achieved with a combination of soloists, with the concerto grosso of the earlier part of the century offering exchanges between a small group of instruments and the larger ensemble, or the sinfonia concertante later in the century, in which the small group would be more an assemblage of soloists, retaining their distinctive voices. Another possibility could be double or triple concertos, functioning more like solo concertos but with more than one instrument taking the solo lead, and this type remained appealing to composers well into the next century. Mozart himself explored all of these possibilities (the older concerto grosso had been superseded by the sinfonia concertante by his time), aside from the piano writing concertos for violin, oboe, flute, bassoon, horn, and eventually clarinet, as well as ones for more than one instrument, such as two pianos, three pianos, and flute and harp.

CONCERTO AS DRAMA

Much has been written about Mozart's concertos, and all too often writers have been hung up on the perplexities of form, since despite being a prime type of instrumental work, concertos do not use the same formal schemes as symphonies, quartets, or sonatas. Most obviously Mozart's concertos have only three movements instead of the usual four for symphonies and quartets, but more strikingly the first movements do not use sonata form, the foundation for drama in instrumental music. Obsessing about form in concertos may be of academic interest, but for listeners who wish to enjoy these works and get something meaningful from the experience, there are more important matters. Still, for us in the twenty-first century, to get the most from that experience, it is useful to look for metaphors or images that make it relevant to us, while at the same time connected to the age in which Mozart wrote them. Writers both then and now like to think of these concertos as works of drama, but defining that in the absence of sonata form, with its inherently dramatic essence, can be fairly treacherous. The fact that an individual voice interacts with a group suggests the basis for the drama, but what exactly does that mean?

In order to call that interaction dramatic, we generally assume that there must be conflict, but do we find conflict in concertos between the one and the many? And if we do, do we take that conflict to be a struggle between the individual and society, or more specifically between Mozart and his own social or even musical milieu? If we doubt that conflict characterizes the musical events of concertos, then do we instead call it a type of dialogue? Are there other genres or media that provide a model for the concerto, such as opera (either arias or ensembles), or even the theater? All of these possibilities and in fact many more have been explored, in some cases with interesting results. Most seem to agree that the fact that these works are instrumental does not mean we should treat them as absolute music, with no psychological or social meaning beyond the music itself. On the other hand, maybe Mozart was just having a good time designing a suitable venue for his virtuosic (but not vapid) display as a pianist, and we should simply sit back and let the glorious sounds waft by. The sense of drama, though, seems inescapable, and coming up with a good way of translating that into modern experience seems fairly crucial if we wish to go to the next step.

In looking for current parallels with the dramatic essence of Mozart's concertos, at least two factors need to be placed in some sort of balance: the nature of the exchanges between the solo and the group, and the kind of structure that this happens in, however loose that structure may be. Even with sonata form, as we discovered earlier, the term "form" is inappropriate, since although we have certain expectations about sections, key changes, and themes, composers treated this as a dynamic process, very much alive and able to be flexible. This is even truer of the structures found in concertos, although typically Mozart, in first movements, for example, will follow a general format for the presentation of sections, which means that deviation from it will strike us more forcefully, as happens with the early entry of the piano in K271. The pattern of sections in first movements—the nature of the exchanges between the group and the solo—looks more or less like this:

> Part 1: Group introduction
> Solo response
> Return of group to close part 1
> Part 2: New section with solo responding to the previous group
> Combined section, with group and solo
> Final section for group

One writer, Karol Berger, has suggested an interesting way of looking at this arrangement, taking the sections as stories in which we have the same story told three times with three different versions. In the opening introductory section, the orchestra tells the story from its point of view, while the next section, the solo's response, then gives the story in a new version, told from a different perspective. When the solo and group come together in the second part, there may be an attempt to reconcile the two versions of the story, although it could also include new material, yielding a third telling of the tale. Running through the plot we find similarity, especially with the first story recurring, but at the same time with differences that alter each version.

Before dismissing this as a poor way to tell a story, we should keep in mind that some very fine films, one of them a great masterpiece of the twentieth century and another a highly appealing recent film, do exactly the same thing. The masterpiece, *Rashomon*, Akira Kurosawa's postwar 1950 film, gives us four different versions of the same story of a rape and killing, each time told from the vantage point of a principal character or observer, leaving questions because of the differences about who is lying and why. Coming as this did shortly after the defeat of Japan, Kurosawa may very well be creating an ancient parable for modern Japan, exploring the denial taking place in the Japanese psyche. The more recent film I have in mind, which clearly owes a debt to *Rashomon*, seems to come closer to Mozart's approach in his concertos, in fact with some notable structural parallels. Both films use music in very striking ways, with *Rashomon* drawing heavily on Ravel's *Bolero*, and underline the possibility that cinematography and music have much in common. One suspects that had Mozart lived two centuries later, he might have been a great filmmaker, not only because of the cinematic nature of his operas, but, in a more abstract way, because of his concertos as well.

The film I wish to explore as a type of metaphor for the drama in Mozart's concertos, perhaps surprisingly because of the type of music it uses, is Tom Tykwer's highly successful *Run Lola Run* (*Lola Rennt*, 1998), a film with a tight fusion between cinematography and Tykwer's own techno music. The most conspicuous comparison with Berger's enticing description of concerto structure lies in the format of *Run Lola Run*, with an introduction followed by three different tellings of the same story, each one starting in a similar way but then diverging sharply as chaos theory takes hold, with misalignments of no more than a second early on causing exponentially earth-shaking shifts as each twenty-minute episode unfolds. The introductory section sets the stage for the three episodes: after some unusual visuals we see an aerial shot of Berlin, and then a telephone call from the small-time smuggler/courier Manni (Moritz Bleibtreu) to his girlfriend Lola (Franka Potente) about the mess he finds himself in because she did not pick him up where she usually did (someone stole her moped). While on the U-Bahn (without a pass), Manni evades the inspectors and forgets his bag with 100,000 marks. A derelict picks it up and makes off with it. Manni has twenty minutes to replace the money or face death at the hands of his unforgiving boss, and Lola believes she can come up with the money.

When episode 1 begins, the focus shifts almost exclusively to Lola, the individual now with the greatest challenge of her life—to rescue her boyfriend (she believes love can conquer all) by coming up with a hopeless amount of money in twenty minutes before he does something rash such as rob the Bolle grocery store across from his phone booth. Deciding that her banker father offers her the best prospect for the cash, she runs through Berlin streets to the bank, with the camera focusing on her exclusively at first, her pace paralleled by the techno music, and then showing encounters with people of the city, some known to her and others simply random passers-by. At the bank she confronts her unsympathetic father, interrupting his deep discussions with his new lover, and he has her thrown out of the bank. Without the money she runs to find Manni, hoping to stop him before he robs the store, and some of her brief interactions with other people are friendly while others are not. She arrives seconds too late and has no choice but to join Manni with gun drawn in the store, now as his accomplice. With the bag of cash they run for it, but when cornered by the police, Manni throws the bag high in the air, just like Lola earlier throwing her phone receiver in her room, and a stunned policeman inadvertently shoots Lola in the chest.

Like a Mozart concerto we have now had the group introduction and the solo response, and what comes next in the film does not follow the format exactly but perhaps provides a type of hybrid mixture. In the drama of the concerto we would move on to the next two versions of the story before arriving at the slow movement, but in *Run Lola Run* Tykwer inserts immediately after Lola being shot what has all the appearances of a slow movement. Lying on the street and near death, Lola experiences a type of flashback of her life, in a twilight state of redness a post-coital discussion with Manni about whether he loves her. For this moment of visually privileged tenderness all traces of the fast-paced techno beat give way to slow and even funereal music, both musically and dramatically exploring the type of content that a slow movement of a concerto might, whether in a minor key such as K271 or major as in most other concertos. In Tykwer's format, the slow movement, as it were, comes as part of the first movement, and will be repeated, very differently of course, at the end of the second episode. With a dissolve back to the dying Lola on the street, she gets a reprieve and a return to the point at which episode 1 began (the flying phone); this now becomes the start of the second episode.

Without going into all the details of episode 2, it starts more or less the same, but all it takes is a second of delay, perhaps created by the cartoon dog owner tripping her on the stairs from her room, to create an entirely different outcome. This time she becomes defiant at the bank, and instead of leaving in tears, she snatches the guard's gun, takes her father hostage, and steals the money from the bank. Again she runs to meet Manni, but this time the ambulance she ran beside in episode 1 hits Manni (after hitting a large pane of glass it had avoided in the first episode), leaving him as the one dying in the street. The fast-paced movement again gives way to the slow post-coital session, this time without music and Lola asking the questions about what he would do if she were to die—and how quickly he would get over her and move on to someone else. Again the bag of money flies in the air, the phone lands on the receiver, and the third episode begins.

Episode 3 in a sense becomes the fast-paced finale, the happy Hollywood ending that leaves us incredulous as Manni gets his money back from the derelict and Lola wins the same amount of money at a casino, leaving the lovers alive, happy, and rich; this one ends unlike the other two versions with nothing slow and serious. Needless to say the format does not work exactly the same as a Mozart concerto does, but with changes here and there, it may very well give a useful parallel to the nature of the drama that occurs in a concerto. Aside from retelling the same story in different ways, the film also strikes a balance between the individual and the group, with Lola as the individual of interest—the one who runs with a sense of purpose—and the group consists of the people she comes into contact with, including family members, her boyfriend, a family friend, people at the bank, people on the street, the ambulance driver, and even the dying man in the ambulance in episode 3 whose life she saves merely by holding his hand. Her encounters with these various people can be confrontational, friendly, or neutral, just as in the interaction of the solo with the ensemble in a concerto; in neither case must we insist that there has to be conflict for the drama to be carried forward. Perhaps in some small way the drama of a concerto can be made more accessible by thinking of it in a similar way.

EARLY PIANO CONCERTOS (K271)

Concertos could come into being for a variety of reasons, and for Mozart the most likely involved the fact that he played the solo instrument in question and wished to have them for his own performances. Aside from that, they could be written for other highly skilled players, in some cases pupils, or as the result of commissions, but this would not prevent Mozart himself from playing them if he played the instrument. As a virtuoso on two instruments, piano and violin, the young Mozart wrote concertos using these instruments before he left Salzburg. His earliest efforts for the piano were not original compositions, but show him cutting his teeth on the medium by making arrangements of other composers' works, usually adding new solo sections. In Salzburg, where his primary duties involved church music, he had limited opportunities to perform concertos, especially for piano, but that did not stop him from writing for others, with the assumption that he could perform the best of these during his trips to other cities, where they could be done with much better orchestras. Shortly before leaving on the extended trip starting in the fall of 1777 and lasting almost a year and a half, with stops in Munich, Mannheim, Paris, and elsewhere, he composed four piano concertos, including one for three pianos, and one of these stands head and shoulders above the others.

That outstanding piano concerto, in E flat (K271), needs to be looked at closely, since a case can be made that Mozart launched his brilliant career with this work, going far beyond what he had done with most other types of composition, in fact creating a work that has stood the test of time as one of the great works of the repertory. While some of the earlier ones reveal great promise, this one shows arrival for the twenty-one-year-old composer to the level of maturity that made him the extraordinary genius that we all recognize him to be. We know little about the circumstances of this work, aside from the fact that he composed it for the French pianist Mlle. Jeunehomme, sometimes referred to as Jenomy in the family correspondence, who spent time in Salzburg while on a performing tour in December 1776. We know nothing of her performance of the work, but a Mozart letter dated 6 October 1777 confirms that he played it two days earlier along with K238 and K246, and he may have played it in April of 1781 in Vienna.

Because of when he wrote it, near the end of his painful existence in the hometown he detested so much, with its disagreeable ruler—the archbishop—and its petty, provincial residents, it's tempting to look at some of its unusual features connected to the exasperation Mozart felt at this time, although any such assumptions are purely speculative. Whether one can make these assumptions or not, it may be useful to do so as a way of getting at the strange drama that hits us at the beginning of the work and continues throughout. We expect a concerto to begin with an extended introduction by the orchestra, with no sign of the solo, but in this one, the piano enters halfway through the second bar, completely tripping us up with the brashness of this intrusion. The way it responds to the brief opening flourish by the orchestra catches our attention most strikingly. The orchestra of strings, oboes, and horns tries to be assertive, all playing in unison at a forte level; after an opening note held for half of the first bar drops down an octave, it then rises in a much more punctuated way, outlining a triad. With only three notes giving the tonic triad, there's not much musical substance here aside from a bit of bluster, suggesting it oversteps its own sense of importance, with very little to back it up. Before the orchestra can answer this initial fanfare, the piano leaps right in, with a line that could not be more different, in a cheeky kind of way that seems to undermine any seriousness that the orchestra may have attempted, in fact sounding very much like a snub with its rhythm and trill giving the impression of thumbing its nose at the orchestra. The orchestra takes some offense to this and cuts the piano off, tossing off the same fanfare, only to be made fun of again with exactly the same insult from the piano; with this the piano drops out and the orchestra continues with the lengthy introduction that we expected.

Just under a decade later, in *The Marriage of Figaro*, Mozart connects this kind of music with a character who may give us some clues as to what he's up to here. This happens, to be described in more detail in chapter 7, in the aria near the beginning of the opera sung by Dr. Bartolo, the older man who wanted Rosina as his own bride in the prior work of this trilogy, *The Barber of Seville*, but Figaro and Count Almaviva—who marries Rosina—outmaneuver him. The fatuously pompous Bartolo still fumes in anger in this aria, and his declamation of revenge at the beginning comes on notes that do not go beyond the outline of the triad, and in fact even have a rhythm not unlike the beginning of K271, with a long note followed by shorter notes. He sounds tough as he starts, but it doesn't take long for things to unravel, set to music that shows his true blustering colors, with Mozart using descending octaves and clipped lines along with some very silly-sounding patter to mock his opinion of his own cleverness.

While this may hint at the stance of the orchestra in K271, a scene in *Don Giovanni* gives an even better idea of the kind of drama being suggested, one that happens in the finale to Act 1, to be described in chapter 8, now with a specific interaction between a group and an individual. Just after being caught with his pants down trying to have sex with Zerlina, exposed as the guilty one by her husband and the righteous ensemble looking for retribution, they tell him in no uncertain terms that he, the miserable wretch, should tremble since his immoral actions have now been discovered and punishment awaits him. They do not specifically use the outline of the triad to make their point, although the rhythmic pattern of long notes followed by short notes achieves a similar effect. As they catch their breath to hurl the threat at him again, Giovanni blurts out (backed up by his valet Leporello) that confusion has now set in, and does this to music completely opposite of the group's, with very short notes and a jerky rhythm, certainly a gesture of irreverence and defiance, simply not taking the group seriously and even mocking them. Opera may be a useful way of getting at certain aspects of concertos because of the musical features that the two share—and the fact that actions in operas help to confirm the nature of the music being used. This may bolster some of the other parallels that have been drawn between concertos and opera, for example some of the formal procedures in concertos that come very close to certain types of arias.

If we accept that an unusual type of dramatic exchange happens in these opening passages from K271, one that appears to set up the orchestra as fatuous while the solo replies in cheeky defiance, we can easily imagine the parallels to Mozart's own situation in Salzburg at this time. We need not look far to find someone fatuous from Mozart's point of view (and even his father's): the archbishop and the social order he represented. Shortly after leaving on the long trip in late 1777, Mozart said in a letter to his father exactly what he thought of the archbishop: "the Mufti H. C. [Hieronymus Colloredo] is a prick [Schwanz]." Leopold did not disagree, but it was much too dangerous to say so openly since letters could be intercepted, and besides, Leopold hoped to publish them eventually as an epistolary biography of his son in which he could espouse lessons in morality. Considering Mozart's relationship with his father, whose advice and moralizing he had progressively less use for as this correspondence progressed, he may by association have lumped him in the same group with the archbishop, perhaps also invoking the generation gap. Of course it's risky to try to make concertos personal in this sort of way. I am not suggesting that the work should be taken as a program for events in the composer's life, but by drawing the parallel, one can get a sense of the dramatic dimensions of this type of instrumental work. Even though the concerto starts out with some defiance, that does not necessarily set the tone for the rest of the work, where group and solo can happily coexist in a cooperative relationship.

The disagreements in the first movement, though, do not just fade away. When the orchestra gets on track for its introduction, it does seem to have tinges of the "Mufti" in it, with passages that seem to overstate the case, and rapid contrasts between loud chords and quiet recoiling, as well as some fairly comical passages, such as those just before the piano returns. In fact, it's during these comical bits that the piano seems to get impatient, not waiting for a break in the action to come in but barging in on a high trill in the middle, which seems to shut the orchestra up before the piano throws in something new. The orchestra tries to pull itself together, cutting off this insolence from the piano with the same fanfare as at the beginning of the piece, which the piano answers even more cheekily than it had earlier. Having no rejoinder this time, the orchestra steps aside as the piano continues on its own, not with any themes previously introduced by the orchestra, but instead a variant of what the piano had used to cut off the orchestra when it found it too longwinded. Unlike the *Lola* type of sequencing described above in which the solo tells an established story from its point of view, the solo now proceeds with a new story, only somewhat later reinterpreting the orchestra's story. When part 2 comes in the dominant key, with its first section shared by the solo and the group, the return of the opening opposition between the two leaves the orchestra as a poor competitor to the solo, and with occasional dips into its lowest register, the piano still seems in a mocking mood.

With the return of the fourth section and the home key, a delightful little twist happens: the orchestra propels things to the return of the home key, but instead of continuing with the opening fanfare, the piano grabs it, forcing the orchestra to answer as the piano had earlier. We may think they have gotten over their disagreement, able now to exchange roles, but for the repetition—the orchestra wrests the fanfare back, and the piano's response now becomes strung out, pushing its cheekiness further and further. Even after the cadenza, where we expect the orchestra to conclude the movement on its own, the piano breaks back in, with the same interrupting trill it had used earlier, and it ends the movement very much as the predominant voice. The drama here has not fit into what we expect from a concerto where the solo's strings are pulled by the orchestra; the orchestra tries to do that here, but the solo will not comply.

The next two movements are every bit as stunning as the first, each one with its own distinctive features that disrupt expectations. The second movement, after the fairly jaunty atmosphere of the first, turns serious, and not only because it uses the relative minor key (unusual for Mozart's slow movements). Here he infuses the strongest affective quality of the minor to do this—the pulling of the sixth degree of the scale against the fifth (a semitone in the minor)—which he presents as early as the first bar. Before the end of the short orchestral introduction he goes even further with that type of semitone pulling, doing it in a more broadly harmonic way as well with a shift to the Neapolitan (a non-harmonic chord a half step above the tonic), and he prolongs that for a few bars, leaving us in a state of suspension, before resolving in the expected way to the tonic by way of the dominant. Both piano and orchestra share the darker tone of the movement, including in the middle section in E flat, showing, as he does with the Countess's E flat cavatina in *Figaro* ("Porgi amor"), that he can achieve a grave tone in a major key just as well as in a minor one.

Third movements can begin with either the solo or the orchestra, although if the solo leads off, it's typically a fairly short passage; in this one the solo has an unusually long introduction, so long that it stops feeling like a concerto. In this presto rondo, in alla breve to make it even faster, the piano starts with a display of brilliance, but despite that, not all vestiges of the darker middle movement have been shed, with pauses for breath that leave some tension in the air, in one case with syncopations and elsewhere with appoggiaturas. The most striking feature of the movement happens in the second episode of the rondo form where, after things grind to a halt with a repeating motif and a mini cadenza, a cantabile minuet comes in. With its much slower tempo, graceful melody, and 3/4 time, it seems entirely out of place, but is no mere passing event, as it takes up roughly one-third of the movement. Led off by the solo voice, with the orchestra very much an accompaniment when it does come in, the minuet also has something in common with *Figaro*, the aria that Figaro sings immediately after the opening duets with Susanna when she clues him into the fact that the Count intends to have sex with her before she and Figaro get married. The usually resourceful Figaro sings to the Count in absentia, a minuet—the courtly dance that the Count would dance—and Figaro challenges him to dance to his tune. In fact, Figaro makes it impossible to dance to by adding an extra phrase that breaks the essential symmetrical pattern for dancing a minuet. In K271, almost a decade before *Figaro*, Mozart does something similar, after seven four-bar phrases throwing in a two-bar phrase, and then doing the same thing a few bars later. Perhaps if we go back to the hypothetical scenario of Mozart and the archbishop explored in the first movement, we could look at this minuet as we do the one in *Figaro*, where he throws the aristocrat a curve, presenting him with an undanceable dance. With the predominance of the solo throughout this work, and late in the work an apparent dig at the aristocracy, it may very well be the exceptional treatment of drama in this concerto that sets it apart so brilliantly from anything he wrote before it.

VIENNA PIANO CONCERTOS (K466)

It's the 16th of February in 1785, and you, a resident of Salzburg, have come to Vienna on business, despite the miserable weather. Your dear friend Leopold Mozart also arrived in Vienna a few days earlier to visit his son, now the toast of the city, and Leopold, never one to pass up an opportunity to impress a fellow Salzburger, has invited you to join him that evening at a subscription concert, where the young Mozart will play one of his new piano concertos. You're a little surprised that concerts now take place during Lent, something that until recently would not have been permitted—and certainly would not happen in Salzburg—but you suspend any traditional religious objections you may have and go with the flow. At the concert you greet Leopold warmly, and you take your seats, just two boxes away from the Princess of Würtemberg; the large number of aristocrats attending, all of whom have paid handsomely—a souverain d'or or three ducats—have made it clear to the promoter they would come only if Mozart played. For the time being these concerts have assured Mozart of a tidy income, but they have left the elder Mozart struggling to keep up since at least one takes place every evening, and some in the afternoons as well. You knew about Leopold's rage when Mozart opted to leave the employment of the archbishop, as well as his relief that his son now had an income— allowing him to pay off his debts sooner. Before the concert begins, Leopold leaned over to whisper that the ink had not yet dried on the musical parts, and because Mozart had to supervise the copyists, he had not yet had a chance to play through the third movement. It didn't matter, since he had it all in his head.

When Mozart stepped onto the stage to play his concerto, the audience burst into rapturous applause, and silence immediately fell over the hall when he sat down at the piano and raised his arms to lead the orchestra in. You quickly glance over at Leopold and see the tears of joy in his eyes, not only because of all this attention directed toward his son, but also because of the quality of the orchestral playing, far superior to anything in Salzburg. The first thing that strikes you is that this work starts in a minor key, and not just any minor key, but D minor, a key often associated with storms and even death. Mozart does not always put his most serious music in minor keys, but in this case you have little choice as to how you respond: the orchestral introduction to the first movement clearly bears bad news. Aside from the key of D minor, the ominous aura hits you immediately as it starts in the low strings with the persistence of syncopations and builds toward a climax with the accelerating harmonic rhythm; there is the gradual addition of wind parts, the dynamic shift from quiet to loud, and eventually chromatic passages with their destabilizing effect. Then in the unusual conclusion to this introduction, Mozart switches into counterpoint, adding a level of complication and intensity, as though the three fates have appeared to whisper of an unwanted destiny. In this work, unlike K271, which you heard a few years earlier, the piano waits its turn in the usual way to come in. Setting it apart from the earlier Vienna concertos, the piano enters on what certainly sounds like a new theme, although in no way contradicting or interrupting the atmosphere now in place. This sedate entry of the piano appears to be probing, perhaps looking for a way to address the ill winds that have been blowing, and its theme has a distinctive nature, starting with the leap of an octave and then symmetrically moving inward to a midpoint, in fact suggesting a kind of inward turning. While this theme has not been heard before, it resembles a motif you have already heard from the orchestra, first given by the flute, with an octave leap followed by motion to the middle, played three times by the flute a step higher each time. The solo may be searching within itself for something that will release it from the dark grip of the orchestra, but the orchestra seems to resist this possibility, leaving the solo no choice but to accept its fate.

Immediately after the solo's opening statement, the orchestra returns with the D minor syncopations, and the solo tries to soften this with passage work that lacks the syncopations, but to no avail as it eventually arrives at a variant of the chromatic motion previously introduced by the group. In this work, unlike the defiance noted in K271, we have something much closer to the format of *Run Lola Run*, with the retelling of the same or similar story from a contrasting perspective, as the drama now focuses on the differences instead of outright opposition. That becomes confirmed right after the chromatic motion in the piano and a few bars of the orchestra by itself, when the orchestra prompts its own inward-turning motif with the three setup chords used in the introduction, and the piano then plays the identical motif, rising a step higher for each of the three presentations previously given by the flute. Now the solo finds itself completely integrated into the fabric and atmosphere of the group, and continues throughout the remainder of the first movement to share the ominous view of the group in telling the tale in only marginally altered ways. After the cadenza the orchestra returns to its own introductory remarks, without the syncopations, but very much with the ominous counterpoint, bringing the movement to a close.

Mozart never came to the point that Haydn did in his late symphonies of weaving thematic integration among the movements, or that Beethoven did so spectacularly in almost all of his instrumental works after the Fifth Symphony; Mozart nevertheless cultivated a type of dramatic continuity that did not require overt thematic ties. In this work he actually does give thematic links from one movement to the next, making its drama all the more special. The second movement, a "Romance," somewhat surprisingly starts with the solo giving a simple but beautiful melody, suggesting something nostalgic, or a longing for the good old days before things became complicated. That nostalgia may very well point to a time prior to the bad news of the first movement, a time of simplicity and joy that may have been lost but hopefully can be recovered. It appears also to have been a time of complete harmony between solo and group, as the opening phrases of the piano blend seamlessly into the orchestra, which repeats what the solo just said, and then blends as smoothly back to the solo. The two of them now speak as though with one voice, not together but separately, and when they finally come together, the piano gives a variant of the inward-turning motifs from the first movement, making a definite motivic connection to that movement. This may be a portent of complications to come, even negating the possibility of this type of nostalgic return to a better time and place. Throughout the remainder of this opening section of the romance, the piano's line becomes even simpler, at times sounding like something written for a child just learning to play the instrument. Some hushed whispers in the house complain about this sounding boring, but they have missed the point; Mozart intended to evoke the nostalgia of child-like simplicity.

After all this simplicity in the key of B flat major, you are jolted out of complacency by what happens in a new section in G minor, with an outburst in the solo part involving rapid figuration, hand-crossing, and harmonic tension (aptly described as an "eruption of violence" by Charles Rosen). If the previous section had been nostalgia, this new one wreaks havoc as a force of destruction, in no uncertain terms quashing the retreat to a calm past, which has now been relegated to an illusory state. One of Mozart's great admirers of the next generation, Schubert, would explore this type of procedure as far as it would go, in numerous slow movements (for example the String Quintet in C, the Piano Trio in E flat, and various piano sonatas), and in songs as well, such as "Der Lindenbaum" and "Frühlingstraum" from *Winterreise*, where the texts by Wilhelm Müller give strong clues about the meaning of this format in instrumental works. No piece by Schubert shows this procedure as well as the slow movement from the Piano Sonata in A (D959), with a simple and beautiful melody dominating the A section, a long B section that could not be more destructive and violent—bordering on what can no longer be described as music—and a return to the first section that attempts to re-establish the opening melody but fails since things have been forever changed by the destruction.

Some of the figuration Schubert uses in his middle section reminds us of Mozart's treatment of the piano in this concerto, and Mozart may very well be providing a model here for what Schubert took to a new level. The dramatic essence makes itself clear: nostalgia may appear to be a good escape, but this will be demolished by the things that actually happen to us or by psychological angst, and when we try to recover what we loved at one time, we discover that we cannot because it has been tainted by the intervening destructive forces. For Schubert the impossibility of finding the original state of grace reveals itself in the intrusion of motifs from the middle section into the final section, and Mozart moves that way as well, for example with the encroachment of passage work—some of it chromatic—which had not been in the first section. Also, the return of the first section lacks the amiable exchanges between the solo and the ensemble, as the solo must go it alone for much longer than it had earlier, and the distinctive inward-turning figure has now been eliminated altogether. The movement ends with some awkward leaping motifs in the right hand of the solo that did not exist in the first section but seem reminiscent of passages from the middle section played very high by the left hand. Mozart appears to have recognized what became something fundamental to Schubert's way of thinking—that a happier past cannot be restored.

After a first movement with mostly bad news and a second that prevents a return to the good old days, you wonder if the third, as in *Run Lola Run*, will give a sugar-coated ending. Mozart seems somewhat ambiguous about this, perhaps allowing us to take either possibility depending on our inclination. The piano leads off exuberantly with the theme, a rising figure outlining the chord, but of course back in D minor, with as much descending as rising. If you look for a sign of hope here, it vanishes as the orchestra quickly takes over, going on four times as long as the solo had, taking the theme through harmonic and contrapuntal complexity, in fact with passage work that may remind you of part of the destructive section of the previous movement. The solo responds to this with yet another variant of the inward-turning figure, which it backs up with a return to the main theme, but this time with expansion that digresses into some harmonic instability. When the orchestra brings in a new inward-turning motif, now in the relative major key (F), and the solo gets to repeat it, we may think the happy ending to be at hand, but this key shift proves to be ephemeral, as things shortly land back in D minor with the opening theme. As the orchestra expands on this, it does so with prominent syncopations and tonal flux, in a way taking us back to the spirit of the beginning of the first movement. Also, the inward-turning motif, which the solo continues to play, balances the complete opposite, an extended outward-turning passage that leaves one note static (A) while the higher voice moves further and further away from it with chromatic motion.

After the cadenza and the piano's quick restatement of the main theme, Mozart puts the conclusion in D major, now seventy-four bars of relative stability and lightness with emphasis on the inward-turning motif, but can we take this as the Hollywood ending? After all that has happened in the entire work, with integration unlike most others, this may be a ruse, like the musical silliness of the moral being sung at the end of *Don Giovanni* in D major. Since Mozart ends almost all of his mature operas with the type of ruse which will be described in *Don Giovanni*, you should be wary about leaving your seat feeling cheerful and satisfied with an instrumental work that has so much in common with opera. The emperor, who also attended this concert of what we now know as the Piano Concerto in D minor, K466 (at least it may have been this work), seemed well contented, waved his hat, and called out "Bravo, Mozart!" (Leopold's own description of the event can be found in MLL 499–500.)

The concert you just witnessed came while Mozart stood at his zenith as a composer/performer of piano concertos. After K271 he wrote no solo piano concertos until he had settled permanently in Vienna in 1781 and had written his first opera for that city, *The Abduction*, in 1782. Wishing to present himself to Viennese listeners as a composer of dramatic music which would engage them as actively as possible, he now shifted his energy to instrumental drama in a way that would involve himself most directly. Striking parallels were already apparent in K271 between the concerto and opera, and now in Vienna, one of the opera capitals of the late eighteenth-century world, it should not surprise us that his next fifteen concertos should go even further in behaving like music dramas for the stage. As fine as the first few for Vienna are, presented in 1782 and 1783, they get even better with the six written in 1784, leading to the exceptional pair from 1785, K466 (D minor) and 467 (C major), written within a month of each other early in that year, and the wonderful K482 in E flat from the end of the year (K488 in A from 1786 is every bit as appealing). Two more written during 1786, K491 in C minor and K503 in C major, while marvelously appealing, seem to have shifted the balance somewhat toward intellectual challenge; he wrote only two more after these, and his career as a composer/performer of piano concertos seemed to come to an abrupt end. The pair from the beginning of 1785 could not be more different, and even the keys of D minor and C major reinforce the differences, although curiously these two keys actually do form a kind of odd couple pairing, much explored by Beethoven and Schubert, and even by Alban Berg a century later. The discussion of *Don Giovanni* in chapter 8 will show vividly how ominous D minor can be.

Some have speculated on why these concerts more or less came to an end in 1786, but the answer will remain elusive. It could be that Mozart successfully shifted his focus back to opera, or he got tired of the constant concertizing (or the audience got tired of his concertos). A more likely explanation has to do with the economic situation in the capital: a recession brought on by the heightened military activities caused by revolts in various parts of the Habsburg Empire, and mounting tensions with France (the execution of Emperor Joseph's sister Marie Antoinette a few years later certainly did not help). During the four years that piano concertos replaced opera in Mozart's scheme of things, he put much of his energy into composing and performing these works, and curiously, despite the highly public character of these concertos, intended for the enjoyment of audiences, this public mode of expression also lent itself well to touches of intimacy. That can be sensed in the heartfelt nature of some of the music itself, but it can go beyond that, to the dramatic essence of the works.

LATE: CLARINET CONCERTO IN A (K622)

With only two piano concertos after those written for Vienna in 1786, and not his most exceptional ones, concertos for that instrument had ceased to be a priority for Mozart. Throughout his life he had written concertos for various wind instruments, either for friends such as the horn concertos for Ignaz Leutgeb, or on commission—in one case taking an existing oboe concerto and passing it off with some reworking as a flute concerto—but little of this came late in his all-too-short life, with the exception of the clarinet concerto, written for his clarinet virtuoso colleague Anton Stadler. The instrument in one form or another had been around longer than is sometimes reported, since the beginning of the eighteenth century, but by the time of Mozart's concerto it still was an instrument in progress, and would continue to be well into the nineteenth century. Stadler himself made improvements to it, adding low notes that could not be reached on earlier ones, and Mozart wrote the concerto for this instrument in progress, the basset clarinet, which soon vanished with further developments. The autograph manuscript for this work has not survived, which has forced editors into a certain amount of guesswork to come up with the definitive edition. Mozart clearly fell in love with the instrument, considering the wonderful way that he used it here and elsewhere, recognizing its lyrical quality—at least in the hands of a player such as Stadler—which could be translated so effectively to the exploration of profound emotions. In a curious way it seems fitting that this work for an instrument not yet fully developed should be his last instrumental work, and aside from the little Masonic Cantata (K623), the last work of any type that he would complete before his untimely death. We cannot know if the tone of this work emanated from any type of recognition of his impending end, but the emotional depth he achieved, especially in the middle movement, far surpassing that of the late horn or piano concertos, suggests he may have written it as much for himself as for Stadler.

Unlike the piano concertos of the mid-1780s, which achieve drama in part through a certain amount of tension between the solo and the ensemble, in the clarinet concerto the two work together in complete harmony. Even the orchestration supports that accord, as the orchestra complements the lyrical quality of the clarinet by lacking oboes, trumpets, and timpanis with their more punctuating or prominent sounds, leaving it, aside from the strings, to the gentle blending of flutes, bassoons, and horns. With this absence of tension between solo and ensemble, the first movement behaves in a traditional way, letting the orchestra have a fairly extended opening section, to which the solo responds with the identical theme first given by the ensemble. More than the piano concertos just described, this concerto comes much closer to the model compared to *Run Lola Run*, as the solo now explores the themes presented by the ensemble from a new although not radically different perspective, occasionally darkening the tone somewhat with excursions into the minor, exploiting the very lowest register of the clarinet, or with passage work that can be chromatic. Near the end of the movement the solo bows out to allow the ensemble to have the final say, which it does in an entirely amiable spirit.

That amiable tone in the first movement gives way to perhaps the most serious second movement that Mozart ever wrote, with a much slower than usual adagio tempo, and an exquisite melody in the clarinet from the beginning, supported at first by strings only. Despite the lack of an orchestral introduction, the movement can certainly be thought of as an aria, with the singing tone of the clarinet in place of a mezzo soprano; not until well into the movement do we hear passage work from the solo—the beginning of the middle section of this three-part aria—and some of this could be thought of as ornamentation to the melodic flow, although more for affective purposes than display. Not only aria-like, the nature of the melody can be compared with certain of Mozart's opera arias that profoundly probe heartfelt matters, such as the two sung by the Countess in *The Marriage of Figaro*, "Porgi amor" and "Dove sono," the first of which will be discussed in some detail in chapter 7. In "Porgi amor" Mozart even features two clarinets as the chief obbligato instruments, and they contribute much to the tone of the Countess's lament about the loss of love. This aria offers a superb example of Mozart exploring the deepest possible sadness in a major key, and this concerto movement does the same, in D major.

The start of the melody for the clarinet in this movement has much in common with the opening of the Countess's, as they both have short sub-phrases separated by rests, each has a rising gesture followed by a falling back, they have similar rhythms, and in the larger phrases they each have an overall rise followed by a descent to or below the starting point; in the aria the clarinets make their entry immediately after this first full phrase. Because of the great similarities, we can assume that the two also probe similar emotions, although a concerto will not have the specific associations that an opera with a plot has. Still, it can possibly have its own drama, of a personal nature. It's tempting to speculate that Mozart may have been pondering the potential brevity of his own life as he now stood at the apex of his musical powers, knowing that he had much more to say to the world but fearful that he may soon be silent. He wrote this work two months before he died, and while his health vacillated at the time, only in the last few weeks did his end seem imminent. The uncertainty of his health may, though, have prompted such musings. The third section returns to the beginning, with its later emphasis on descending figures in both solo and ensemble, and solo with orchestra conclude together in a spirit of quiet resignation. The third movement, a rondo, tries to lighten things up a little, putting a good face on the regret just expressed, but in spite of its efforts it cannot escape the darker tone entirely, again occasionally slipping into the minor or using the lowest register. The orchestra gets the final say, and as loud and cheerful as it may attempt to be, it cannot shake loose the memory of the previous movement.

6

SALONS

Solo Keyboard Works

Taking piano lessons became common for boys during the twentieth century, but in previous centuries that would have been unheard of, since the piano was almost exclusively the domain of women. In Mozart's time families with the means to do so would insist on their daughters studying this instrument, as a crucial part of their finishing education. These women, usually amateurs but often exceptionally talented, would play for their own enjoyment, for small circles of family or friends, and for audiences that could fit into the drawing rooms of their homes—as private concerts or as a part of musical salons. Men who played the piano more often than not were professional musicians, and when invited to play at these home concerts, as Mozart often was, they would display the quality of playing that talented amateurs could aspire to but not likely reach. Usually composers as well, these professionals occasionally played their own sonatas, or possibly that of another composer, but generally preferred instead to improvise at the keyboard, producing music that appealed to the emotions, with rapid changes of mood, or by telling a musical story, in some ways not unlike music for silent films early in the twentieth century. Improvisers for films often evoked topics or associations, summoning the emotions underlying the visuals through these associations. The professionals during the eighteenth century used topics as well, but also played in ways that would show their virtuosity, astounding their listeners with their ability to make up such things right on the spot. Instead of sonatas, these improvisations came closer to resembling fantasies, themes and variations, rondos, or other miscellaneous types not as structured as sonatas.

If we compare Mozart's sonatas with his other major works for keyboard—the concertos—we notice very quickly that the sonatas do not reach the same high level, but that should not cause us to undervalue them. Mozart wrote all of his mature piano concertos for himself to perform, and for that reason they could be demanding in the extreme. He did not compose sonatas for himself, even though he did occasionally perform them at private concerts; he wrote them for the large number of amateur women players, which meant he intended them for publication, so as many amateurs as possible could get their hands on them. They also served another purpose, to be used for teaching, and for Mozart, like any other teacher at the time, most, if not all, of the pupils were women; some of the sonatas incorporate technical matters that aspiring pianists need to address. The sonata market boomed in Vienna in the late eighteenth century, with publishers well aware that good money could be made, composers issuing a steady stream of sonatas as a means of keeping body and soul together while working on long-term and financially riskier projects such as operas or symphonies, and women with means eagerly awaiting the latest sheet music to hit the stores. Composers published not only sonatas, but also fantasies, variations, and other types, providing variety for their devotees as well as pieces that would make these players feel more like the composers themselves, coming from an improvisational mindset.

At the age of ten Mozart composed a few piano sonatas, presumably as compositional exercises and no doubt with Papa's help (all of these are now lost), but then did not touch the medium again for almost another decade. Unlike his early start on just about every other type of composition (first symphony at the age of eight, first sacred work at ten, first opera at eleven), his apparent avoidance of piano sonatas until the ripe old age of nineteen reflects on the situation in Salzburg, where the market for publication scarcely existed. In fact, he wrote the sonatas from the late 1770s mainly for himself to perform while traveling. As for the later sonatas, we know from a number of sources that the amateurs who played them were predominantly women—from information about the identity of pupils, the almost invariable dedications to women on the published music, the social phenomenon of piano playing as a part of the finishing education of young women, and the role of women in the musical salons. Another source, in fact one of the most interesting and illuminating, comes from literature, and the use of the piano as a powerful image with feminine associations in novels and poetry. Some writers themselves excelled as musicians. Jane Austen, for example, incorporated piano playing and music for that instrument into some of her novels, while others simply recognized how potent an image the piano could be. Friedrich Schiller, for one, makes that central to his poem "Laura am Klavier" (Laura at the Piano), in which he reinvents Petrarch's muse Laura as a modern, erotically provocative voice through the piano, but still with her sense of spiritual mystery. She keeps this mystery with her angelic harmonies, "like new-born seraphims from their heaven," but Schiller also labels her "Zauberin" (enchantress), able to entice and tempt with "ein wollustig Ungestum" (a sensual impetuousness). Other poets shared this fascination with Laura, but in Schiller's language she could sing with the seductive silvery tones of the piano.

Perhaps the most striking treatment of the piano as a feminine seductive force came from Johann Wolfgang von Goethe in his novel *Die Leiden des jungen Werther* (*The Sorrows of Young Werther*, 1774), in which Werther's unrequited love for Lotte smolders because of the way her piano playing arouses him. Since propriety prevented portrayal of an actual relationship between an engaged or married woman and another man, Goethe needed to find a way to bring this illicit passion near to the surface, and for this the piano served his purposes perfectly. In this epistolary novel, Werther sums up his feelings this way: "Why couldn't I throw myself at her feet? Why couldn't I counter with an embrace and a thousand kisses? She escaped to the piano and sang to her own accompaniment in her sweet, low voice, and so melodiously. Never were her chaste lips more enchanting. It was as though they parted thirsty for the sweet tones that swelled forth from the instrument and only a furtive echo escaped them." Lotte has some inkling of the effect her playing can have, and she draws a parallel with dancing: "If passion for dancing is sinful, then I cheerfully admit to it. . . . When something is troubling me and I can sit down at my poor old piano and play a *contredanse*, everything is all right again" (the seductive nature of the contredanse will be discussed in connection with its usage in *Don Giovanni* in chapter 8). Goethe's treatment of the piano as an image raises an interesting possibility for Mozart's sonatas—that they are not only the province of women but they may have an element of seductiveness as well. Women played them not only as pleasant entertainments, but also as a means of attracting husbands (or lovers, depending on the circumstances), and some of that appeal may lie in the music itself.

PUPILS AND SALONS

Mozart wrote half of his piano sonatas, all of his fantasies, and most of his variations and other types of solo keyboard pieces during the final decade of his life while living in Vienna, and as a resident of the capital he had special and often warmly familiar relationships with the women who would be the market for these works, as pupils, as friends, at private concerts, and in the salons. There were risks involved in moving to Vienna, a city where taste could be fickle, especially since he lacked a court appointment when he came. Before he could knock the Viennese out with his operas or piano concertos, he had to earn a living the only way he could, by taking on pupils and by publishing music for which a market already existed. When Leopold came to visit him in 1785, he complained to Nannerl back in Salzburg about the pace of the private concerts and salons, and now as a widower, he was not entirely disinterested in some of the women who held salons. Never one to shy away from giving advice, even after the fairly disastrous breakdown of the father-son relationship in 1778–1779, Leopold always emphasized the need for pupils, something Mozart knew perfectly well, in spite of the time they would take away from composition.

Teaching could be a fairly tedious business, but if he enjoyed the pupil—or even better, her whole family—it could go down much more easily. One such possibility arose on the extended trip in 1777–1779, while in Mannheim, where he hit it off with Christian Cannabich, concertmaster and conductor of the famous Mannheim orchestra, and the rest of his family, which included Cannabich's daughter Rosa, who briefly became his pupil. About his goings-on with this family he sent a delightfully facetious letter to his father, putting it in the form of a confession:

I, Johannes Chrisostomus Amadeus Wolfgangus Sigismundus Mozart, plead guilty that yesterday and the day before (and already
many other times) I did not arrive home before midnight; and that
from ten o'clock until the designated hour at Cannabich's house, and
in the presence and en Compagnie of Cannabich, his wife and
daughter [Rosa] . . . I frequently, without difficulty, but with ease,
spouted rhymes, and, in fact complete garbage, namely, about dirt,
shitting and arse-licking—and actually in thoughts, words and—but
not in deeds. I would not have behaved so godlessly, though, if our
ringleader, namely the one named Lisel [Elisabetha Cannabich—
Rosa's mother], had not incited and agitated me into it; and I must
confess that I heartily enjoyed it. I confess these sins and transgres-
sions of mine from the bottom of my heart, and in the hope of having
to confess them often, I strongly resolve to improve on the sinful life
I have embarked on. Hence I beg for the holy dispensation, if it can
be easily secured; if not, it's all the same to me, for the game will
carry on anyway. (MBA ii 123–24)

Leopold may have been amused, but not about Mozart squandering
valuable time; he would have been much happier about the fact that
Rosa took piano lessons from Mozart, and even more about the description of this teaching, involving the Sonata in C major (K309), which
Mozart wrote for her:

We finished the opening Allegro today. The Andante will give us
most trouble, for it is full of expression and must be played accurate-
ly and with the exact shades of forte and piano, precisely as they are
marked. She is very smart and learns very easily. Her right hand is
very good, but her left, unfortunately, is completely ruined. . . . I
have told her too that if I were her regular teacher, I would lock up
all her music, cover the keys with a handkerchief and make her
practice, first with the right hand and then with the left, nothing but
passages, trills, mordants and so forth, very slowly at first, until each
hand should be thoroughly trained. (LMF 374)

In another letter, Mozart indicated how a sonata could actually be
much more than a teaching piece, suggesting that Rosa "is exactly like
the Andante," making the expressive slow movement a musical portrait
of her. He no doubt enjoyed teaching her, but also found it demanding.
In Vienna a few years later his pupils included the likes of Countess

Wilhelmine Thun-Hohenstein, Countess Marie Karoline Rumbecke, Maria Thérèse von Trattner, Barbara von Ployer, and Josepha Auernhammer.

Of the various salons Mozart attended, he probably most relished those of Countess Thun, a highly sophisticated and intelligent woman, and, of course, his own pupil. Coming from the upper nobility, she attracted impressive gatherings, and even the emperor himself, who may have done some things for Mozart's career at her urging. She promoted and supported his career with enthusiasm, and in all probability he performed his sonatas K330–332 at her salons. While Mozart's association with her appeared to be beyond reproach, his relationship with another of his friends (and probably a pupil), Baroness Martha Elisabeth von Waldstätten, took a somewhat different turn, certainly with a seductive or at least naughty side to it. She went out of her way to assist both Mozart and Constanze, facilitating their marriage ceremony, providing a lavish meal, rescuing Constanze with a place to live before the wedding, and even pleading the appropriateness of the marriage to Leopold. Her promiscuity was no secret in Vienna, and when Mozart wrote to Leopold that "I am under a great obligation to the baroness. . . . I should very much like to give her some pleasure," there may be more here than meets the eye. He warned Constanze about the baroness's behavior, urging her not to emulate her in any way, but that apparently did not stop Mozart from having his own fun with her. Immediately after a masquerade ball, and not long after the wedding, he wrote this to the thirty-eight-year-old baroness:

> Now, in God's name; I have taken her and must keep her! What is to be done?—I must praise her—and imagine that the praise is true! . . . All right then, courage!—I would like to ask your Ladyship that—pfui, the devil—that would be too indecent! *A propos.* Does your Ladyship not know the little song?
>
> A woman and a jug of beer,
> How can they hold together?
> The woman owns her own supply
> Of which she points an ample pair at me.
> Then they hang together.
>
> Didn't I bring that in very neatly? But now, *senza burle.* If your Ladyship could give me a pair this evening, you would be doing me a great service. For my wife is—is—and has urges—but only for beer

prepared in the English way! Well done, little wife! I see finally that you really are good for something. My wife, who is an angel of a woman, and I, who am a fine specimen of a husband, both kiss your Ladyship's hands a thousand times and are eternally your
faithful vassals,

Mozart magnus, corpore parvus,

et

Constantia, omnium uxorum pulcherrima
et pruddentissima. (MBA iii 234–45)

Was Mozart simply playing an epistolary game, or was he as much a hypocrite as the ones he portrays in *The Marriage of Figaro* and *Don Giovanni*? Certainly his relationships with his pupils could stray into ribaldry, and we should not be too surprised if sonatas written for them push some boundaries as well.

TOPICS, EMOTIONS, AND URGES

When is a sonata only a sonata? Are sonatas just nice pieces of music for the enjoyment of those who play them, or can they have other meanings, perhaps personal for the composer, or maybe even for the public? At one time observers assumed that instrumental music from the eighteenth century belonged to a category known as pure or absolute music, meaning nothing beyond itself but simply standing as music that could be understood only in musical terms. Few still hold to that position since far too much has been discovered about the ways composers, including Mozart, imbued their works with extramusical meaning. One of the more interesting approaches to this has come from Leonard Ratner and students of his such as Wye J. Allanbrook: the identification of *topoi*, or topics, namely associations that certain musical passages will evoke derived from dance types, street songs, folk music, or any other source where the music itself makes the identity of the association clear. If the composer uses a theme that sounds like the *Dies irae* plainchant, and follows that with one that has a folk dance flavor associated with weddings or spring growth, as Haydn does in numerous of his late symphonies, we have a self-contained dramatic contrast playing the forces of death and life against each other. Mozart uses these kinds of topics consistently in his works, and they can add levels of meaning in operas or generate drama that can be understood in more than musical terms in instrumental pieces. One especially good example of this in the piano sonatas K332, nicely illustrated by Allanbrook, will be explored in the next section.

While topics give us a very useful insight into what Mozart may have been up to in some of his sonatas, other ways can also be found to get at these possibilities, in some cases coming from the composer's own comments, or, more often than not, there are connections of music with specific emotions, states of mind, actions, or urges that happen in operas, where the texts confirm the associations. For a comment by the composer, the one he made about the slow movement from the Sonata in C, K309, proves to be especially useful, a movement, as just noted, which Mozart claimed to be a musical portrait of his fourteen-year-old pupil Rosa Cannabich. This becomes even more interesting when we consider how Mozart described her to his father, as "a very pretty and charming girl. . . . She is serious, does not say much, but when she speaks, she is pleasant and amiable" (LMF 408). On this extended trip Mozart consistently bent the truth in letters to his father, and listening to the music of the movement in question, we would simply not come up with the description provided for his father. The music is playful, pert, full of mischief, and sassy, and one suspects in light of the fun he had with her family, including the apparently naughty behavior of Rosa's mother, that the musical description comes much closer to the truth. As often happens with Mozart, including in operas where contradictions exist between music and text, Mozart tells us what we really need to know in the music itself. In a movement such as this we have a connection between Mozart and his pupil, with the composer writing her into the music itself, revealing what he probably most enjoys about her, and while she was innocent because of her age, there may have been similar, less innocent connections with some of his older pupils.

Since Mozart linked no other sonatas with a pupil, we need to get at the possible associations between music and people by other means, possibly through the use of topics, but in different ways as well, such as with the help of opera. The linkage of music and emotions goes back to the origins of opera, especially in arias, where we consistently find rage, love, regret, joy, hope, longing, disdain, and numerous other emotions portrayed clearly using distinctive music. If the composer then employs similar music in instrumental works and builds in contrasts or interaction with other musical emotions, we can get the sense of something unfolding that may prompt us to experience the music in fairly complex ways. For some of Mozart's pupils there may have been special layers of meaning. This can go far beyond the simple emotions of happiness or sadness, also straying into seduction, desire, teasing, practical jokes, deception, and a host of other possibilities. All of these can be found in his operas, usually associated with specific characters, and I will refer to some of these in the discussion of specific keyboard works that follows. The music that turns up in sonatas will of course never be the same as that used in the operas, but there can be passages or styles sufficiently similar to give something of the same sense, and suggest that Mozart may be playing some musical games not unlike the ones he played with words, for example with Baroness Waldstätten, or, even more so, with his amorous cousin the Bäsle.

PIANO SONATAS, FANTASIES, AND MORE

Mozart's piano sonatas written before moving to Vienna, often quickly sketched while traveling, appear—with the exception of ones written for a temporary pupil such as Rosa Cannabich—to have been produced as performance pieces for himself, with the appropriate level of difficulty. Much changed in Mozart's career when he moved to Vienna in 1781, and that included his approach to piano sonatas, since he now lived in the city of salons and well-heeled pupils—both youthful and more mature. He could of course continue what he had already been doing much earlier with expressiveness, especially in slow movements; some of the pre-1781 sonatas have middle movements labeled "andante amoroso," "andante con espressione," or "andante cantabile con espressione." While the labeling may not have changed all that much, the nature of the writing did, with the expressive character of the Vienna sonatas very much surpassing the earlier ones, and not only in slow movements. He clearly did not compose these sonatas for himself, and since he now knew many of the women who purchased and played his sonatas, he wrote them in ways that could establish musical relationships between himself and the players. He also knew that these women played the sonatas in settings that would help to reveal themselves as potential future spouses to a suitable man in the salon audience. As with

Goethe's descriptions of the effect a woman's playing could have, the appeal could be playful and even seductive, without being spelled out specifically and therefore not breaking any rules of decorum.

The first three written for Vienna, K330–32, stand out as possibly the most appealing of all his piano sonatas, and the publisher Artaria published them as a set in 1784 just shortly after Mozart wrote them, making them available as quickly as possible to the intended players. The andante cantabile middle movement of the first of these, the Sonata in C, K330, seems to capture something of that alluring flavor, as he tells the player that it should be not only singable, but also dolce (sweet), starting it with a melody that fits both of these descriptions. It opens with four repeated notes that gently, by way of a turn, lead to a small leap of a fourth, and when for the second phrase that same iterated pattern recurs, he breaks the expectation with a leap of an octave, repeating that immediately in the next bar. That upward leap, propelled by a grace note from below, seems not unlike the leaps used in *The Magic Flute* by Tamino near the beginning, underlying his desire for Pamina as he looks at her picture, or the one she sings in Act 2 as she ecstatically embraces him. These leaps become the most striking feature of this movement, suggesting something more than a song-like and sweet melody.

The second piece, in A, K331, may very well be the best known of all Mozart's sonatas, certainly the two outer movements if not the unusual minuet between them. Instead of the usual sonata-form movement at the beginning, Mozart leads off with a theme and variations (his approach to variations will be described in the next section), and the theme, possibly fairly well known at the time, comes from the Czech folksong "Hořela líp, hořela," in Austria known with the German words "Freu dich, mein Herz, denk' an kein" (Rejoice, my heart, think of no one else). The sumptuous variations on this theme take the rejoicing to new levels in each of the six variations, giving musical embellishment possibly on the exclusiveness of the attraction implied in the text, especially in the delightful fourth variation in which the left hand plays the upper melodic lines. The spirit continues in the minuet and trio second movement with lots of chromaticism and compact phrases that one writer has characterized as "yearning phrases"; continuing the enjoyment of the fourth variation from the previous movement, the trio also places the upper melody in the left hand, with the crossing over of hands perhaps suggesting what sometimes happens in piano four-hands writing when physical contact results from hand crossing. The third movement, Alla Turca, the Turkish march, known to almost everyone, stands as one of those classical pieces that have entered popular culture in our time through advertising, films, and other hearings. Mozart wrote this at about the time of his Turkish opera *The Abduction from the Seraglio*, and of course Turkish operas were all the rage at the time, apparently also prompting new styles in women's fashions (a point the film *Amadeus* probably got right). We can easily imagine a woman at a salon playing this sonata wearing the latest low-cut neckline and a plumed Turkish hat (as the singer Caterina Cavalieri played by Christine Ebersole does in *Amadeus*).

While not quite so well known, the third of this trio of sonatas, in F, K332, may in fact be the most fascinating of all, keeping player and listeners in the first movement on the edge of their seats with its rapid-fire shifts from one theme or topic to the next. Back in sonata form, this one confirms that we should abandon all preconceived notions about the number of themes any sonata-form movement should have; textbooks usually say two plus a closing theme, but this one has no fewer than seven—more if we include the new material within some of the themes and the fact that the so-called development starts with a new theme. Wye J. Allanbrook has outlined the different topics that these various themes embody, starting in a singing style with a shift to the learned style in the first theme, moving to a minuet, then a sturm und drang (storm and stress) rant in D minor no less, on to another minuet, a contrast to this with disruptive syncopations and even hemiola (changing the meter from 3/4 to 2/4 by the offbeat placements of forte and piano), yet another minuet, and then ending the exposition with a fantasy-like closing theme. Trying to develop all of this would be impossible, so Mozart leads off the development with an eighth theme, and then comes back to the syncopated material from the exposition. The recapitulation restates the exposition as precisely as it can, with no change other than the tonal one keeping the section in the tonic key. As delightful as the tour of topics may be, Mozart seems to be playing with his audience here, turning everything upside down with themes that seem mismatched, with fairly violent outbursts in the stormy key of D minor after sedate minuets, and more dislodging of the regularity of the 3/4 meter of the minuet with something that loses the meter. After all this the closing theme seems like a nose-thumbing gesture, not unlike the ones at the end of *Don Giovanni* or *The Magic Flute*, responding derisively to what has been going on. The opening singing style and the minuet—the courtly dance that belongs to the class of most of Mozart's pupils—in a way defines the conventional expectation of these women's place in society, but Mozart has given them a very cheeky comeback, allowing them to mock their traditional roles and behave with impudence that sets them free, as do women from his operas such as Susanna, Zerlina, Despina, and Pamina.

The slow movement, very slow in this case (adagio), evokes emotions in much the same way that the Countess does in her first number of *The Marriage of Figaro*, "Porgi amor," using similar devices of rising and falling back, gentle syncopations, and propulsion to a climax. Even the parallel thirds that follow this climax and then abound remind us of the obbligato clarinets in thirds that accompany the Countess. As the discussion of that opera will confirm, that cavatina gives the Countess special status, setting her apart from the fray by opening up the second act, and despite the comedy of the work, gives us a sense of the profound regret she feels as a result of the Count's promiscuity. If the first movement of this sonata points to the restrictive role of women in eighteenth-century society, the second movement may be looking at it from a more serious angle, with the sense of regret that women could rightly feel; these social issues will be discussed in much more detail in the chapters on the late operas. The third movement may fit into the scheme as well, with its opening bravura that breaks down after twelve bars and gives way to a dolce melody that does not stay dolce for long, since it in turn yields to syncopations, angular passages, and very large leaps. Again from operas we recognize these types of large leaps as key to defining the strength of character for women such as Donna Anna (courage) in *Don Giovanni* and Fiordiligi (honesty) in *Così fan tutte*.

Mozart did not write many piano sonatas, only eighteen as far as we know, and the ones that follow this wonderful set of three do many of the same kinds of things, with some that in their simplicity appear to be teaching pieces, while others challenge the skills of the most able players. One of the easy ones, the Sonata in C, K545, Mozart listed in his own catalog of works as being "for beginners," although as simple and charming as it may be, it can play tricks with the memory. After the opening four bars of the theme it launches into a sequence of five scale passages, each one starting a note lower than the previous one. I once heard one of the great pianists (a noted Mozart interpreter) performing this at a concert, who forgot when to come out of the sequence, adding a sixth which of course threw the whole thing off miserably, forcing the pianist to stop and start over again. Maybe the professionals should leave these to amateurs, and keep these pieces off the concert stage. One writer has suggested that the andante middle movement of that sonata more or less resembles the aria "Dalla sua pace" sung by Don Ottavio in *Don Giovanni*, an opera Mozart wrote in 1787, just a year before this sonata. Whether one hears that or not, the idea of connections between operas and sonatas is not farfetched.

If Mozart's output of piano sonatas seems a little thin, he more than made up for it with other types of solo keyboard works, including variations, fantasies, rondos, minuets, fugues, different dances, and others that have no title aside from allegro, andante, or adagio. The traditional sonata at the time wore something of a straightjacket, with an opening sonata form movement, a slow movement—usually andante—and a quick rondo finale, and Mozart went out of his way to liberate his sonatas from this mold, sometimes starting them with variations, using minuets along with a singing style for middle movements, ending with rondos, and here and there infusing them with writing that veers toward fantasies, fugues, or other dances. These other types of compositions, then, written equally before and after the move to Vienna, are closely related to sonatas. He wrote most of the later pieces for the same players as the sonatas, and with many of these pieces enjoyed the same kind of playful relationship with these women.

Some of the other smaller solo keyboard pieces are real gems, such as the Rondo in A Minor, K511, from 1787, with a theme that immediately pushes the chromatic envelope, at times has a distinctive vocal character, and finds climaxes through leaps just like characters such as the Countess or Fiordiligi in the operas. As noted in other chapters, Mozart does not need minor keys to generate sadness in operas, but in a keyboard piece for salons, the emotions perhaps need to be worn more directly on the sleeve. At the point where a dolce melody appears, he shifts to the parallel major, and then stays there for a very long time, ending that middle section with fantasy-like flourishes. For the return of the first section that fantasy-like character has become much more engrained. Fantasies could stand alone as distinctive works or coexist with other pieces, such as the Fantasy and Fugue in C, K394, or the Fantasy in C Minor, K475, published in 1785 with the sonata in the same key, K457. Even though fantasies shared some common ground with sonatas, they did offer a somewhat different type of experience to those who played them, since their extended flourishes had an improvisatory quality, as in the Fantasy in C Minor, K396, from 1782. They gave the player some sense of the type of experience enjoyed by a great improviser like Mozart, who could play this sort of thing from the top of his head for hours, of course with levels of difficulty far exceeding anything written down. Fantasies also had that quality of rapid shifts in character and emotions, allowing the player to manipulate the listener as though on a string, as in the Fantasy in D Minor, K397, also from 1782, which has distinctive sections progressing through andante, adagio, returns to the original tempo interspersed by presto flourishes, allegretto, and finally back to the first tempo. Within these all types of contrasts can occur, from harsh repetition and chromaticism to highly vocal dolce melodies. Perhaps with these pieces more than any others, the players could get a glimpse of how Mozart's musical mind worked, reveling in the boundless creativity that set him apart from all others.

VARIATIONS

It's a brisk autumn day in Vienna in 1785, and you, in your late teens, have been invited along with your mother to attend a musical salon at the luxurious home of Maria Thérèse von Trattner, whose husband Johann had this home built on the fashionable Graben, not far from the Stephansdom (St. Stephen's Cathedral). Maria started studying piano with Mozart shortly after his arrival in Vienna in 1781, and holds salons monthly in which she plays along with some of his other pupils. Mozart himself occasionally attends, and of course he would be asked to play at the end, which he would do by taking the theme of a sonata and improvising on it in the most ingenious way. On this occasion he could not attend, and neither could your mother, but you happily come because an attractive young woman whom you have met socially on a few occasions, only slightly older than yourself, will be one of the performers. At those previous meetings you thought there might be something developing between the two of you, but it was still too early to tell. This woman, Barbara Ployer, had just started studying with Mozart the year before, and she plays exceptionally well. She has a look of mischief in her face, and when at the most recent meeting she told you to call her Babette, you were not quite sure if you should take this as a new level of intimacy, or if she was just teasing you.

Her turn comes, and before she starts, she takes a quick and quizzical look at you before announcing that everyone will recognize the theme for the variations by Mozart that she will play. Of course you recognize it immediately, and unlike some of his other themes for variations, taken from popular operas by Salieri, Sarti, Grétry, Paisiello, and Gluck, this one jumps out at you with the delightful two-part simplicity of the theme's setting. Not only well versed in music, you are also well traveled, having been as far afield as the Loire valley of France, where you had spent a happy summer a couple of years ago, living with a family in the picturesque wine village of Sancerre to improve your French. While there, you heard children singing folk songs, one of which Barbara now plays, the nursery-rhyme song "Ah, vous dirai-je, maman" (Ah, would I tell you, mom [known to us a couple of centuries later as "Twinkle, twinkle little star" or "Baa, baa black sheep"]). After the uncluttered theme, the variations that follow cleverly rework the theme, always keeping the theme recognizable in the variations. Depending on the nature of the variation, this transforming of the theme could inject levels of humor, facetious sadness, amazement, or just plain fun. Unlike what Beethoven would do with variations a generation later, Mozart followed a fairly standard format in his, which he would deviate from if improvising variations himself in performance; in published ones such as this he wrote what talented amateurs could play. With this one, fairly typical of his published variations, the music follows this pattern: theme; variation 1) sixteenth-note embellishment of the right hand melody; 2) sixteenth-note embellishment of the left hand harmony; 3) triplets in the right hand; 4) triplets in the left hand; 5) alternating between hands; 6) harmony in the right hand and embellished melody in the left; 7) scale passages in the right hand alternating with broken figuration; 8) the minor key, with suspensions and chromatic lines; 9) back to the major, still with suspensions; 10) hand crossing, with treble melody played by the left hand; 11) adagio, with syncopations and appoggiaturas; 12) the allegro finale. It had just been published a few months earlier, although he wrote it shortly after settling in Vienna in 1781.

Having taken the study of French seriously, as any well-educated young person in Vienna would (in higher society French always trumped German at this time), you knew that the children's version parodied a French love poem. You could imagine that not only was Mozart playing a game with this, but Barbara, with her glance at you, appeared to be up to something as well. The words for the nursery rhyme you had heard went like this:

Ah! Vous dirai-je Maman	Ah! Would I tell you mom
Ce qui cause mon tourment?	What torments me?
Papa veut que je raisonne	Papa wants me to be reasonable
Comme une grande personne	Like an adult
Moi je dis que les bonbons	But I say that candies
Valent mieux que la raison.	Have more value than reason.

All very cute, but you knew that the love poem from which the parody comes, with the title "La Confidence," starts with the same two lines but then moves on like this:

Ah! Vous dirai-je, maman,	Ah! Would I tell you mom
Ce qui cause mon tourment?	What torments me?
Depuis que j'ai vu Clitandre,	Since I saw Clitandre
Me regarder d'un air tendre	Look at me so tenderly;
Mon cœur dit à chaque instant:	My heart says every second:
"Peut-on vivre sans amant?"	"Can anyone live without a lover?"

It has five stanzas, and by the fourth stanza it has come to this (different variants of it exist):

Il rougis et par malheur	He blushes and sadly
Un soupir trahit mon cœur.	A sigh betrays his heart.
La cruel avec adresse,	The cruel with emphasis

Profit de sa faiblesse:	Exploit his weakness:
Hélas, Maman! Un faux pas	Alas, Mom! One silly mistake
Me fit tomber dans ses bras.	Makes him fall into her embrace.

Thankfully your mother has not come to witness this, since Barbara seemed to be directing it straight at you, and you would certainly not tell such things to your mother. Barbara clearly was exploiting your weakness for her and for music, and if she didn't before, she now has you exactly where she wants you, using the variations to snare you with their swings from sheer delight to crocodile tears. In a way, the variations even seem to take the love song through a similar type of progression, although not with any fixed link between text and music. Still, the variation in the minor has something of the tone of the fourth stanza, of course with a touch of silliness considering that the lad, something of a mommy's boy, tells this tale of woe (or happiness?) to his mother. The mother/son relationship of course lightens the whole thing up, but the torment here seems to have more to do with lovesickness; by the end all can have a good laugh, prompted by the allegro finale immediately after the woebegone adagio. After the performances end and you enjoy a good glass of wine, you hope for more than the bemused chuckle that you get from Barbara; she apparently expects you to figure it all out from the music.

7

REVOLUTIONARY THOUGHTS ABOUT WOMEN AND POWER

Figaro and Così

The Marriage of Figaro (Le nozze di Figaro) remains one of the most popular works in the entire operatic repertory, and for good reasons. Aside from the facts that the characters engage us as real people and the music is wonderful and memorable, the work takes on issues that are as relevant to our time as they were to Mozart's, namely the obnoxious way that some people in authority throw their power around, and the way especially that this affects women. *Così fan tutte* may not have quite the same traction with opera managers as *Figaro*, but it addresses these issues as resoundingly, although much more subtly, which may account for it not being as popular. For both of these Mozart worked with the same librettist, Lorenzo Da Ponte, who appeared to be the ideal collaborator for the socially conscious Mozart intent on getting his views on these subjects into the public domain. In fact we know little of what actually went on between them, unlike the composition of *Idomeneo*, during which a regular stream of letters flowed between Mozart and his father in order to get what he wanted through his father's intervention from the relatively inexperienced and conventional Giambattista Varesco back in Salzburg. In Vienna Mozart now moved in the most sophisticated literary and artistic circles, and it was inevitable that the best composer in town should connect up with the most progressive librettist there. Da Ponte stood at an entirely different level than Varesco, and the two of them appeared to hit it off nicely, without the kind of tensions encountered previously. Mozart would have insisted that the libretto be prepared exactly as he wished, and Da Ponte either gave in readily on these points, or perhaps, as a man of considerable experience, persuaded Mozart occasionally to set things up his way. Regardless of how they went about it, we have two of the most spectacular operas in the repertory, packed with social criticism that has lost little of its edge more than two centuries later.

THE MARRIAGE OF FIGARO

The power politics in *Figaro* concern the relationship between the aristocracy and those beneath them, but in the twenty-first century we do not need to assume the situation has vanished because that kind of class distinction no longer exists—with the exception of countries such as Great Britain which have retained the monarchy. Some people in Britain, to say nothing of the Commonwealth countries and even the United States, still get very excited about the monarchy, but for many it's simply a source of amusement, comparing the British with their "Palace" to Americans with their "Dallas." Following the antics of the Queen's offspring has given us much to laugh about, at times with embarrassment, although in parliamentary democracies instances continue to exist when the regal can exert actual power, for example in the dissolution of parliament or the forming of new governments. Protocol still demands a bow or curtsy in the presence of royalty, but for the most part, the monarchy has little or nothing to do with our lives, in contrast to Mozart's time. With the decline of the royals, certainly in authority if not in actual existence, it did not take us long to find substitutions. Wealth has become the new royalty, and along with wealth, other types of stratification remain equally well defined, most notably with the relationships of bosses and employees, which in many cases look very similar to the old feudal arrangements of the *ancien régime*, lacking any kind of democratic input from below. Probably most of us can recognize the Count from *Figaro* from our workplaces, from his eagerness to throw his weight around as our superior, but all too often as well with what he thinks he can get away with as a sexual predator. *Figaro* could just as easily have been written at the beginning of the twenty-first century, and we would recognize the characters as people we know or have heard about.

The sexual aspect of this opera takes on a special urgency, since almost everything that happens hinges on what the Count claims he has done to bring his estate into line with new enlightened standards: he has abolished the repugnant old feudal *droit de seigneur*, which allowed the lord of the estate to deflower the young servant women in his domain just before they got married. No one has demonstrated that this practice ever actually existed, or if it did, if it involved some sort of financial instead of sexual payment, but whether it existed need not concern us in the slightest: for this plot it does exist, and the story would fall flat without it. Some have even suggested that Caron de Beaumarchais, whose play *Le mariage de Figaro* Mozart and Da Ponte based the opera on, invented it himself, but that too does not matter. Here we have it, and it defines the hypocrisy of the Count, who claims to be enlightened enough to abolish it, but he has every intention of putting it back into practice because he cannot resist Susanna, the Countess's servant, who will soon be marrying Figaro, the Count's valet. The principal action centers around the Count's attempt to get Susanna to meet him in the garden that night for sex before she gets married the next morning, and the main subplot depends on it as well, involving the housekeeper Marcellina's claim to get Figaro as her husband if he cannot repay a loan from her.

The intrigues that take place will amuse us to no end, especially as we watch the Count out-maneuvered at first by Figaro and then most effectively by Susanna and the Countess, but despite the comedy—and even farce at times—a darker side lurks as well, one that keeps this work completely relevant to our time. This concerns the double standard that exists between the sexes, one that gives men the clear advantage in the way they can treat women and in the social perception of their actions. The very notion of the *droit de seigneur* underlies this: it's the lord of the estate who has the right to have sex with his female servants, and certainly not the lady with the male underlings. Some eighteenth-century literature of course explores the possibility of the latter, but very much under the cover of secrecy: for men it's assumed that they will take mistresses, and for women it's expected that they will remain faithful to their husbands. These notions of sexual conduct were deeply ingrained in feudal practice, and during Mozart's time enlightened writers such as Beaumarchais finally challenged them. Have these notions fundamentally changed in the past two centuries? Perhaps at least to some degree in Western society they have, but clearly not in many other cultures, often with horrific consequences for women.

Beaumarchais's *Figaro* stands as the second part of a trilogy, and much of the audience at the time would have known the first work, *The Barber of Seville*, perhaps not from the play itself but more than likely from the opera based on it by Giovanni Paisiello, which had its premiere in 1783—only three years before Mozart's *Figaro*. With the exception of Susanna, most of the main characters turn up in both works, and it's useful, although not essential, to know them from *The Barber*, which today we probably do from Rossini's setting. In that work Rosina (now the Countess) is the ward of Dr. Bartolo, and despite their age difference, he intends to marry her, but with the help of the scheming barber (Figaro), Almaviva (the Count) wrests her away from Bartolo's confinement and marries her, leaving Bartolo fuming. In *Figaro*, though, set a few years later, we will have difficulty recognizing Almaviva as the ardent lover of Rosina, since he now neglects her and hunts women almost the same way he does hares.

Some comparisons need to be made between Beaumarchais and Da Ponte/Mozart in their working of the story, the characters, and the issues, since in many respects they are very different, involving the treatment of the plot, and even more importantly what we learn from the music. Whether or not Mozart and Da Ponte would have wished to set the play as is, the length simply precluded that, since it would have ended up longer than an opera by Wagner. Not only did they not wish to set it as it stood, but they could not, since censorship in Vienna would have prevented inclusion of some of the more politically charged speeches, such as Figaro's in the final act when he dresses down the Count as a nobleman, as someone with only a fraction of his own intelligence and ingenuity but who stands as superior by the mere fact of his birth. Other parts were not especially well suited as operatic settings, such as the court scene, in which Marcellina presses her legal claim against Figaro to get his hand in marriage if he can't produce the money he owes her. That occupies Act 3 of the play, and much of it can go, leaving the opera with four acts. Similarly many details that work in a play had to be trimmed for a musical setting; essential dialogue can be included in recitatives, but that of course is the least important part of an opera. Just because some of the more politically biting speeches have been excised, we should not imagine for a second that the political sting is gone. For the censors, much better able to comprehend words than music, the work appears to have been softened sufficiently to win their approval, but Mozart seems to have pulled the wool over their eyes— and certainly their ears.

In the hands of a composer such as Mozart, we should fully expect that the music will turn the work into something very different from what Beaumarchais had in mind, and the music can make this happen in both relatively straightforward and extremely subtle ways. That difference does not so much concern politics as it does other factors— certainly the depth that can be given to characters, but also the way in which the issues of power and sexuality can be addressed. If Mozart wishes to ridicule a character, he can do that with music, although he will never hit us over the head with it. If he wishes to give a character substance he can ably do that, giving her depth that we may not have suspected from the play. And, if he wants us to leave the theater not simply laughing at the delightful turn of events at the end, but intuiting the more serious aspects of the issues, as happens in the relationship between the Count and the Countess, he can achieve that as well with the music, going beyond Beaumarchais's cheerful conclusion, leaving at least a thread of lingering doubt about whether the Count has been reformed. To achieve this he may ask us to apply our capacity for musical memory, recalling certain key things that have happened earlier when we hear similar kinds of music invoked later. This may seem an unreasonable expectation, but music and memory in fact walk hand-in-hand. We may not catch many things the first time, but the mark of a great opera, like a great film, is that it will not only generate as much or more excitement the second, third, or twentieth time we see it, but we will discover new and breathtaking things with each new experience of it.

Overture and Act I

It's Wednesday, 5 October 1977, and after a long day's work, you opt to spend the evening at home and watch a new made-for-TV production of *Figaro* directed by Jean-Pierre Ponnelle on PBS. Opera has been shown on TV for a number of years now, but mainly films of stage

productions in the series *Live from the Met*. This one, recorded in
Vienna and shot in London, has been designed for TV, using a set
instead of a stage; unlike the cinematic versions that started a few years
later (such as the *Don Giovanni* to be described in the next chapter),
here we have lots of close-ups of the singers, appropriate to a TV screen
instead of a large screen with its greater possibilities for an elaborate
mise-en-scène. As the overture begins, you watch with delight as the
names of the singers scroll by: Dietrich Fischer-Dieskau (the Count),
Kiri te Kanawa (the Countess), Mirella Freni (Susanna), Hermann Prey
(Figaro), Maria Ewing (Cherubino), and also strong secondary roles.
Aside from the extraordinary voices, this cast includes some of the finest
singing actors in the business, especially Freni and Ewing. The titles
make it a little difficult to concentrate on the overture, but you do
notice the fast pace that prepares us for the rapid-fire action about to
unfold. Conflict seems to be generally lacking, and any contrast that
does exist emerges subtly. Some punctuated offbeats give hints of tension, as does a passage heard twice (in different keys) with a rising
chromatic line underlying some counterpoint with more chromaticism
and appoggiaturas that seems slightly out of place, but even here he
gives the rising line to the bassoon, an instrument often associated with
buffa patter.

It may surprise you that Mozart then begins Act 1 with a simple little
duet between Figaro and Susanna, with the two of them doing completely mundane, apparently everyday things—Figaro taking measure-
ments on the floor and Susanna trying on a new hat. Beaumarchais
starts his play with this too, introducing us to the two most important
characters in the work, but with Mozart's music we learn things that the
playwright could not tell us, namely, which of the two holds the upper
hand. The duet follows a typical format, with the two of them first
singing contrasting themes, and then together; when they come together, they do not do so on neutral musical ground, but Susanna wins, with
Figaro conceding to her theme. Throughout the entire work Figaro
may like to think that he controls things, but at almost every turn we see
Susanna one step ahead of him, understanding what he does not, driving the plot through her ingenuity, and clearly winning the battle of the
sexes. Not only does she have one leg up on Figaro, but she does on the
Count as well, demonstrating the mental superiority over the nobility
that Figaro carps about but cannot really quite manage. While able to

manipulate the Count, she also has a friendship with the Countess that places the two of them on equal terms, which Mozart clarifies in Act 3 with the music of a luscious duet. Mozart sets up the simple musical contrast in the opening duet, as he does so often, with different types of dances, using not actual dances but music with the characteristics of specific dances to define the intended aura, and these already emerge fully in the short orchestral introduction: Figaro, with his choppy lines with large intervals, sings a bourrée, a dance with asymmetrical features, while Susanna, with her melodic, stepwise singing, intones a gavotte, a much gentler type of dance, and her gracefulness wins.

Her curiosity about his measuring yields the answer that this will be their room after marriage, and he's trying to decide where to put the bed. She immediately recognizes the folly in taking this room, and when she doesn't give reasons, he starts the next duet by explaining that it's convenient because of the close proximity to the Count's and Countess's chambers, and how quickly they could come if called, imitating the sound of the Count's bell. She takes great pleasure in mocking the ding-ding of the bell, going absurdly low for the Count, who could be summoning Figaro to go on a three-mile errand which would leave the Count free to "dong-dong" right into the bed just vacated by Figaro. The dance type Mozart uses in this duet, the contredanse, had a bad rap from dance masters of the time, who considered it far too lascivious, even a corruptor of the morals of the youth, making it a brilliant choice here. She then lets the apparently clueless Figaro know that the Count, having grown bored of chasing women outside of the castle, now looks within, and that none other than Figaro's dear little Susannetta has become the target. She certainly knows about the Count's hypocrisy concerning the *droit de seigneur*, but not Figaro, who, despite being the valet, apparently has not noticed.

In the first two duets dance has worked as something implied—an image that gives additional meaning to our understanding of things—but with Figaro's solo cavatina that follows after Susanna leaves, the dance now becomes real. Figaro's ego has been bruised, partly because of his own ignorance, but even more because the Count's dallying directly concerns his own fiancée, and the bedroom he took to be a reward is in fact a setup. No one but the audience hears him sing this cavatina, "Se vuol ballare, Signor Contino" (See if you can dance to my tune, my lord Count), so we see Figaro trying to convince himself that he still has the Count under his little finger, as he did in *The Barber of Seville*. What better way to do this than to call the tune for the Count to dance, and as an aristocrat, the Count dances the minuet, which Figaro now figuratively gives him with guitar and song. Figaro starts out firmly in control, so much so that he gives the Count a clever slip: instead of a balanced phrasing pattern that could actually be danced, Figaro adds an extra four bars, throwing off the symmetry and making it undanceable. The Count would fall flat on his face if he tried. Still trying to be in control, although now with an accompaniment more or less like a static version of the opening of the overture, Figaro tells him to dance the capriole, an upward-leaping (and usually not forward-moving) step in either dancing or dressage. We could well imagine Figaro cracking a whip under the Count's feet to make him jump, or even more vividly, as in some Western movies, someone dancing to avoid his feet being shot. Figaro's control soon degenerates into a presto patter, and even after returning to the minuet, Mozart laughs at him with the presto conclusion by the orchestra.

The women seem to know everything, while the men do not, and Marcellina, who now storms in with Dr. Bartolo, knows all about the Count's plan for Susanna. This does not suit her purposes, since she intends to get Figaro for herself, and if the *droit de seigneur* goes forward, it means there will be a marriage between Figaro and Susanna. The Count must be stopped, and Bartolo, still chafing about having lost Rosina because of Figaro's pulling of strings, thinks it would be a just punishment for him to be stuck with the old hag Marcellina. Every opera needs a vengeance aria, and Bartolo now gets his, with "La vendetta," but like Figaro in "Se vuol ballare," the middle section degenerates into patter that simply makes him look foolish, all the more so because he tries to sound legally clever (lawyers are often the butt of eighteenth-century jokes). Marcellina and Susanna have little use for each other, and Mozart now gives them a duet in which each one compliments the other with dripping irony, with some of the edge infused by the unevenness of the bourrée-like character.

All the main characters except for the Countess appear in Act 1, and the deliciously gender-bent Cherubino comes next. Just barely post-puberty, Cherubino cannot restrain his sexual impulses for any woman who crosses his path, and while the women, including the Countess, for whom he languishes most of all (and he envies Susanna's job of undressing the Countess at night), find him amusing, the men—and especially the Count—do not. Cherubino has a knack for being in the wrong place at the wrong time, especially where the Count's conquests are concerned, and the Count finally banishes him to the military front, which Figaro mocks mercilessly at the end of Act 1 with "Non pui andrai," recounting the heroism and horrors of military life, and the end of playing Adonis. The role of the barely pubescent boy must be played by a woman, and while this offers a delightful gender twist, it gets wrenched even further in this work when they attempt to disguise him as Susanna to go in her place for the assignation in the garden. That plan falls through, but Susanna's cousin Barbarina actually does dress him as a girl later on to avoid his military commission. Susanna and the Countess have great fun with the boy played by a woman disguised as a girl, but the Count and Barbarina's father, the gardener, find no humor at all.

In Act 1 Cherubino has an aria, "Non so piu cosa son," in which Mozart musically portrays his newfound sexual ebullience and confusion. It's difficult to imagine the role played better than it is by Maria Ewing, a genuine show-stealer as she flits about through much of the work looking like a deer caught in the headlights—especially during Figaro's "Non pui andrai." In her aria "Non so piu" you are surprised to see her mouth shut as the singing flows, of course voice-over being an impossibility on the operatic stage. For TV, though, you ask yourself why not; opera moves back and forth frequently between action and contemplation, and if it's possible, why not have contemplation coming from the head instead of the mouth. Ponnelle uses this often in this production—maybe a little too much. Unlike the musical attention bestowed on all the other characters, when the Count finally makes his appearance, Mozart relegates him to a comic role in a trio, bordering on farce as the Count relates how he found Cherubino in Barbarina's bedroom (when the Count was himself looking for some intimacy with Barbarina), and he now finds him the same way in Susanna's room, much to the delight of the music master Don Basilio and the chagrin of Susanna.

Act 2

Unlike Beaumarchais's Countess, thrust into the fray in the middle of Act 1, Mozart and Da Ponte delay her entrance until the beginning of Act 2, with a cavatina, "Porgi amor qualche ristoro" (Bring me, love, some relief), not preceded by any recitative, bestowing on her grace and dignity reserved only for her in this work. Mozart may have felt compelled to write this sort of number for a prima donna, Caterina Cavalieri in this case, including her much larger aria "Dove sono" in Act 3, but he always easily rose above this type of necessity with the virtue of creating a number that stands as essential to the drama and tone of the work, unimaginable without it here, and with profound implications for the way we should understand the end of the opera. With simple elegance Mozart crafts this number to realize the emotional void the Countess now finds herself in, deprived of the Count's love which only a few years earlier had been so ardent. The slow tempo sets the tone, and in the lengthy orchestral introduction for such a short number, Mozart lavishes his finest melodies and orchestration, featuring obbligato instruments such as the paired clarinets (an instrument featured in some of his most emotionally charged instrumental works such as the clarinet quintet and concerto), all to an uncluttered, poignant harmony. The melody, introduced by the strings and then taken up by the Countess, works its magic with the simplicity of a rising step which falls back slightly, followed by a rising syncopation to give a little more of an edge before again falling back, and then a descending line with musical emphasis on the words "duolo" (sorrow) and "sospir" (sigh). The climax arrives at the highest note reached through a rising passage on "morir" (death), the death she would prefer if love cannot be restored, and toward the end the syncopations become more urgent, all the while with her plaintive voice precariously supported by the obbligato clarinets. After this number she may be thrown into the midst of the schemes to trap the Count, which happen quickly with the plan to disguise Cherubino as Susanna, but we cannot forget the fact that her wellbeing depends on the outcome.

As much as I would like to discuss every musical number of this extraordinary opera, space precludes that option, and I will limit myself to just a few from the rest of the work. After the seriousness of the Countess, the remainder of Act 2 gets on with the comic business of the plot to trip up the Count, with Susanna and the Countess disguising Cherubino as Susanna, and the crumbling of that scheme when the Count turns up at the most inopportune moment. They hide Cherubino in a closet, but the Count demands the key, and when he leaves with the Countess to get one, Susanna slips into the closet while Cherubino leaps out of the window, smashing some of the gardener's flower pots in the garden below. The Countess fully expects to find Cherubino in the closet when she returns with the Count, and she makes her confession when the finale to Act 2 begins. As wonderful as the arias in this work may be, the ensembles trump them, with this finale giving us a staggering twenty-three minutes of continuous musical action—something even Wagner could not imagine. Ensembles can be either small or large, and we have already had a taste, with the duets in Act 1 and especially the trio with its lively action leading to the discovery of Cherubino by the Count in Susanna's room.

The brilliance of these ensembles lies in a type of counterpoint that allows the characters a musical independence separating each one from the other(s), and the possibility of having them all sing at once. This would be unimaginable in a play, since everyone speaking at once would simply create a jumble of sound that prevents anyone from being understood. With the type of counterpoint used in ensembles the characters can all speak together, and because of their musical separation, we can understand them. There is, of course, a limit to how many can be layered in this way, since the ear and brain can stretch this only so far, with three or four a likely maximum, as in the trio with the musical layering of Susanna's agitation, the Count's anger, and Basilio's gleeful response to their predicaments. The action will not necessarily go on continuously, but can pause for moments of reflection, in a musical tableau, as happens in the trio, when each character reflects, simultaneously, on the implications of the actions that have just occurred. In the finale we have a progression toward something bigger, starting with the Count and Countess alone as he threatens her with reprisals if Cherubino turns up in the closet, their amazement when Susanna emerges, which now gives the women the upper hand over the invariably unforgiving Count, the arrival of Antonio the gardener, angry about his broken flowerpots and Figaro's claim that he was the one who jumped, and finally the arrival of Marcellina and Bartolo, eager to get on with their lawsuit to force Figaro to marry Marcellina.

As these different actions take place, the ensemble breaks down into sections in different meters and tempos, and with the final piu allegro sections, all seven characters (Basilio has replaced Antonio) at times sing simultaneously, but not as seven separate musical entities, which would be too much for even the most sophisticated listener. They now align musically into groups with common objectives, with Susanna, the Countess, and Figaro forming the front wanting Figaro and Susanna to marry, and Marcellina, Bartolo, the Count, and Basilio expecting Figaro to marry Marcellina. The two groups are musically contrasted, but occasionally voices may be given individuality within their respective groups as their thoughts deviate somewhat from those of the rest of the group. The finale ends prestissimo, with lots of noise as Da Ponte tells us in his *Memoirs* that finales should conclude, and only in the last ten bars of singing do all voices come together homophonically, not because their objectives have been aligned, but merely as part of the noisy convention for ending the act.

Act 3

The third act has some wonderful numbers, including the Countess's "Dove sono," a chorus of female servants that includes Cherubino disguised as one of the girls, and a finale with a march and fandango, but the centerpiece of the act, and perhaps the focal point of the entire opera, is the sextet "Riconosci in questo amplesso" (Recognize with this embrace). The court case has been omitted, except for the crucial need of Figaro to establish his more elevated heritage despite having been abandoned as an infant. When he shows everyone the spatula tattooed on his arm, Marcellina gasps in recognition, acknowledging Figaro as her son and Bartolo as his father. Nothing seems to be going well for the Count, and clearly there can be no marriage between Figaro and Marcellina; on the upside for the Count, he can get back to his earlier plan for an assignation with Susanna in the garden since that marriage is on again. Susanna has not been present at these proceedings, but has gone off to get money to repay Figaro's debt, and on her return she knows nothing of these new developments. The musical construction of the drama sets this sextet apart from all other ensembles, in fact achieving it with sonata form in a way that compactly demonstrates most ably the dramatic essence of this instrumental form; vocal and instrumental forms clearly can have much in common. Not only did earlier composers use sonata form in operatic ensembles, including Pergolesi in *La serva padrona* (1733), but Haydn and others routinely used the form for arias.

The sextet begins with Marcellina, Figaro, and Bartolo wallowing in their newly discovered familial joy, with tension added, as often happens in sonata form, by Don Curzio (the lawyer) and the Count, whose immediate plans have been thwarted. When the five of them break off, three against two, Mozart modulates to the dominant key, and Susanna enters in the dominant on a new theme, with money in hand ready to pay off the debt—now the second group of the sonata form. She sees Figaro embracing Marcellina, and can't believe her eyes, thinking that the two of them have worked out their differences and will get married; Susanna shows her anger with a few neatly placed slaps on Figaro's cheeks. The forces in conflict now pit the happy familial trio against Susanna, who knows nothing of the new arrangement, along with the irate Count with Curzio grumbling that things have not gone their way, and this yields a development section with all the appropriate contrasting counterpoint. Mozart releases the tension with a modulation back to the home key of F, and that key arrives with Marcellina by herself leading off the recapitulation, to the identical accompaniment as the beginning of the sextet, resolving the tension with Susanna by giving her the happy news—using a theme only somewhat altered from her first theme. With Susanna integrated into the happy family, the sextet concludes the recapitulation in the home key with her incredulity mollified as she stammers "his mother" and then "his father," first uttering these in disbelief, and then with the joy of acceptance. The Count and Curzio continue to mutter their disapproval, while Susanna's line soars above the happy trio, making the recapitulation in the best sense of the form a musical reconciliation of the drama with some lingering tension still in the mix.

Act 4

Aside from being tripped up, the Count remains decidedly mean-spirited, carrying on with the assumption that he can behave as badly as he likes, but if anyone crosses him, and especially his unfortunate wife, there will be hell to pay. The trap for the Count remains the focus of the last act, but instead of Cherubino going in place of Susanna, it will be the Countess herself disguised as her servant. The Countess and Susanna cook this one up on their own, leaving Figaro in the dark about it, leading to a rant from him about women when he sees what he thinks is his fiancée in the garden with the Count. When he then sees Susanna dressed as the Countess, he quickly recognizes her voice and facetiously plays a seductive game with her, at first to Susanna's chagrin. They settle their differences easily (although Figaro seems not to realize how completely he has been out-maneuvered by Susanna), but not so the Count and Countess. He is on the prowl, trying to get Susanna to a secluded spot where he can seduce her, and after Cherubino and various others pop up in the wrong places, he finally succeeds in getting her (his own wife in disguise) alone. Because of all the other people lurking about, however, the Count sends her into an enclosed gazebo alone to wait for him. While alone he sees Figaro making advances toward a woman he assumes to be the Countess, and ever the bloody-minded hypocrite, he raises the alarm, shouting for all to come and see the traitorous iniquity he has discovered. All appear, and amid their pleading of mock forgiveness to his reviling of their treachery, he refuses with many repetitions of "No!"

All of this has sprinted along in allegro assai in the most delightful finale ensemble writing, but the appearance of the real Countess throws all for a loop after his last "no," and he of course realizes he's been had. The rapid-fire motion stops, and in andante he can do nothing, having been exposed for the duplicitous snake that he is, but ask her for forgiveness. Her reply, set apart from his with a pause, comes as an extraordinary musical moment, in fact nothing short of an epiphany, stopping everyone in their tracks, and most certainly the audience: her words offer forgiveness, but the music does much more than that. The nature of her line, with its rising fifth falling back slightly followed by the same gesture repeated with a gentle syncopation and a tender ornament as the whole line descends, can only remind us of the first time we heard the Countess, in "Porgi amor" at the beginning of Act 2. There she sang of regret for lost love, and with the same musical tone, we must believe that she now tempers her forgiveness with regret, considering how wretchedly the Count has acted to the last second before she emerged; when the next opportunity arises, he will probably act the same way again. Beaumarchais lets him off the hook, but not so Mozart, whose music unites all on stage to take up the Countess's tone, recognizing that something deeper has gone on here. The issue of how men treat women will not likely be brushed away easily, and Mozart in fact will come back to it consistently in his remaining operas. This has been no ordinary evening of TV.

COSÌ FAN TUTTE

Chronologically *Don Giovanni* comes next, but it merits a full chapter to itself; *Così fan tutte* and *Figaro* have enough in common that they stand together nicely in one chapter. *Così* may be the most puzzling of Mozart's operas, since on the surface it gives the impression of being a misogynist diatribe, but after *Figaro*, with Susanna and the Countess as the ones in control, that seems an unlike stance for Mozart and Da Ponte to take. Unlike *Figaro*, at least for the first three-quarters of the work, Mozart's music in *Così* does not seem to make the characters come alive as flesh-and-blood people; because of this, some have been inclined to judge it as inferior to the other two operas on which Mozart collaborated with Da Ponte. Jumping to any of these conclusions too quickly can be risky, since Mozart usually runs a step or two ahead of his cleverest interpreters. The point of the opera appears to be to demonstrate that women will be unfaithful to their lovers, and Don Alfonso, aided and abetted by the women's servant Despina, goes to great lengths to reveal to his young friends Ferrando and Guglielmo that their fiancées Fiordiligi and Dollabella will not be faithful if put to the test. The young men protest with swords drawn that their lovers could not possibly be unfaithful, but unable to explain adequately what constitutes that constancy, they accept Alfonso's bet to see if it can be proved otherwise in the course of one day. It certainly sounds like misogyny, but if we imagine that to be the point of the work, we have probably missed some of the most important signals.

The first and strongest signal is this: what moral authority do men have to make this judgment about women? Very simply, they have none. They have nothing other than the convention that says men can be as promiscuous as they like, but not so women. The authority with which the men speak here does not differ in the slightest from that of the Count in *Figaro*, who spends the entire opera trying to get Susanna into bed, but throws a fit when it appears to him that the Countess may be enjoying a little of the same. In taking up this subject again in *Così*, Mozart presses forward with the subject of his two previous operas, a subject in fact thoroughly familiar from the novels and plays of the time. *Così* soon focuses on the inequality of the sexes, and as often happens, the woman from the lower classes, Despina, sees through the hypocrisy of men and tries to persuade her ladies that their notions about this, which conventional society has burned into their consciences, should be dispelled. She assures them that their men will certainly be philandering while at the military front, and what's more, she herself has two lovers that she secretly plays off of each other. Her ladies at first seem horrified, and the act of rebellion does not come easily for them, especially for Fiordiligi, but finally it does come; the lesson at the end of the opera is not the unfaithfulness of women, but instead the equality of the sexes in every possible respect.

But why would Mozart develop this theme in such a sophisticated way with an opera that despite the beauty of the music at first seems to give us cardboard cutouts instead of characters with real warmth and emotions? In place of genuine feeling we get symmetry, in fact a staggering amount of it, first with the pairings of the characters: three men and three women, two sets of lovers who will be reversed in Act 2, and another man/woman pair who will be the facilitators. That symmetry pushes the extreme in Act 1, with the skeptic Alfonso and his willing collaborator Despina pitted against two men who cannot imagine their lovers being unfaithful and two sisters who cannot imagine betraying their men. In that act the music takes a similarly rigorous approach to the symmetry, with each character getting one aria, two quintets and a sextet more or less at the center of the act, trios for the men at the beginning and near the end, and a finale to round out the act. That symmetry appears to represent the established order of things—that all is well with a world in which lovers behave as they should and morality remains intact as the women fend off temptations and maintain the social status quo. Not only does all appear to be well with the world, but Mozart has given the essence of a musical work of comedy with the balance of arias and ensembles, with six arias and a much larger number of ensembles—really the stuff of *opera buffa*—in fact eleven in this act (two duets, five trios, two quintets, and two sextets), plus a chorus for good measure. Musically in these ensembles we have little or nothing to define character, as the sisters typically sing a third or sixth apart while the men diverge by larger intervals for no reason other than the placement of the tenor and baritone voices. Even the arias have more to do with standard operatic types instead of definition of individuality. In fact, it can be difficult to remember which of the lovers is which in the original pairings, and even Mozart, who may have had the best memory of any person to live in the past two centuries, got it wrong in one of his letters. Similarly, a prominent libretto published in the early 1960s made Guglielmo the tenor and Ferrando the baritone.

Everything changes in Act 2, to the point that we may wonder if we are still in the same opera. Of the thirteen numbers in the act, the arias now outnumber the ensembles, with seven; most of the six ensembles come in the first half of the act, four of them, leaving only the finale and one duet to break up the almost continuous stream of arias in the last half. Unlike the arias in Act 1, some of these now go much further in defining character and expressing genuine emotions, especially Fiordiligi's "Per pieta" in the middle of the act, with the heart-searching it unleashes not only in her but the other astonished lovers as well. While Act 1 belongs to the men and their social conventions of normality, that clearly shifts in the second act as Despina now takes over, persuading her ladies that they needn't be so prudish but should enjoy themselves, as their lovers would if left alone. She leads off with an aria that explains what any girl of fifteen should know, which is how to manage men with ruses, laughing, and crying, how to tease and confuse them, being clever, wily, or affectionate—in short, how to wrap them around her little finger. With this proclamation of what women can do, apparently unheard of by Fiordiligi and Dorabella, she sets the tone for the act, and the more the sisters think about it, the more they concede that a little playfulness to relieve the boredom of having been left alone will not do any harm, especially if their fiancés know nothing of it. Playfulness soon turns to passion, first for Dorabella with relative ease, and finally for Fiordiligi after much agonizing, and the issue changes from a little diversion to marriage to the new lovers, of course the old ones in disguise, now with the partners reversed. It's simply tough luck for their former lovers, who may have been killed in battle anyway; they imagine they will be safely gone with their new husbands long before their fiancés return. With this act of complete destruction of social decorum they have won the battle of the sexes, despite the embarrassment of having been duped by the men in disguise; it seems fitting that at the point that Fiordiligi gives way to her new sexual freedom, she wears the disguise of a man, dressed as a soldier ready to go to the front.

Act I

Like *Don Giovanni*, despite being a relatively long work, *Così* has only two acts, and this seems likely because of the distinctive character of each act, and the damage that would be done to the need for contrast between them if intermissions were to break them up. Having used the overture in *Don Giovanni* not only to set the tone of the work but to quote key thematic material at the beginning, Mozart follows suit in *Così*, beginning with a short andante section of fourteen bars, concluding it with the five-note motif that later in the work states the title: "Co-sì-fan-tut-te." When that happens in a very prominent moment just before the beginning of the Act 2 finale, with Alfonso gloating in his success and his two young friends licking their wounded egos, Alfonso first gives it as a solo, and his friends reluctantly join in as a chorus in three-part harmony, echoing the fateful words "so do they all." Men may bemoan this about women, but in reality their one-sided world of moral speciousness had ended. After this interjection in the overture, the tempo changes to presto, where it stays for the rest of the overture, establishing the lightness of tone for what will happen in the first act.

In the first three trios a similar pattern holds, with Alfonso set apart musically from Ferrando and Guglielmo, the two of them bragging about their virtuous lovers and typically singing together homophonical-ly in tenths and even at times in octaves. Occasionally all three come together despite their obvious differences. Just as the men present themselves to us in ensemble, the sisters do the same, in a duet, first singing separately although with little to distinguish them, and then together, generally a third or a sixth apart. Alfonso's first aria, short in the extreme, tells us nothing about him, but in a minor key he feigns sadness before telling the sisters the details that their soldier lovers have been summoned to the front. The quintet that follows brings all five of them together to rue their departure, and the crocodile tears of the men mix with the alligator tears of the women. Balancing the sister's duet, their lovers now have one, with more crocodile tears, and a chorus set to a military march, interspersed by a quintet with more facetious lamenting, sends them on their way. Knowing full well what a soldiers' life entails, the sisters exhort their lovers to be faithful while gone, an appropriate irony for what will follow, and Mozart then gives the best music so far in this act, in a trio about the wind carrying the lovers safely to their destination. Despina finally makes her first appearance, in recitative not unlike that of Leporello in *Don Giovanni* complaining about the working conditions of a maid, having to serve sumptuous drinks and chocolate but getting none for herself.

Dorabella gets the first chance to vent about the sorrow of her loss, and Mozart gives her a good agitato aria, but nothing that goes beyond the stock emotions of the situation, and certainly nothing that leaves us any the wiser about her character, since she simply reacts as she should. When Despina finally discovers what has happened she mocks them for their naiveté, assuring them in an aria that their men will not be faithful, so why should they? Alfonso recognizes an ally, and despite her quip that an old man like him can do nothing for her, he gets her on his side with limited information about the plot to further his plan. Finally all characters sing together in an ensemble as the men disguised as Albanians make their first appearance, leaving Despina amazed by these eccentric characters (she has not been told who they are) with handlebar moustaches and exotic costumes from Turkey or further afield; the sisters cry foul, wanting nothing to do with them, still grieving the departure of their lovers.

The aria that may most get our attention in this act comes from Fiordiligi, as she reacts in horror to the intrusion of these strange men into the sanctuary of virtue which she occupies with her sister. She has another big aria in Act 2, with similarities to this one, preceded as it is with an extended accompanied recitative in which she sets out her moral territory in no uncertain terms, leaving her fiancé Guglielmo clearly satisfied by her steadfastness. With the Act 1 aria, "Come scoglio immoto resta," starting andante maestoso no less, Mozart lets her vent, crowing how like a boulder she cannot be moved. Of course she will be moved in the next act, and Mozart pulls a classic musical "the lady doth protest too much" here, using wildly large leaps—sometimes as distant as a twelfth—in her lines that make her sound anything but immovable. The absurd leaps and forced high notes give way to a fairly unconvincing allegro still with incongruous leaps, and when the pace picks up even more, to piu allegro, she lapses on "barbara speranza" (crude hope) into coloratura that, because of how low it stays, sounds anything but heroic. If Mozart doesn't believe her, neither should we, and this stands in marked contrast to the genuine emotions of her aria in the second act.

Alfonso seems fairly inept at moving his plot along, unable to get the sisters to budge in the slightest, so Despina steps forward, telling us that things get done when she throws her weight behind them. She instructs the men to pretend to take poison, feigning suicide as their only alternative to the women's disinterest, hoping this will at least move the women enough to offer some physical comfort to the dying lovesick aliens. With a little prodding the ploy works, and the next problem is to revive them with a mystifying antidote. For this Mozart and Da Ponte settle on a delightful solution, involving one of Mozart's friends from his childhood visits to Vienna, a man who had become a celebrity for all the wrong reasons. This was Franz Anton Mesmer, a name still indirectly known to us now because of the word "mesmerize," derived from Mozart's friend's name. The Mozart family would visit and even stay with the Mesmer family in Vienna, and in 1768, the twelve-year-old Mozart's opera *Bastien und Bastienne* may have received its premiere in the garden of the Mesmer home. Franz Anton completed a degree in medicine in Vienna, but his practice soon changed from conventional medicine to something that wealthy patients found more appealing, involving a magnetic apparatus that patients, holding hands in a group, would latch onto, and through the power of suggestion believed that this could cure all their ailments. The ruse worked for those willing to pay the exorbitant fee, but it did not go down well with the Viennese medical board, which stripped him of his license and sent him packing from their fair city. He moved to Paris, where gullible "patients" happily paid much more for the service than the Viennese had, making him fantastically wealthy before the crackdown from the French authorities. Despina now bursts in as a doctor, and after muttering some Latin to appear authentic, she pulls out a large magnet which she presses to the foreheads of the stricken lovers, and explains what's going on: "I will use this piece of Mesmeric magnetic stone which originated in Germany, and has become spectacularly celebrated in France."

Mozart has some fun here with an in-joke that his audience at the time would catch, but not likely audiences today. Some productions try to update this with other references, as Peter Sellars does in his version from 1990, in that case using a Die Hard battery which Dr. Despina attaches with jumper cables to the men's crotches. In 1990 this gave rise to some laughs, but unfortunately over two decades later few will catch the reference to that type of battery or for that matter the Die Hard movies; since the performance has survived on DVD, we therefore find ourselves stuck trying to grasp these references instead of Mozart's even funnier ones from his time. Act 1 ends with a large comic ensemble that includes the Mesmer scene and relatively fruitless attempts to change the sisters' attitude toward their suitors.

Act 2

The change that takes place in the second act happens on more than one level, and these different possible levels, as in *Figaro*, depend on the capacity of the music to give the substance. At the simple and straightforward level the sisters give in to the advances of their new wooers, as Alfonso bet they would, and of course we would not have much of a story if this did not happen. Of much greater interest than the fact that it happens is how it happens and the emotional and moral implication of this; here Mozart's music plays the leading role. Things unfold as they should in a comic work up to a certain point, with Dorabella easily falling for her preferred Albanian, but more crucially than fulfilling Alfonso's prediction, she readily embraces the rebellious spirit instilled by Despina—that women have as much right to this type of behavior as men. Mozart keeps this at the appropriate comic level with a duet between Dorabella and Guglielmo, in which he gives her a heart as a token of his love (and tries to substitute it in her locket for her portrait of Ferrando), with musical representation of the pitapatting of their hearts. Mostly they sing together or singly on similar motifs, although occasionally they stray off alone, with her chuckling about the game she now plays with him, while Guglielmo bemoans Ferrando's loss but gloats that he has avoided it happening to himself.

Things do not move so smoothly for Fiordiligi, and at first this may simply play into the comedy, establishing a little bit of difference between the sisters, but it soon becomes something else entirely. Ferrando tries to break her down with an aria, still in the mode of those from Act 1 since it does not convey his genuine emotions, but it appears to work, bringing a reaction from her that musically departs from anything heard to this point in the opera, in fact creating a striking turning point as she recognizes fully the danger of the game she now plays. Before her game-changing aria, she leads off with an accompanied recitative, in which she clearly lays out the scope of her transgression, taking her reaction outside the boundary of comedy. Blaming it on the person trying to seduce her will not do since she is clearly the guilty one for giving him any signs of hope, and she knows she deserves to be punished. For Guglielmo she offers true and perfect love, but with this stranger only her passion has been aroused, and this passion bereft of virtue evokes a string of self-inflicting invective: "è smania, affanno, rimorso, pentimento, leggerezza, perfidia, è tradimento!" (madness, pain, remorse, regret, faithlessness, wickedness, and treachery), with her high held note on "perfidia."

We get the point in the accompanied recitative, but not the depth and sincerity of the emotions, which can only come in an aria of the stature of the one she now sings: "Per pieta" (Have pity). She asks her real lover, Guglielmo, for forgiveness for the faith she has broken, and hopes with the fatalism of one who knows it to be impossible that her betrayal by giving into temptation will remain a secret for which she can privately atone. The words may be moving, but Mozart gives her music which, unlike that of "Come scoglio" in Act 1, makes the emotion genuine, starting adagio on a descending pattern with rhythms that accent her instability, and often with a flowing melody. This aria occasionally has leaps as large as "Come scoglio," but never gratuitous as they had been there; these come much less frequently, emphasizing words such as "orror" (horror, atrocity), "vergogna" (disgrace), or "ascoso" (secret), the key words of the aria, bringing them to life even more vividly with syncopation or sustained upper notes. A new section shifts to allegro moderato, with a preponderance of passages that are downward-moving, the direction of her emotions, and a small amount of coloratura near the end serves as a launch for the climactic high notes that bring the conclusion. With "Come scoglio" we could easily recognize the crocodile tears, but here the music leaves no question that the tears are real, emphasized even further with the obbligato lines for clarinets and other woodwinds. Sellars has his Fiordiligi strip off her blouse as this aria moves to the end, with absolutely nothing sexy about it as her near-nakedness reveals a physical vulnerability to parallel the emotional one.

Mozart has now drawn a line in the sand, and nothing can be as it was before, as the emotions of *opera seria* have encroached on the previously neatly symmetrical comedy. Ensembles, with the exception of the finale, become scarce as we move through the second half of the second act, now leaving it to arias to carry the drama which has shifted from comedy to a test of the emotions. Not surprisingly, the two jilted lovers do not get it, as they react in conventional ways without anything of the depth introduced by Fiordiligi. Guglielmo, Fiordiligi's original lover, has the first go at it with an aria, and he can muster nothing more profound than to condemn women outright for their treachery—after men like himself have put them on pedestals of virtue. Ferrando quickly follows with something at about the same level, regretting the defeat but not ready to give up loving his Dorabella. Unlike the emotional depth of Fiordiligi, Mozart makes their arias almost trivial in comparison, as if to underscore the fact that they do not get it—that their lovers unequivocally have established for themselves the right of women to behave as men do routinely.

The social order has been transformed, not to the liking of the men, as a new world of equality has dawned, one that Alfonso knew about and Despina already practiced, and one now available not only to radicals prepared to snub convention but to everyone regardless of social background. The opera needs to be brought to the comic conclusion set up by the earlier events, with the sisters embarrassed by their inability to keep the faith, and even Despina's regret about being a pawn in Alfonso's plot. While the conclusion with the lovers returning from the front to uncover the fraudulent double marriages will evoke a few laughs, something else has happened because of Fiordiligi's earlier straying outside of the boundaries of comedy. She has agonized over her choice, understanding fully the implications of her actions, and for her equality has clearly come at a cost, with moral pangs and emotional scars. Because of this, her transformation is all the more believable, not merely the flick of a switch as it was for Dorabella, but an equality for which she has paid dearly. The conclusion may look like a conventional happy ending, but in light of what has happened, we probably should not speculate about the future for these couples, now that the men no longer hold the trump card of inequality.

8

CARNIVAL VERSUS LENT

Don Giovanni

It's a rainy Sunday early in December of 1979 in Cincinnati, and you decide to go to a movie. You enjoy opera, having had the pleasure of being an usher for summer productions at the zoo in your youth, and in recent years you have seen broadcasts from the Met on PBS, which seemed okay but suffered from the size of your thirteen-inch TV screen and poor sound quality. But now something different has come up, a screening of *Don Giovanni* at the Hyde Park Theater on Erie Avenue— not a broadcast from an opera house, but a cinematic production that does not use a stage at all, instead set like any other movie with both indoor and outdoor scenes. The idea seems intriguing and innovative, and although you know nothing about the director Joseph Losey, you decide to give it a try. Armed with a bag of popcorn, you settle in, and it starts like any other movie, with the logo for Gaumont films flashing across the screen. The titles follow, with no sound other than the wash of waves against a shore, and you're pleased to see the names of some very well-known singers, including Ruggero Raimondi, Kiri te Kanawa, and Teresa Berganza. When the conductor's name, Lorin Maazel, comes on, the music of the overture begins, and after director Losey's name, you see various characters walking toward the camera through narrow passageways between ancient buildings, curiously followed by scenes of nothing but open water and a stormy sky. The dark sky seems fitting considering the gloomy opening of the overture, and when the tone of the music changes to something much lighter, so does the scene, now with all the characters on a boat which enters a canal just off a lagoon, clearly in Venice.

The boat docks, and as the characters disembark—on their way to a glass-blowing factory—in full eighteenth-century costume, you notice that some of them wear or hold distinctive Venetian carnival masks, identifying exactly when the action takes place. They file in to view the spectacle of the glass blowing, and the large open fire the blowers use appears especially striking; you may even be concerned when one of the characters (whom we soon discover to be Don Giovanni) stands precariously close on a plank almost directly above the fire (by the end of the opera we fully understand this scene at the beginning). The overture ends, the scene changes, and so far it could be the beginning of any movie, with longer-than-usual titles, music, and some unusually vivid visuals. This film, first released in Paris a month before it came to the United States, can still be found on DVD.

The new scene that follows the overture starts in a most puzzling way, and as it continues, it moves from puzzling to downright distressing. This work, which near the end summons the most cataclysmic forces to blow away the unrepentant Don Giovanni, begins with Giovanni's servant Leporello complaining about his working conditions and moaning that he cannot enjoy the life of his master. Somehow it does not seem right to begin this way, starting things off clearly in the mode of comedy, especially considering the nasty business that directly follows. After Leporello's bellyaching, a short musical transition sets the tone for something more serious, and this brings Donna Anna and Giovanni on stage, she screaming that he will not escape, and he trying to calm her down while concealing his identity. It soon becomes clear that he has attacked her in her bedroom, and that she has mustered every ounce of energy she has not only to fend him off but now to hold him until the rest of the household can come to her rescue. In this high drama, a heinous crime has been narrowly averted, and the intended victim demands that justice be done; from raw comedy the scene has menacingly shifted to the stuff of tragedy.

If we have any sense of decency, we should recognize the seriousness of the situation and take Anna's side, but Mozart prevents us from doing this, musically compounding the puzzlement of the shift from comedy to tragedy. As Anna pursues Giovanni, trying to rouse the house, with Giovanni attempting to quiet her with threats, Leporello gives us his own peculiar running commentary, turning the ensemble into a trio, mostly singing a light patter against their serious lines, about the pickle the master finds himself in and not wanting to be there. Things get worse: her father, the Commendatore, roused by her screams, emerges, challenging Giovanni to fight, which Giovanni in deference to the old man's age refuses to do; goaded on by accusations of cowardice, he accepts the challenge and kills her father. The trio continues, the Commendatore replacing his daughter, and as the high drama races ahead, Leporello keeps his silly commentary going, wishing he could disappear. The trio ends, with the Commendatore gasping his last breaths and Leporello chattering on about what he has seen. Leporello, after establishing that his master has survived, comments in recitative that this was pretty good for one evening—to violate the daughter and then butcher the father. Why on earth would Mozart take something as monumentally serious as this and make light of it, as he does with the music he gives Leporello?

This question, not only about the opening scene but about much that happens later on in the opera, has troubled commentators for over two centuries. If we take a moralistic view of it, and of course the Don Juan story comes from a tradition of morality plays in the Middle Ages, we could perhaps assume that framing Giovanni as overly callous at this point, and even interjecting tomfoolery into the scene, will make his demise all the more satisfying at the end. When we come to the end, though, we will see that Mozart removes this as an option, since when Giovanni's victims sing a moral about what happens to evildoers at the final moment of the opera, Mozart gives them music, to be described in detail later in this chapter, that makes them sound foolish doing it; apparently Mozart does not side with the moralists. But if he trips up the moralists, does that leave us only one choice—that he actually condones the most grievous of crimes? If we transport this to our time, we will have exactly the same problems with it. Religious moralists will conclude that Giovanni gets what he deserves in the end with divine retribution, while secular moralists will come to the same conclusion based on his treatment of women, and both will take the singing of the moral at the end literally, not catching what Mozart does with his musical treatment of it. Surely we should not construe this opera as an endorsement of crime.

Perhaps, though, we are being too literal about it, and other options may exist if we suspend our disbelief, as we must with opera, questioning if the action of the opera represents real life at all. Mozart brings most of the characters very much to life with the music he gives them, although curiously he does not do that for all of them, and especially Giovanni himself. He gives the women—Anna, Donna Elvira, and Zerlina—strong defining features with their arias, but the men—Giovanni, Leporello, Don Ottavio, and Masetto—pretty much all come up short on that, as they for the most part inhabit the ensembles. Ottavio may seem an exception to that with the two fairly substantial arias given to him, but curiously he was intended to have only one, and Mozart wrote a second one for him because the singer doing the role in Vienna could not sing the aria written for the premiere in Prague; performances today typically include both arias. Giovanni has three arias, but we search in vain for anything in these that may help to define his character, as the first one exhorts Leporello to round up more women for the party of peasants, in the second he serenades a servant girl who never actually appears, and in the third, while disguised as Leporello, he instructs the peasants with Masetto on how to capture the villain (himself). We may all feel that we know someone like Giovanni, although probably not as extreme, but Mozart gives us nothing in his music that actually lets us know who or what he is (Søren Kierkegaard cleverly argues that the music given the other characters defines Giovanni's sensuality).

Losey appears to have come up with a possible solution about what Mozart may have been up to in this work, picking up many of the clues that the composer and Da Ponte leave us, and reveals this from the beginning with the carnival masks we see during the overture. Masks become even more prominent in the finale to Act 1, when Elvira, Anna, and Ottavio come to Giovanni's party as masqueraders, wearing masks, as the libretto requires, making this party a carnival ball. Having picked up on that, much more happens that places the entire opera as a carnival event, such as the crossdressing in Act 2, with Giovanni disguised as Leporello and vice versa, trotting out the social reversals common during these festivities, and certainly the amount of seduction that becomes normal during carnival. Excessive drinking of course becomes part of it, and Giovanni's first aria, the champagne aria, sets the tone. In fact, the *mise en scène* for this aria resembles the painting *Battle be-*

tween Carnival and Lent by Pieter Bruegel the Elder (1559), which shows revelers led by the king of carnival riding a large wine barrel; Giovanni, calling for wine and women, could very well be the king of carnival. In general, opera during the eighteenth century was most often performed during the extended carnival period, with the season ending temporarily for Lent. More specifically to the Don Juan legend, there was a theatrical version of it performed in Naples in the 1660s during carnival that actually included a catalog of Giovanni's conquests, not unlike Leporello's catalog aria for the benefit of Elvira. During carnival, just about anything goes, along with seduction, drinking, mixing of the social classes, insults thrown at those in authority, and every other imaginable overindulgence; this all comes to a grinding halt at the beginning of Lent, with its religious piety and physical restraint.

As for Mozart and carnival, we know he loved it in the extreme, and he often indulged in carnivalesque behavior in and out of the season. We see that most clearly in the pranks he got up to with his merry cousin Anna Maria Thekla Mozart (the Bäsle) in Augsburg, in the insults they enjoyed hurling at the clergy, their naughty scatological letters to each other (of which his have survived), and the likely probability that the two of them had sex. In one letter, after an endless stream of "Muck! Tasty! Also terrific, muck, and lick muck," he gets on to something else: "During carnival time, did you really live it up? In Augsburg one can certainly have a much better time of it than here [Mannheim]. I really wish I were with you, so that we could hop about together and do it right." (MBA ii 308) This came from Mozart in his early twenties while traveling across Europe, but he had no less enthusiasm for carnival later on, as we see in this letter to his father, who also loved carnival, from 1783:

> You no doubt know that it is carnival time, and that there is as much enthusiasm here for dancing as in Salzburg and Munich. So, I would really like to go as Harlequin (but not a soul must know about it)— because here there are so many genuine asses who attend the Redoutes [dance halls]. Therefore I would like you to send me your Harlequin costume. But it must arrive as soon as possible. . . . Last week I gave a ball in my apartment. . . . We got started at six o'clock in the evening and finished up at seven.—What, only an hour?—No indeed—until seven o'clock the next morning. (MBA iii 251–52)

Even more than going as Harlequin, he told his father that "during the last carnival days we will put together a company of masqueraders and perform a little pantomime, —but I beg you, do not give us away" (MBA iii 257). A month later he described this pantomime in detail, and in fact a fragment of the manuscript has survived.

Considering Mozart's passion for carnival, it should come as no surprise that he might incorporate it into a major work, although not necessarily in as overt a way as the little pantomime performed in 1783. That appears to have happened with *Don Giovanni*, and the opening scene just described, keeping in mind the features of the season, could be a type of little carnival play. It starts with Leporello grumbling and wishing he could be of the class of his master, normal behavior during carnival, and doing this in a comical way. Giovanni wishes to enjoy the seductive climate of these pre-Lent days, so he tries his luck with Anna, who later admits, without being overly distressed, that she thought Ottavio had entered her room. When Giovanni's behavior made it clear he was not Ottavio, her moral upbringing at the hands of the Commendatore kicked in, and she resisted with all her might, even trying to be the moral punisher. Despite the season, not everyone got into the spirit, since some moralists had no use for the risqué fooling around of masquerading, and Giovanni just happened to run into one of these well-brought-up young women, who may not object to a gentle prank from her fiancé, but certainly would not tolerate it from a stranger. As the opera progresses, we find other women much more amenable to these types of advances, especially Zerlina.

With the entry of the Commendatore, we have the classic authority figure who gets insulted during carnival, and in fact Goethe, in "The Roman Carnival" from his *Italian Journey* (1788), lets non-Italians know exactly how these insults sounded. The favorite insult, "Sia ammazzato" (death to you, or to hell with you), becomes a type of password, added to all jokes and even compliments, or shouted by a boy at his father or a priest. The more the old man scolds him for his behavior, the more the boy claims the liberty of the evening and curses even more vigorously. When the Commendatore persists in dressing Giovanni down, insisting on a duel, Giovanni insults him using words fairly similar to the ones noted by Goethe: "Misero, attendi, se vuoi morir" (you've asked for it, miserable wretch, if you want to die). The death here may be something more figurative, not unlike the insult "Sia ammazzato," and at the confrontation near the end with the statue of the Commendatore, who commands that Giovanni repent, the response is even more insulting than it had been earlier: "No, vecchio infatuate!" (absolutely not, you stupid old jackass). Since the statue speaks from the otherworld, the insult extends to heaven as well.

With any great work one cannot neatly tie up all the loose ends, and that, I will concede, certainly applies to my idea that this has more to do with carnival than a realistic type of representation. As I go through the work, I will draw out the numerous spots where it does seem to work, and much of this, as in the other operas, has to do with Mozart's music, which at times tells a different story than the libretto. In *The Marriage of Figaro* we noted that the literary source, Beaumarchais's play, had a bearing on the opera. The same holds for *Don Giovanni*, although this time we have not just one work but a long tradition of street plays, three plays by noted playwrights, and an opera that came out just before Mozart's. The early tradition of *commedia dell'arte* and street theater, including morality plays with titles such as *The Atheist Struck Down* or *The Stone Guest*, appears to have been absorbed to some extent by the three playwrights, the first of whom, the Spaniard Gabriel Téllez, better known to us by his pseudonym Tirso de Molina, called his 1630 play *El Burlador de Sevilla y Convidada de Piedra* (*The Trickster of Seville and His Guest of Stone*). In the discussion that follows occasional references will be made to these plays, but suffice it to say for now that in this play he calls for a confessor at the end, unlike the unrepentant Don Juan of the others, linking it to the morality plays of the more distant past. In the next one, Molière's *Dom Juan* of 1665, Juan seems more a free thinker than seducer, with his conquests part of the way he explains his existence. Carlo Goldoni's 1736 *Don Juan*, also known as *Don Giovanni Tenorio, ossia Il Dissoluto* (Debaucher), resisted the supernatural presence of a ghost or stone guest, but indirectly brings that in as Giovanni meets his demise by way of a lightning bolt. All of the characters used by Da Ponte turn up in one or the other of these different plays.

Just shortly before Mozart took on the subject—and we should assume Da Ponte's claim in his *Memoirs* that he gave the idea to Mozart to be self-aggrandizement instead of the truth—an opera by Giovanni Gazzaniga, *Don Giovanni, ossia Il Convitato di Pietra*, with a libretto by Da Ponte's rival Giovanni Bertati, turned up in Venice and quickly spread throughout Europe. There can be no doubt that both Da Ponte and Mozart knew it, although Da Ponte makes no mention of it in his *Memoirs*, since the two operas have far too much in common for the similarity to be coincidental. Gazzaniga's remains relatively unknown (although it gets performed from time to time, and a DVD exists), and that fate appears to be deserved, considering that it cannot be judged as much better than run-of-the-mill. Its interest to us lies in the fact that, despite being in one act and only half the length of Mozart's, Da Ponte cribbed many ideas from it, taking some aspects of plot verbatim, although always better written than Bertati's libretto, and it probably even gave Mozart a few musical ideas. After the prologue, Da Ponte follows Bertati almost exactly. Bertati gives us four female victims, and Da Ponte excluded one of these, Ximena. The conclusion also has some similarities, and these will be noted in the discussion near the end of this chapter.

ACT I

Overtures tell us much in purely musical terms about the operas that will follow, setting the tone or creating an aura not unlike the way title music from films of the 1940s and '50s did, and in fact film composers from that era got their inspiration from opera. Mozart seemed most interested in setting the tone for *Figaro* in the overture with a light and breezy atmosphere, but in *Don Giovanni*, his next opera after *Figaro*, he introduced as the first music thematic material of crucial importance to the conclusion of the opera. He even chose the key strategically, D minor, a key often associated with death or storms in the eighteenth century, and the darkness of the key will often be reinforced with syncopation, suspensions, and dissonant chords such as diminished sevenths. This overture begins that way, with music almost identical to that accompanying the Commendatore's statue when he arrives at Giovanni's feast, as he promised at the graveyard that he would, bringing with him the air of death and foreboding.

After this somber opening passage associated with the Commendatore, the material changes to a syncopated line in the violins, with music belonging to Giovanni, who responds to the statue with surprise and confusion, incredulous that his invitation had been accepted but still focused enough to tell Leporello to bring him a plate. The next passage in the overture gives the knock-kneed Leporello's reply that he dare not because the ghost will kill them. Of course we know none of this action in the overture, but the music itself tells us through its atmosphere as much as we need to know. After this chilling andante opening, the main section begins, still in D minor, and no faster than moderato—in fact, not much faster than andante. We still feel the tension, and even the short passages of a lighter nature are usually set apart by fairly menacing-sounding descending open octaves. When the comical entry of Leporello comes after the overture, described in the previous section, we have not been prepared for anything this light, and Mozart plays with our expectations here, as he does throughout the opera, with the juxtapositions of comedy and seriousness.

After a lengthy duet between Anna and Ottavio, Elvira makes her first entry, singing what sounds like a rage aria as she vents about how she has been jilted by her new husband. Eventually Giovanni and Leporello join in to make it a trio, disarming her seriousness as Giovanni discovers the woman he now tries to console to be his own abandoned wife. Once again Giovanni eludes her, leaving it to the bewildered Leporello to explain why he cannot stay with her now; this results in the catalog aria in which he leaves no illusions about the kind of man she has married, enumerating his conquests throughout Europe (no less than 1,003 in Spain), his lack of social discrimination, his preference of plump ones in winter, and so on. The rage she displays in this act stands in marked contrast to her softening in Act 2, and these extreme swings place her directly in the middle between Anna and Zerlina, stances that could very well measure their responses to the seductions of carnival.

As Elvira leaves the stage, village folk enter, singing and dancing, in what could easily be a carnival event—considering the words that Zerlina, Masetto, and the chorus sing about love and not letting the opportunity slip by. It turns out instead to be their pre-wedding celebration. Giovanni immediately takes an interest in the pretty Zerlina, instructing Leporello, who sees there may also be some girls for himself here, to get rid of the nuisance Masetto—who only happens to be the bridegroom. He does not go easily, and even gets an aria to vent his bitterness about the liberties the nobility can take and his obvious concern about the well-being of his bride with a nobleman whose reputation he does not know but about whom he can expect the worst. To this point the work has had only two arias, both by male servants/peasants, certainly defeating the expectation that these will go to the leading serious characters. Despite some misgivings, Zerlina has agreed to venture off alone with Giovanni, on her wedding day, and like her counterparts in the plays by Goldoni (Elise), Tirso de Molina (Thisbe), and Molière (Charlotte and Mathurine), we may wonder how she can be led down the garden path so easily on the most important day of her life. In the plays some of these women have very low expectations about their future peasant husbands, welcoming a shot at social climbing to nobility even if the prospect does not ring true. With Zerlina we have no cause here or at any later point to question her commitment to marriage with Masetto, nor have we any reason to find her gullible enough to fall for Giovanni's trap. Something else appears to be at play, which could very well be that since this takes place during carnival she plays along with the ruse, fully embracing the spirit of the time—very simply ready to have some risqué fun, unlike Anna, and for the time being, Elvira. Like other members of her social class, notably Despina in *Così fan tutte*, she has a much more flexible view of the world than her more demure counterparts from the higher classes.

Her willingness to indulge in some carnivalesque behavior with Giovanni leads into what may very well be the most sensuous duet in the entire operatic repertory, "Là ci darem la mano" (Let me take your hand). The urgency of the pleasure he anticipates resounds in his gentle opening line, and while her words of reply express some doubts, her music, very similar to his, takes us beyond her words to the same feeling of sexual excitement. As the duet continues with both of them speaking separately, he tries to persuade her with the ruse of her being elevated to nobility, although the music says more about sexual bliss than social class. Her words of misgiving lose nothing of the sensual anticipation. With no real opposition in the music it's only a matter of time until the inevitable will happen, and it does, with him beckoning "Andiam" (let's go), and she replying with the same word, now just as much the aggressor. After this opening voluptuous andante in 2/4, they now embrace musically and physically, in the urgency of allegro in 6/8 time, for most of the remainder of the duet singing together a third (or tenth or sixth) apart, Zerlina more than Giovanni taking the melodic lead. In Losey's production, Teresa Berganza spreads out luxuriously on a bed, and Ruggero Raimondi sinks his face into her ample, now mostly exposed, breasts. While not showing them going all the way, Losey leaves little else to the imagination, although perhaps only in desire, since the sudden arrival of Elvira forces a *duetus interruptus*.

Elvira has found her husband taking advantage of another woman, and predictably she reacts with rage, this time getting an actual rage aria, although a fairly short one, but still with potent flourishes including coloratura passages at the end that drive upward to high As. Her anger carries over to the quartet which she leads off, eliciting a sympathetic response from Anna and Ottavio, contradicted by jabs from Giovanni, who proclaims the poor dear to be completely out of her mind. They resolve nothing, although commiseration lies more with Elvira, and Ottavio concludes they must probe further to find the truth. Following the quartet Anna has a eureka moment, as the sound of Giovanni's voice has brought a great revelation to her, now convinced beyond a shadow of a doubt that this man dismissing Elvira's woes is none other than the killer of her father. After revealing to Ottavio the gruesome details of what happened to her on that fateful night, she launches into a major aria, "Or sai, chi l'onore" (Now you know the guilty one), an aria which bears comparison with the one Ottavio gets right after hers and even more so with his aria in Act 2. Mozart leaves no question as to her strength of character with the forcefulness of the lines he gives her, pushing progressively higher with decisive rising intervals, and a passage that propels her upward to a long, held high A; after speaking of vengeance she exhorts Ottavio to respond in like manner. This music of great resolve carries through to the end of the aria, with her cries for vengeance reaching an acute level of ascendancy.

Ottavio's immediate response misses the mark by a mile, as he ponders how someone high born—from the same club as it were—could be capable of committing such a crime, and he reluctantly concedes that his duty to his fiancée will have to override the possibility that his friend and fellow nobleman could be guilty. His aria, which comes right on the heels of hers, "Dalla sua pace" (My peace of mind), belonging to the Vienna version of the opera, fails to match her strength in the music or the text; he talks of comforting her when she wants nothing but retribution, needing nothing of his wimpy succor. With "Il mio tesoro intanto" (My treasure must be comforted) in Act 2, he comes off as seeming even more inept, reminding us why Brigid Brophy in her *Mozart the Dramatist* called him the biggest milksop in the history of opera. He should be the one to bring Giovanni to justice, and he has more than one chance to accomplish that, but based on the music of these arias we can see why he does not have the backbone to do it. In "Il mio tesoro" he has gentle melodic lines, and when he does have high notes, nothing propels him there in the way that Anna's line does in her aria; Mozart simply leaves him hanging on these high notes in splendid obsolescence while the real musical interest shifts to the accompaniment. He gets to sing coloratura passages as well, and while that may be an indicator of strength for a women, for example the Queen of the Night in *The Magic Flute*, for a man it seems a little more questionable. This aria does not have to be included in Act 2, although it usually is; in some productions he exhorts those around him to console Anna, while in others he evokes this from the gods. Either way, it shows how he fails to understand what she needs, and his inability to provide it.

The scene changes back to Giovanni with his champagne aria, summoning all to the ball at his palace, but ready for the conquest of Zerlina that he just barely missed out on earlier. She has hell to pay—to mollify the irate Masetto—and she shows her true colors in the skillful way she manipulates him, at first lying about not being touched, but then much more effectively while singing her aria "Batti, batti, o bel Masetto" (Beat me, my dear Masetto). He may be a bit of a numbskull, but even if he were not, she would have him eating out of her hand after this number she pulls on him. The beating she refers to we should not take literally as wife beating, and Mozart's music makes this entirely clear; this aria drips with the same kind of sensuality that permeated her duet with Giovanni, and now she offers it explicitly to her dolt of a future husband, speaking an oafish language that he will understand, about blows, pulling hair, or scratching out the eyes of the innocent little lamb that he hates, but to music charged to the extreme with sexual energy and the promise of what will actually come. Of course it works; he readily admits the witch has enchanted him, and that under such circumstances, men simply go all soft in the brain. With the arrival of Giovanni and her wish to hide, he realizes she has duped him.

FINALE TO ACT I

The finale to Act 1 of *Don Giovanni* stands as a great tour de force, and deserves to be set apart from the rest of the discussion, significantly

longer than the Act 2 finale of *Figaro*—stretching to a full half hour of
continuous music drama. The quantity need not concern us; the quality
can only be described as stunning, and it perhaps more than anything
else marks the greatness of this opera. It starts inauspiciously, with
Masetto ready to catch Giovanni in a trap and trip up Zerlina in her web
of deception. Giovanni enters and his call to the peasants and his servants has all the trappings of carnival about it as he summons them to
dancing and drinking in the ballroom. Zerlina tries to hide from him,
and when he finds her, she talks as though they are still together in their
duet, obviously a problem for her with Masetto hiding in the bushes
and able to overhear. Caught by Masetto, Giovanni tries to explain that
he found her neglected, and Mozart underscores the lie with music that
uses the Scotch snap figure (a short note followed by a longer one), an
old comic device in music that in this case exposes the ruse. He brushes
off this little setback by inviting them both to join the dancing. The
carnival atmosphere then gets its strongest affirmation, as Anna, Ottavio, and Elvira make their entry in masks, and as the music becomes a
minuet, Leporello alerts Giovanni that masqueraders have arrived.
With misgivings, they agree to accept the invitation to attend, and amid
dancing, drinking, and flirting, a chorus breaks out to the celebration of
liberty.

Aside from the minuet just heard, the dancing has been somewhat
nongeneric, but now it becomes specific, in the most ingenious possible
way. The ball begins, with Giovanni calling for more music and telling
Leporello to be certain everyone has a dancing partner. Three separate
small orchestras take their positions on stage, and the first one strikes
up the same minuet heard a little earlier; to this courtly dance in 3/4
time the three masqueraders of high birth begin to dance, noting the
presence of Zerlina and exhorting themselves to be strong. Giovanni
and Leporello ironically observe how well everything is going, and as
they do, we hear open fifths from the second orchestra as musicians
tune up before starting to play their dance. Giovanni forces Leporello
to keep Masetto occupied so he can dance privately with Zerlina, and
spiriting her away from the others, they now dance a contredanse,
which the second orchestra plays in 2/4 time, simultaneous to the first
orchestra playing the minuet in 3/4. Dance masters of the eighteenth
century wrote at length about the contredanse, and almost to a person
they had nothing good to say about it, since it lacked the kind of pro-

priety and decorum they insisted on, not least of all because of the face-to-face physical contact it involved. Many of them used very strong language to condemn it, calling it lewd and licentious, certainly not suitable for young people, since it would corrupt their morals. It could not be more appropriate that Giovanni dances this dance with Zerlina, since what he wishes to accomplish with her fits exactly with the way people of Mozart's time perceived this dance from a moral standpoint.

As these two dances continue simultaneously, Leporello urges Masetto to dance, but Masetto, deprived of the partner he expected to have, refuses vehemently, and now we hear the third orchestra tuning with open fifths. It begins to play yet another dance, this time a deutscher (German dance) in 3/8 time, and Leporello forces Masetto to dance it with him. This dance, a rustic one for peasants, lacking the gracefulness of the minuet with its leaps and stomping, could not be more apt for the country bumpkin Masetto being led by the servant Leporello. Mozart has set up a highly complex fusion of three dances in three different meters, which come together as shown in the below figure.

The alignment of these meters creates a certain amount of musical confusion with the three against two and the bar lines with consequent accents occurring at different points, to say nothing of the fact that three distinctively different dance melodies have been stacked up in layers. The confusion underlies the complexity of the different actions unfolding on stage, but yet it all comes together as a unified whole, with the ability of the listener to hear it reinforced by the visibility of the three separate orchestras and groups of characters dancing on stage.

In productions of this work directors do not always recognize the brilliance of what Mozart has achieved, and do not necessarily have the groups of characters dancing the appropriate dances in question. When attempting to place the action in our time, as Peter Sellars has done with Giovanni as a New York drug lord, scenes such as this become

Minuet in 3/4

Contredanse in 2/4

Deutscher in 3/8

fairly incomprehensible as the characters must dance modern dances to the specific dance music that Mozart provides. This hazard of modern productions should not deter directors from trying such things, but it does give them an added headache. In small theaters, such as the Estates Theater in Prague, where Mozart conducted the premiere of the work, and the opera remains a constant fixture of the repertory, the stage is not large enough for three separate orchestras to be placed on it, so for the production I saw there in June 2011, they provided token orchestras with one player for each. It's hard to describe the pleasure of seeing this opera in that theater, knowing Mozart had conducted it there in 1787, but not only because of that; the small size of this theater means that it has an intimacy about it, allowing members of the audience to feel almost that they are right on the stage. The set designed by the great Czech scenographer Josef Svaboda (also the designer of the opera scenes in Milos Forman's *Amadeus*) reinforced that impression, as he made the stage a continuation of the balcony patterns of the house.

The cleverness of this dance scene parallels the shrewdness of Giovanni's scheme—to keep the masqueraders amused, put Masetto out of the way, and get Zerlina for himself, but it backfires as he leads her away to a secluded spot, ready to complete what was left unfinished after the duet. Now Masetto is in hot pursuit. She recognizes the peril, more one suspects because of the prospect of being caught by her angry fiancé than anything else, and under the circumstances, despite her enjoyment of the pleasures of carnival, she does the only thing she can: she screams for help. The dances in separate meters now end, and the new section in a fast-paced allegro assai in 4/4 time brings everyone to her rescue; temporarily carnival gives way to Lent as the masqueraders unmask, identifying themselves, not fooled in the least by Giovanni's ploy of putting the blame on Leporello. A final allegro section reinforces the battle between carnival and Lent as the chorus homophonically berates Giovanni for his treachery, hurling threats at him about the fiery end that awaits him, musically doing this in the strongest possible way using whole notes and then half notes that emphasize the strong beats for the words starting with "Trema scellerato!" (tremble, you vile miscreant). In marked contrast to this, Giovanni and Leporello respond sotto voce as though in bewildered amazement, on quick notes in fragmented and syncopated lines that sound more like chopped-up speech than singing, appropriate to the confusion of which they speak. Despite all the strong-beat pressure, they do not give an inch, continuing to blurt out their disruptive interruptions against the forces of good, sticking it to the moralists who are convinced they have their quarry trapped. Only in the last few bars of the finale do the two opposing groups come together homophonically, and with the victory of capture now seeming to be in hand, exactly at this moment Giovanni and Leporello, having lulled their potential captors into complacent self-assurance, make their escape from the clutches of those who would spoil their (especially Giovanni's) fun.

Act 2

If we should think that anything happened at the end of Act 1 to make Giovanni wish to modify his behavior, we are entirely mistaken, as the beginning of Act 2 sees him ready for new conquests. Leporello may not like this way of life, but a few coins buy his complicity easily enough. For most of the characters nothing much changes at the beginning of the new act, with one notable exception: Elvira. She seemed the embodiment of hell's fury itself in the first act, but now we quickly discover a woman almost unrecognizable from what she had been. To take his new plans forward, Giovanni needs to exchange cloaks and hats with Leporello, since the next object of his amorous attention, the maid of Elvira, he calculates will not respond well to his noble bearing. Leporello objects, but gets no choice in the matter, and now carnival begins anew as seduction hangs in the air and Giovanni uses one of the favorite disguises of carnival—pretending to be a member of the lower classes. The scenes that follow belong entirely in the realm of carnival.

Just as a trio with Elvira, Giovanni, and Leporello came near the beginning of Act 1, the same holds in Act 2, as the two men disguised as each other discover Elvira standing at her window, musing about her wretched husband. He certainly deserves no pity, but the music Mozart gives her contrasts her prior rage completely, now softened up to the point that she may in fact doubt the words she sings. Since Giovanni hopes to find her maid there, he needs to get rid of Elvira; to accomplish this, the changing of clothes turns out to be fortuitous. If the cross-social-dressing had not been enough, this scene becomes pure carnival, as Giovanni sings to her of his newfound love for her, standing behind Leporello in her line of vision disguised as Giovanni. She tries to resist, but Mozart's music will not let her, and to their sniggering amazement, she gives in. At first apprehensive, Leporello quickly gets into the spirit of the deception, and now we have the astounding situation of Elvira spending the better part of the evening with a very mediocre facsimile of Giovanni, apparently so head-over-heels in love that she never once suspects the ruse. Driving them off with a threatening shout, Giovanni gets to sing his serenade to the maid, accompanied by a good serenading instrument, a mandolin. When the deception is finally exposed to Elvira in a sextet, despite the laughter it evokes, we cannot help feeling some pity for the disconsolate woman.

Giovanni's plans again must be put on hold, this time for Elvira's maid (imagine the maid explaining that little fling to her mistress), since Masetto comes along ready to kill the man who may have violated his fiancée, but the Leporello disguise gets Giovanni off the hook. After another aria which tells us nothing about Giovanni himself, in which he sends the other peasants scurrying off in all directions to find the foe, he asks Masetto if a good beating would not be enough, and then inspecting Masetto's weapons, gives the poor oaf a nasty drubbing. Left lying moaning and groaning, he is found by Zerlina, and in "Vedrai, carino," as sexually charged as her aria from the first act, she tells him to come home to receive a mysteriously wonderful healing balm that she possesses, unlike anything an apothecary can brew since she actually carries it with her. Being the dimwit he is, having just been beaten to a pulp with his own weapons, he may be too dense to understand what she now offers him.

After the escapades of the evening, Giovanni and Leporello meet up by chance at a graveyard, exchange cloaks and hats to become themselves again, and discover the statue of the Commendatore as an unidentified voice warns Giovanni he will soon laugh no more. Leporello must read the inscription at the base of the statue about the revenge that awaits the traitor who killed him, and this prompts Giovanni to force his servant in a comical duet to invite the statue to dinner—who accepts with a simple but terrifying nod. Following the carnival theme, this could be a masquerader in a very clever costume having a bone-chilling effect on two susceptibly tipsy revelers standing in a graveyard. Before that dinner we hear again from Anna, this time with a somewhat softer tone in which she chides Ottavio for considering her cruel because she will not return the love that he purports to offer. He still doesn't get it, thinking that by staying beside her he can ease her despair.

After *Figaro* we fully expect that the last finale of an opera will be spectacular, and in *Don Giovanni* Mozart does not disappoint, swinging through delightfully funny sections to terribly serious ones, and even combining the two. A sumptuous banquet has been laid out for Giovanni, so appetizing that Leporello cannot resist a few bites (Giovanni catches him in the act and asks him to whistle with his mouth full); the wine flows freely, we can assume that women grace the table (even though the libretto does not say so), and of course we hear music, provided by an on-stage band. Giovanni tells them to play, and aside from the amusement they provide for the feast, Mozart has his own fun with the audience by selecting well-known excerpts for this table music, at first from the operas of other composers. The first one, identified for us by Leporello ("Bravi! Cosa rara"), comes from *Una cosa rara* by Martín y Soler, a new opera from 1786 with a libretto by Da Ponte; when Giovanni asks Leporello what he thinks of this music, Leporello replies with a touch of irony that it conforms to his master's elevated standards. Da Ponte may very well be having his own little bit of fun with Mozart here. For those who actually know the opera, a connection could be made to *Don Giovanni* since it has to do with the licentious objectives of an aristocrat toward a woman from a lower class. This music continues as Giovanni stuffs himself and Leporello looks both revolted and envious, treated as nothing more than background music—a type of eighteenth-century muzak.

As Giovanni demands more food, the band strikes up the second piece, now from Mozart's old friend Giuseppe Sarti's *Fra i due litiganti* (1782), which the musically literate Leporello once again correctly identifies. In this case there appears also to be a nod to Goldoni, who wrote the libretto for Sarti's opera, and of course whose play *Don Giovanni Tenorio* provided a major source for Mozart's opera. As with the prior excerpt, this one also has a more specific bearing, with the passage in question using a text about a lamb being led to the slaughter, an event just around the corner for Giovanni, although considering the action currently taking place, with Leporello stealing some pheasant to satisfy his own appetite, we should not imagine any sort of dark premonition here. The third excerpt, so well known that Leporello does not have to name it but simply comments that he has heard it excessively, is Mozart's own "Non più andrai" from *Figaro*, with Figaro scoffing at Cherubino as a soldier no longer able to flit about as a butterfly capturing pretty girls; Giovanni's days of chasing women are also about to end.

On the last note of "Non più andrai" Elvira bursts in, not hell-bent on his destruction, but throwing herself at him with the offer of one last chance to accept her and mend his ways, a prospect so foreign to his being that he mocks her and invites her to stay and eat if she likes. Flashes of the old abandoned Elvira return as she stomps off, jeering at him to go ahead and wallow in his iniquity—a reprobate surely doomed. Leporello expects his master to be moved by this display of anguish, but Giovanni simply toasts wine, women, and song, brushing her off with his own priorities. On her way out she lets fly a bloodcurdling scream, and when prompted to investigate, Leporello does the same, announcing the arrival of the statue with an imitation of his steps—Ta, Ta, Ta, Ta; he refuses to answer the door and dives under the table. The statue makes his entry with the music from the beginning of the overture, described earlier in this chapter, and, not interested in the food for mortals offered by Giovanni, launches into his graver reasons for coming.

The trio that ensues will remind us of the trio at the beginning of the opera, with Giovanni urging the statue to get on with his message since he has limited time for this, the statue assuring Giovanni in longer tones that he stands at the brink of death, and Leporello jabbering in the same type of patter he had earlier, chattering in uncontrollable fear. His patter at the beginning of the opera defused the seriousness, and once again it has that effect, infusing the scene with the spirit of carnival. As noted earlier in the chapter, Giovanni has nothing but contempt for this symbol of ultimate authority, hurling the insults of the season at him as a son would at his father or a skeptic would at a priest or even God. He may be dragged literally kicking and screaming to hell, but he goes without fear, with no intention of repenting his way of life, and even blaspheming as he descends. We get a good pyrotechnic show here, but certainly not anything that will give moralists satisfaction; only repentance can do that, as happens in Tirso de Molina's play but not any other versions of the work since then. Whether we like it or not, we are forced to admire Giovanni's resoluteness in the face of the most harrowing arm-twisting. Instead of a moral victory, we have something much closer to the end of carnival and beginning of Lent, putting an end to wild behavior with the striking of midnight on Mardi Gras, but reminding us that the craziness will return next year.

The opera could end at this point, as it did for the first performance in Vienna in contrast to the premiere in Prague, but we miss something important if we think that it could stop here. Part of the misunderstanding lies in the fact that most conductors—including Maazel—refuse to perform the final moral the way Mozart wrote it, and they therefore try to add an element of seriousness that Mozart did not intend. As the scene begins, Leporello brings those in pursuit of Giovanni up to speed on what has happened, barely able to blurt out the words about his astonishing demise. In a court of law his fantastical evidence could be picked apart with ease, but the others buy it without much effort, Elvira confirming that she actually saw the ghost, and the others echoing her words but looking inept since they had nothing to do with punishing him. They look even more foolish as Mozart then turns it into vaudeville, with characters coming forward singly or in pairs to explain how their lives will unfold. Ottavio, the one who should have apprehended Giovanni, looks especially feeble, as he goes on and on about getting married soon, but Anna puts him off for another year; if we bring Goldoni into it, she may simply be looking for a ploy to ditch him altogether. Elvira will go to a convent, which in Tirso's play is where Don Juan stole her from in the first place, Zerlina and Masetto will return to domestic simplicity, for the moment going home to dinner, and Leporello will try his luck at getting a better master at the local tavern. Some of them then come together to say he should be left to rot like Proserpine in Pluto's hell, but apparently as ignorant of myth as inept at retribution, they do not seem to know that Proserpine inhabits both the lower world and the upper one she came from before being abducted by Pluto.

Then comes the moral, and they introduce it cheerfully with the call for good people to be jolly and sing the oldest song that exists. Gazzaniga ends his *Don Giovanni* in a similar way, but instead of a moral they simply sing and dance joyfully, in fact pretending to be instruments of the orchestra to back up the dancing. The presto singing of the moral written by Mozart, with words to be wary of how you live since a miserable fate awaits sinners, uses a pseudo-liturgical style, led off by the most self-righteous of the lot, Anna, with a fugato theme, briefly backed up by the chorus, and then answered by Zerlina, the least righteous of the group. The chorus then takes over, but on the key part of the text, "E de' perfidi la morte" (the treachery of sin results in death), Mozart, in carnival style, makes them sound foolish singing it, with solecisms that turn it into an example of how not to write in a semi-liturgical style. All the wrong syllables get accented for the beginning of text: E(p) de'(f) per(p) fi(f) di(p) (p=piano: quiet; f=forte: loud), and if these dynamics are sung as they have been written, the results will be absurd. To make it even more farcical, the accented syllables (which in any normal way of speaking would be the unaccented ones) are on short notes off the beat in contrast to the weak syllables on long notes on the beat. On "morte" (death), the most serious word of all, Mozart does something even sillier, as he makes the singers hold the first syllable for an absurdly long time—four full bars with four tied whole notes, and then clips off the second syllable with a mere quarter note, making it only one-sixteenth the length of the first syllable (at presto a quarter note goes by very quickly, sounding like a hiccup).

I have seen this work performed many times, and have heard it many more times on recordings and DVDs, but I have never yet heard a performance in which "morte" is performed the way Mozart wrote it (although Nikolaus Harnoncourt in a production with the Opernhaus Zürich comes fairly close). Most conductors hold the quarter note at least the length of a whole note, if not longer, and that results in something that sounds normal instead of absurd. Mozart knew what he wanted, and wrote it; trying to make this sound normal does a disservice, and certainly misses the point of what Mozart wished to achieve. As the chorus continues, Mozart simply does not let up on the intentional mistakes; for example on "è sempre, è sempre, è sempre ugual" (and always the same) he drags out the first part on a long chromatic descending line with some syncopations which could sound appropriately menacing, but that descent ends with an incongruously clipped "pre ugual," even placing "pre" and "u" together on a mere quarter note. With all of this "bad" writing, if we still didn't get it he gives the opera a jaunty little twelve-bar instrumental conclusion after the chorus cuts out, leaving a sound in our ears of anything but seriousness. It appears that Lent has not been the winner.

9

A FELLOW PRANKSTER AND A STRANGE COMMISSION

The Magic Flute and Requiem

During the last year of his life Mozart's writing continued to be as prolific and diverse as it had been in most previous years, including almost every type of composition except for symphonies. We have no indications other than the last few weeks before he died that he may have anticipated his end, and the numerous fragments and unfinished works, some that he undoubtedly intended to return to when time permitted, suggest that he believed his future looked bright. Among this late music we find a healthy balance of serious and comic works, assuring us he had not lapsed into a morbid state of the contemplation of death, and his letters to his wife and certain friends do the same, with some of the most irreverent ones coming during 1791. He had not written any large-scale works on spec for a long time, and that continued to be true now, with the two operas of this year, *La clemenza di Tito* (Tito's Clemency) and *The Magic Flute* written either on commission or with the assurance that performances would take place. The same proved true of the Requiem, a mass for the dead of fairly large proportions, which he wrote because of the unusual commission that arrived at his doorstep. More myths surround the composition of this work by Mozart than just about any other, including that he became obsessed with it, believing it to be his own requiem because of his imminent death. He received the commission in the middle of 1791, roughly six month before he died, and it's unlikely that he saw his own future as anything but rosy at that point. In fairly urgent need of money at the time because of his necessarily extravagant lifestyle, the commission was for enough money to make it worthwhile, and his recent appointment as the adjunct director of music at St. Stephen's Cathedral (which would become a well-paying position when the current director died) meant that a requiem would be useful to have in his arsenal of works.

Even without the myths about the Requiem, the story of its commission is nothing short of bizarre, putting Mozart indirectly into contact with a genuine crackpot, Franz Count von Walsegg. Something of a musical dilettante, he had the peculiar habit of commissioning composers to write music and then passing these works off in performance as his own, with no copyright laws at the time to restrain him. His wife Anna died in February 1791, and even with the seriousness of the occasion, he remained up to his old tricks, sending the commission to Mozart anonymously (probably by way of a clerk employed by his lawyer in Vienna). Mozart was unable to complete the work before he died, so his widow asked various other composers to finish it since she did not wish to lose out on the second installment of the handsome commission, and some details of this will be described below. When Walsegg received the completed work, he copied the entire score in his own hand to give the impression he had composed it, and then had it performed two years after Mozart died (by all indications it had been performed previously, including as a fundraiser for Mozart's family). Mozart would have been aware of none of these details, and even Constanze did not know who had commissioned it until 1800, but Mozart may very well have been curious about the cloak of mystery surrounding the way Walsegg's agent approached him. Had he known any of this, he would not have been pleased about someone trying to take credit for his work, but the rest of the intrigue could very well have bemused him.

THE MAGIC FLUTE

The Magic Flute came about in a very different way, although few details are known of the request and the collaboration. Mozart's old friend Emanuel Schikaneder moved to Vienna in 1789 with his theatrical troupe, and the two of them appeared to pick up where they had left off in Salzburg a decade earlier when Schikaneder lived there. Schikaneder had participated in a game played by the Mozart family and some friends called Bölzlschiessen—shooting with air guns at targets painted to represent people in this circle, or known to them, in compromising situations. After the word got back to Salzburg about the fling Mozart had with his cousin the Bäsle, someone painted a target showing Mozart bidding his sad farewell to her. Another one had Schikaneder two-timing with a young woman on one side of a tree while another woman waits for him patiently on the other side, an apparently not uncommon activity for him. On his extended trip starting in 1777, Mozart wrote to his father about an idea he had for a target, which should show "a small man with light hair, stooped over, revealing his bare arse. From his mouth come the words: *good appetite for the feast*. Another man should be shown with boots and spurs, a red cloak and a splendid, fashionable wig. He must be of medium height, and precisely in the position that he can lick the other man's arse. From his mouth come the words: *oh, there's nothing to top that*." (MBA ii 103) Of course we do not know who they are, but possibly the short man could be Mozart himself and the well-dressed one the archbishop. Mozart's scatological language, especially in his letters, is well known, and attempts to put this down to something pathological are misplaced in the extreme; in southern Germany and parts of Austria many people indulged in this type of language, with "Leck mich im Arsch" almost as normal as "cheers" or "top of the morning to you." Mozart also wrote canons using such language, two starting with the phrase just noted (K231 and 233), followed by some delightful extensions of lavatory humor. Schikaneder shared the enjoyment of off-color humor and risqué behavior with Mozart, and the two of them undoubtedly got up to all sorts of frivolity both in Salzburg and later in Vienna.

Schikaneder's troupe performed not at the sophisticated, centrally located Burgtheater but at the much more rough and tumble suburban Theater an der Wieden, which he now directed, with entertainment aimed at a more rustic audience, including a genre called *Zauberoper* (magic opera). Schikaneder presumably suggested to Mozart that he write one of these, basing it on the fairy tale "Lulu, or the Magic Flute" by A. J. Liebeskind. Schikaneder prepared the libretto, of course with

Mozart's watchful support, and the two of them must have had an enormous amount of fun with this collaboration, each trying to outdo the other with off-the-wall zaniness. Schikaneder wrote the part of Papageno, the bird catcher who wants nothing to do with seriousness, for himself. Not unlike the part of Osmin in the German opera Mozart wrote a decade earlier, Papageno has all the attributes of the apparently banned Hanswurst, with overindulgence in food, wine, sex (if he can get it), and general tomfoolery. The opera has a serious side too, with the Queen of the Night, her daughter Pamina, who has been abducted, the prince Tamino, who takes it upon himself to rescue her, and Sarastro, who presides over an order that the Queen considers to be evil but turns out not to be.

Much has been made of the possibility that this order represents Freemasonry, of which Mozart was an active member, and that the peculiar shift between the two acts moves from the negative perception of Freemasonry in Act 1 to the proper one as an exemplar of truth, beauty, and brotherhood in the second act. I'm entirely prepared to agree that the order portrayed in the opera is Freemasonry, but to presume that we should take an entirely positive view of it in Act 2 misses what Mozart tells us in the music. Despite his continuing involvement with and composition of Masonic music, Mozart could see the flaws in the order which purported to be the voice of reform in the so-called enlightened despotism of the Habsburg Empire, certainly its blatant misogyny, but also its attitudes to key social issues of the time such as the use of torture and slavery. Schikaneder also subscribed to Freemasonry, but this did not always go smoothly for him; when he tried to join a lodge in Regensburg shortly before moving to Vienna, the lodge asked him to avoid meetings for at least half a year because of reports about his sketchy private life. Both he and Mozart were unlikely to let Freemasonry get by unscathed in this opera, and very clearly they do not. For the most overt indicators of this, we need only compare the musical treatment of the characters both for and against, along with the one who appears to go through a transition; as with his previous operas, Mozart uses his music to tell us what is most important. The Queen, the greatest enemy of the order, gets the best music in the opera (along with her daughter Pamina), and Papageno, who has no use for the high-mindedness of the order, completely steals the show with his delightfully engaging music. On the other side, Sarastro gets fairly stuffy music, always hymn-like in his solo numbers, and even worse, Mozart makes him a bass, with some passages as absurdly low as the ones given to Osmin in *The Abduction*, in which stateliness can turn to satire if pushed too low. The man in the middle, Tamino, gets a very good aria at the beginning, but his first proves also to be his last, as Mozart relegates him to ensembles after that, increasingly marginalizing him as the work proceeds. At the end, after we have heard the last from him, Mozart lavishes the final show-stopping aria on Papageno, as if to say that the Hanswurst-like character has come out on top.

Aside from the extent to which Freemasonry should be taken seriously, the other issue over which much ink has been spilt concerns the apparent misogyny of the work, and that of course ties in with the refusal of Freemasons to accept women as members. If one simply reads the libretto, which unfortunately has happened all too often with those who claim misogyny, it appears that women should be regarded as nothing but second-class citizens, a rant that mostly comes from Sarastro and his priests. In Act 1 a priest chides Tamino for being beguiled by a woman—the Queen—and believing her view of Sarastro's evil; later in the act Sarastro tells Pamina that only a man can guide her and a woman must not exceed her rightful place. This gets even worse in Act 2, with two priests warning Tamino to be wary of the duplicity of women (the first maxim of the order), and not be blinded when they should resist, because otherwise there will be dire consequences. Some productions omit this duet, and for those that emphasize the seriousness of the opera, one can see why; Mozart gives them music for the last line that makes them sound ridiculous, and this will be described in the section on Act 2. Tamino and Pamina can also usefully be compared. While he becomes more marginalized, she receives the exact opposite treatment, with one of the greatest arias of the entire operatic repertory, "Ach, ich fühl's," in Act 2. Even the libretto paints her as superior to Tamino, with his apparent inability to face the trials of initiation prompting her to take the lead, guiding him through them. The contradictions of text and music have often been of more interest to stage directors than musicologists, and some productions, including the one that you will attend, address them in fascinating ways.

Act I

It's 29 July 2006, and the Salzburg Festival has gone all out to celebrate the 250th anniversary of Mozart's birth, staging all twenty-two of his completed and incomplete operas. You have come to Austria to see *The Magic Flute* on this night, and having attended excellent productions of this opera previously, you hope for the best with the often all too conservative Austrians. You have reason to be concerned, since a highly controversial production at the festival staged by Graham Vick in 2005 had been withdrawn and replaced (with essentially the same cast) by Pierre Audi's production first shown at the Netherlands Opera in Amsterdam in 1995. Riccardo Muti will be conducting the Vienna Philharmonic in the pit, and that too gives you some concern, although not for the musical quality. For this opera, which addresses the rights and even value of women, you wonder if the orchestra, as was true a couple of decades early when you last heard it, will still be made up of men only (who argued that women distracted them in the serious business of music making). You breathe a sigh of relief when the orchestra makes its way into the pit of the Grosse Festspielhaus and a handful of women take their places. When the orchestra plays the opening three large chords, you feel somewhat reassured by the image projected onto the curtain of an abstractly conceived naked woman playing a flute; after moving into the fast part of the overture, needless to say the flute gets some prominent lines, along with other woodwinds. Halfway through the overture things stop for another sounding of the big chords, this time amounting to three times three, evoking Masonic symbolism (you can refresh your memory with a readily available Decca DVD of this production).

The curtain rises as the overture ends, and a delightfully unrealistic serpent, with an oversized papier-mâché head and two headlights on the side, menaces the hapless Tamino (Paul Groves), who, incapable of taming the beast, can do no better than call for help. In some ways this opening scene tells us what we need to know about Tamino: by himself he can accomplish little, and he has no chance of succeeding without the help of others. Aid comes from the mountain side, in the form of the three women who serve the Queen, decked out in Tyrolean hats and coats, and they take an immediate liking to the young prince, competing with each other to be the one left standing guard while the others should hasten off to tell the Queen. The music they sing not only plays on the comedy of the situation but also suggests their sexual arousal. After the whimpering Tamino in need of being rescued, the dreadlocked bird catcher Papageno (Christian Gerhaher) then makes his splashy entrance, riding in a VW-like convertible pushed by strangely yellow-clad sprites, as other green ones buzz around in the air. In the original production this was Schikaneder's opportunity to make his breezy appearance, and there have been some side-splitting ones in recent times, such as at the Sydney Opera House in 2008, where Papageno, resembling a well-known television comedian, came onstage carrying a smoldering barbie with steaks broiling. His delightful aria identifies his profession and merry inclinations, but laments that he lacks a woman, whom he thinks he should be able to catch the same way he does birds. This focuses on his most persistent urge throughout the opera, and gets a little bawdy too, as he describes what he would do with a woman if he had one.

After Papageno meets Tamino and the three ladies punish him with a padlock on his lips for lying about killing the serpent, Tamino responds amorously in his first aria to the locket with an image of Pamina given to him by the ladies. The Queen expects him to rescue her, but from this tenor Mozart gives us something comparable to Don Ottavio's arias from *Don Giovanni*, raising doubts that he will be up to the task. Strength seems called for, but for that we must wait for the next aria, sung in glorious coloratura by the Queen, who rises from the ground clad in bright green, like a mythical mother earth. You are delighted that Diana Damrau as the Queen stands entirely up to the task of the vocal gymnastics this extraordinarily demanding part requires. When anything serious happens in this work, such as this outpouring from the Queen, Mozart and Schikaneder quickly defuse it, in this case with Papageno humming desperately because he can't sing with locked lips.

The three ladies dispatch Tamino on his way to rescue Pamino, with the reluctant Papageno in tow, providing the prince with a magic flute to get him out of nasty situations, and magic bells for Papageno for the same purpose. The scene now changes to Sarastro's realm, and we get our first introduction to it not by way of the grandeur of the order, but from a group of slaves, bemoaning the cruelty of the chief slave Monastatos. Based on their comments we get the impression that the depiction of him does not invoke something more broadly racist, but that he is simply a bad apple within his race. We may be surprised that this order of goodness and brotherhood keeps slaves, but considering the time, perhaps we should not: the great enlightened American, Thomas Jefferson, a ceaseless advocate of human rights, apparently had no qualms about owning slaves his entire life. Unlike England and America, slavery had more or less escaped the radar of the Habsburg Empire, and while Sarastro's position may seem hypocritical to us, it probably did not disturb many in Mozart's audience. The use of torture, though, is quite another matter, since this had been banned in the empire not long prior to this opera, and Sarastro's use of it to punish Monastatos—the seventy-seven lashes on the feet—gives a strong hint that his order may not quite be what it claims to be. This production clearly makes something of the dubious nature of the order, first of all putting Sarastro (René Pape) in a kind of whiteface, but much more strikingly, giving facial makeup—white faces and blackened eyes—to those in his entourage that makes them look as though they just escaped from the set of the best known of all zombie movies, *The Living Dead*. The production that had been too controversial for the festival from the previous year had portrayed Sarastro as the ignoble one, and considering his presentation here, you conclude that Audi had a similar inclination.

The opera seems so full of contradictions that at a certain point you stop trying to enumerate them. The most obvious ones involve the shift between the two acts, with the villain Sarastro transformed to the hero, while the wronged mother becomes the reprobate, and Tamino seems willy-nilly to follow the one who directs him. It probably makes better sense not to try to make sense of such things, but simply go with the flow. As becomes very evident in the second act there appears to be a struggle unfolding between the powers of rationality on the one hand and magic or the irrational on the other, and judgment needs to be reserved about which force wins. While the opera has many extraordinary touches, one that stands out especially is the presence of the three boys, played in this production by three members of the Vienna Boys' Choir, entering like mythical aviators, and their existence in both acts certainly joins the contradictions just noted. They originally come from the Queen, charged with the task of protecting Tamino, Papageno, and Pamina, but as they do this in the second act, rescuing both Papageno and Pamina from possible suicide, and giving Tamino direction, they could be thought of as helping the new forces. Still, the magical aura about them never wanes, like the flute itself, and perhaps they help to bridge the gap between the irrational and rational forces in conflict, with both sorcery and wisdom. This works most strongly not through what they say, but instead through the music, which in its simplicity and charm provides some of the most memorable and moving music of the opera.

Act 2

The second act places the focus squarely on Sarastro's temple, beginning with a march of priests followed by the three times three chords from the overture, and then a council of priests, with Sarastro expressing some very high-minded sentiments about the order and the difficult initiation lying ahead for Tamino. These remarks happen in spoken dialogue, not music, perhaps reminding us of what we imagined to be high-mindedness coming from Pasha Selim in *The Abduction*. Unlike Selim, Sarastro does have a singing role, and after exhorting the priest to follow his lead, he puts his lofty sentiments into song in the first of his arias (with a chorus of priests) in which he calls on the Egyptian gods Isis and Osiris to lead the pair seeking wisdom. For this hymn-like song Mozart gives him some of the least interesting music of the opera, and makes certain that he gets to sing some absurdly low notes. In the spoken dialogue prior to this, Sarastro lays out in no uncertain terms the conflict which will unfold, between the superstition wielded by the Queen, a woman, against the rationality, virtue, and wisdom of the male order, and much of what happens in the remainder of the act will play these off against each other. While the libretto does this on one level, the music adds another dimension, and we, along with directors like Audi, must decide which way the music takes it.

The scene shifts to Tamino ready to start his trials (along with the reluctant Papageno), and the next musical number, a duet sung by two priests, starts them off on the test of silence, all the while reinforcing the message from Sarastro about the treachery of women and what odious things will happen to them if they allow themselves to be swayed by women. Feminists cry foul at this point, but they all too often do this without listening to the music, which takes the priest's words seriously for the first two-thirds of the duet, but not after that. For the last line of text, "Tod und Verzweiflung war sein Lohn" (Death and damnation was his fate), Mozart has them singing sotto voce, accompanied by staccato bassoons, trombones, and low strings in a jaunty little march rhythm, with a repeat, and again with the same music for the orchestral conclusion. This music, completely incongruous for the text, clearly pokes a hole in their misogynist rant, mocking the seriousness of their words and deflating their so-called wisdom. Tamino's test of silence now conveniently removes him from much of the music to come, immediately after his confrontation with the three ladies in a quintet.

Monastatos, despite the seventy-seven lashes, has not given up on his sexual quest for Pamina, and just as he moves in to strike, the Queen emerges to rescue her just in the nick of time, and presents Pamina with a dagger which she should use to finish off Sarastro. The Queen now gets her second big aria, a classic vengeance aria with spectacular high notes and coloratura, musically one of the high points of the entire opera. When she exits Monastatos tries to pick up where he left off, and receiving nothing but Pamina's scorn, he takes the dagger left by the Queen and raises it to kill her. This time Sarastro intervenes and now shows something of his true colors, the great humanist gloating about how he will get his revenge on the Queen and force her to grovel in shame. He follows this up with his second aria, right on the heels of the one just sung by the Queen, "In diesen heilgen Hallen kennt man die Rache nicht" (In these hallowed halls revenge is unknown to us). If this strikes you as contradicting what he just said before launching into his hymn-like piety, you have not missed anything. Aside from his blatant hypocrisy, musically his arias cannot hold a candle to the stunning beauty of the Queen's, and Mozart may very well be asking us to make a choice by placing them side by side.

While this battle between the heavyweights goes on, with Tamino not uttering so much as a peep, the character who, along with Papageno, commands our greatest attention in Act 2 comes forward: Pamina—sung spectacularly in Salzburg by Genia Kühmeier. Ready for the love that has been promised, she manages to find Tamino, but he will neither speak to her nor gesture why he cannot, and this prompts her to sing the great aria "Ach, ich fühl's, es ist verschwunden" (Ah, I feel it, the loss of love). Mozart now moves to another musical dimension, beyond the rage of her mother or platitudes of Sarastro to the most profound and deeply felt emotions, known to us from the likes of the Countess or Fiordiligi in earlier operas. These emotions come through

with uncluttered lines, strategically placed leaps, and even some coloratura, although not at all like her mother's: on the word "Herzen"
(heart) a brief coloratura drives the line upward, giving the falling back
an even greater sense of pathos. She sings to Tamino, but from him we
have had no indication now or earlier that he could possibly comprehend the profundity of her feelings.

Later in the finale, after their prolonged separation which takes her
to the point of suicide, a priest finally brings Pamina to Tamino, and her
greeting that accompanies their embrace, simple in the extreme with its
rising leap on his name into her upper register, has such power that we
hear it as something of an epiphany. His reply, with a smaller leap, falls
a little flat in comparison. The lead she now takes follows the two of
them through the remainder of the opera, as Sarastro allows her to
accompany Tamino on the final trials of fire and water. Tamino seems
incapable of facing these on his own or knowing how to navigate them,
so she takes charge, leading him and handing him the flute to be their
guide, the instrument Tamino had received from the Queen. Here we
have perhaps the most delightful contradiction of the opera, with the
trials that should lead to the ultimate enlightened wisdom in fact being
conquered by the power of magic emanating from the Queen, made
possible by a woman, the Queen's daughter. In fact, the magic invoked
here counteracts the cold reason that Sarastro represents, and the music, the glorious solo flute passages that lead them through the trials,
takes the lead in determining the stronger of the forces.

A chorus leads the happy pair to the temple, but not surprisingly, the
music of most of the remainder of the opera belongs to those on the
irrational side, and Papageno most of all. The trials have been no more
than an annoyance to him, as he wants nothing but good food and wine,
and the pretty wife promised earlier—hopefully not the old hag who
has befriended him and claims to be his Papagena (Irena Bespalovaite).
When she does not materialize, he comes to the end of his wits and
decides he would rather not live than be without a wife, although he
will at least count to three before putting the rope around his neck.
That count of three, sometimes prolonged with fractions, serves as a
cheeky parody of the somber three counts heard since the beginning of
the overture, and musically Mozart follows this with crocodile-tears
usage of the minor key for his last lament. The three boys come to his
rescue, and remind him that he should us his magic bells; these bring

his future wife out of hiding, the old hag now shedding her disguise and emerging as the nubile beauty he had hoped for. The perky duet that brings the two of them together simply bursts with sexual energy as they both stutter out their names with multiple repetitions of pa-pa-pa-pa. . . . Those repetitions become the harbinger of all the little Papagenos and Papagenas that they will have, and the music seems to leave no question that they will spend all their time trying, as Mozart prolongs this on and on. We may think we should be contemplating serious matters at this point near the end of the opera, but instead the music gives us the delights of procreation.

Not to be left out of the finale, the Queen makes her last stand, with Monastatos and the three ladies in tow, and their defeat seems to have more to do with magic than truth and virtue. I have suggested elsewhere that their end may be a little like the defeat of carnival just before Lent begins, and they will surely rise again when the next carnival season rolls around.

The final scene of the opera presents an interesting challenge for staging, depending on how the battle between the irrational and the rational has been interpreted. The words from Sarastro tell us that light has overcome darkness, and the chorus hails Isis and Osiris for leading the happy pair to the path of virtue and wisdom, although in the last allegro the accompanying music seems a little too cheerful to underscore these sentiments. Most productions, but not all, take the conventional position of Tamino and Pamina being accepted into the temple, such as the one staged at the Met in New York directed by Julie Taymor and conducted by James Levine, also in 2006. In this one the gaudy set, looking like a giant transparent washing machine, emphasized pomp and grandeur throughout, giving Sarastro the nod while not really knowing what to do with Papageno. At the end the lovers happily join the order, with more pomp and ceremony that does not quite fit with the music. The complete opposite of this happened in Prague at the Estates Theatre in the early 1990s (where of course *Don Giovanni* received its premiere two centuries earlier), where the director David Radok could not imagine them wishing to join this sterile order. Tamino and Pamina seem uneasy with the chorus ramming the triumph of the enlightenment down their throats, and as soon as the chorus ends, they run as fast as they can away from the temple to join Papageno and the other common folk.

Knowing the possibility for this going either way, you watch with interest at this point in Salzburg, although you have some inkling of what will happen. It first of all seemed curious that after the Queen's defeat she did not disappear, but was left lying on the stage, suggesting that she and what she represented may not be so easily disposed of. A large artificial beam of light comes down to back up Sarastro's words about light's triumph over darkness, and behind that streams in the chorus, clad in red gowns and headwear, still with white faces and black holes for eyes, looking no less like zombies than they did in the first act. As they sing the solemn andante first part of the chorus, the Queen begins to stir, rising up to a sitting stance from her prostrate dormant position, showing definite signs of life. With the beginning of the sparkling allegro, she quickly stands, abetted by Pamina, who has come to her side, then walks over to Sarastro and gives him a seductive look, to which he does not seem averse. She wanders off amid the chorus, still giving him that look, and he moves away in a different direction, leaving the impression they will meet up when they can give the chorus the slip. While his entourage appears to represent the living dead, certainly nothing the passionate young lovers would wish to join, Audi's Sarastro himself recognizes that he lives a double life and, with the music at the end, goes where Mozart appears to be nudging him.

THE REQUIEM

Those who have seen Milos Forman's *Amadeus* will have a peculiar notion of how the Requiem came into being. Peter Shaffer, who wrote the original play and the script for the film, wished to develop a certain type of fictional relationship between Salieri and Mozart, and he had little interest in historical accuracy. In the film, Salieri arrives in disguise at Mozart's door with the commission for the work, and when Mozart's final illness prevents him from completing it, Salieri, who uses the commission as his method of killing Mozart (from overwork), sits at Mozart's deathbed and takes dictation to finish the task. Of course none of this happened, but what actually did seems almost as strange, and certainly remains shrouded in mystery, prompting one writer to title his essay on the subject "Requiem but No Peace." When Mozart died in 1791, the work remained as a series of fragments with the exception of one section, the opening "Requiem aeternam," while a later section, the Kyrie, was complete except for the details of orchestration. Mozart had been paid half of the commission in advance, and since his widow urgently needed money, she determined to have the work finished with little or no knowledge that others had been involved, both to protect his reputation and to collect the other half. The details of how this happened remain fairly obscure, since most of the people she approached about taking this on, such as former students and friends, said nothing about their involvement publicly, honoring Constanze's wish that the work should be considered Mozart's alone.

It remains unclear how much still needed to be done, and the bits of information that have emerged have not clarified very much. Some writers have speculated that Mozart always composed everything in his head and simply needed to find the time to write it down, in part based on a comment he made in a letter to his father, although with counterpoint involved, as it is for much of the Requiem, with different requirements for working out ideas, that seems unlikely in this case. For a vocal work such as this, Mozart would write the voice parts first, and then the bare minimum of the accompaniment—usually just the top melodic line and a lower bass line, leaving the other parts to be worked out later. Some of the sections have come down to us that way, so someone else had to make those decisions about the inner parts—the orchestration—but for other sections even less existed, meaning some fairly original composition needed to be carried out.

Among those who completed the work, the person who appears to have done by far the most chose not to keep silent about his involvement: Mozart's pupil Franz Xaver Süssmayr. In a letter to the publisher Breitkopf & Härtel almost a decade after Mozart's death, he claimed to be the sole composer of at least three or four movements, which placed Constanze in a fairly awkward spot. She disputed his claim, saying that Mozart had left pieces of paper with sketches that Süssmayr used for his work, and when one of these scraps turned up fairly recently, it gave some credence to her counterclaim. He had worked closely with Mozart as an assistant during the composition of *La clemenza di Tito* and *The Magic Flute*, and as such he had better insight than anyone else into Mozart's working methods. It may very well have been the case that when Mozart fell too ill to work on the Requiem, he discussed it with Süssmayr and perhaps even dictated some passages. We know that he had much to do with the completion, more than Constanze admitted, and needless to say, he has taken much of the blame for writing or orchestration that does not appear to be up to Mozart's usual standard. Some have even suggested that he completely botched the job and have produced their own new versions which they believe come closer to Mozart's original intentions. It's highly unlikely that these add anything better than what we have, since Sussmayr, despite his limitations, had an inside track available to no one else, and the best we can hope for is his completed version. In spite of the flaws, this extraordinary work deserves all the respect it has been shown in the past two centuries, and it stands as a fitting conclusion to Mozart's life.

The requiem mass, or the mass for the dead, has been part of the Roman Catholic liturgy for many centuries, typically in the same form since Pope Pius V regularized it in 1570. The name requiem comes from the words of the opening section, the Introit: "Requiem aeternam dona eis, Domine" (Rest eternal grant to them, Lord). Of the two primary types of masses, the Ordinary and the Proper, this one belongs to the latter, which varies from day to day throughout the church year according to the occasion, in contrast to the Ordinary, which always remains the same. As a variable mass, it omits some of the more jubilant parts such as the Gloria, Credo, and Alleluia, and replaces them with sections of a more mournful nature, usually with these sections (although not necessarily in this order): Introit (Requiem Aeternam), Kyrie eleison (Lord have mercy), Lacrimosa (Day of tears), Dies irae (Day of wrath), Domine Jesu (Offertorium), Sanctus (Holy, holy, holy), Benedictus (Blessed is the one), Pie Jesu (Pious Jesus), Agnus Dei (Lamb of God), Lux aeternum (Eternal light), Libera me (Deliver me), and In paradisum (In paradise). Mozart's Requiem does not follow this exactly but adds certain other sections often used during the eighteenth and nineteenth centuries, including the Tuba mirum (The Trumpet's mighty blast), Rex tremendae (King of fearful majesty), Recordare (Remember loving Jesus), Confutatis maledictis (When sentence on the damned is passed), and Hostias et preces tibi, Domine (Sacrifices and prayers of praise to Thee, O Lord, we offer). While typically sung on 2 November (All Souls' Day) for all deceased, it can also be used at any time in memory of a specific individual.

Mozart wrote very little liturgical music during his final decade in Vienna, in part because the demand for it in the 1780s scarcely existed since the reforms imposed by Joseph II on church music all but put an end to its composition until his death in 1790. He had been a strong patron of opera during his reign, especially comic opera, and Mozart clearly benefited from his enthusiasm. After his death, church music once again became an attractive proposition for composers, and even without a commission Mozart may very well have been inclined to write a requiem now that he had prospects for employment at St. Stephen's Cathedral. In the months immediately prior to starting work on the Requiem, Mozart had poured much of his energy into opera, simultaneously *La clemenza* for the coronation of Leopold II in Prague and *The Magic Flute* for Schikenader, both in 1791. Opera rang in his ears, and while in most respects a requiem has little or nothing to do with opera, following an entirely different type of style, that did not stop Mozart from making his Requiem dramatic, at times actually borrowing some techniques from opera. Even his choice of instrumentation played a role in the drama in order to find the appropriate affective tone for certain numbers, with greater emphasis on lower wind instruments such as basset horns and bassoons, and an avoidance of flutes, oboes, horns, and clarinets. Trumpets and timpani figure prominently as well, along with trombones used mainly as backup for the chorus, but also with some of the most striking solo obbligato writing for that instrument during the eighteenth century. All the usual strings are present, and as would be true of other liturgical music, this one has a basso continuo for organ, which the organist was expected to improvise from the figured bass (a single bass line with numbers that indicate chords and their inversions). Even the distribution of vocal writing plays into the drama, with some of it carried by the chorus while other, more intensive sections go to soloists alone or in combination.

While the title of the work implies peace or rest in the hereafter—a release from the turmoil and burdens of life—much of the text deals with anything but peace, arising from the Roman Catholic notions of the final judgment which will not go in everyone's favor, to be followed for some by the torments of hell. This horrific side of the end comes up in the Dies irae, the Tuba mirum, the Confutatis maledictis, the Lacrymosa, and even to some extent in the parts dealing with deliverance, such the Rex tremendae, where the God of love appears every bit as much a God to be feared. Mozart knew the tradition of the requiem well, having himself performed in the one by Michael Haydn for Archbishop Schrattenbach in Salzburg in 1773, and regardless of whether he held any of these views about God, he did not hold back in exploiting musically the grim side. He certainly knew the attitude of some of the French *philosophes* to God, including the atheistic views of Baron Holbach, and especially the position of Voltaire, the close friend of Mozart's host in France, Louise d'Épinay, who railed among other things at the God who "gave us evil hearts in order to punish us. . . . In all this I do not recognize the god I must adore." Most people in the eighteenth century did not share Voltaire's distain, but whether one did or not, the formidable image of a god as punisher loomed large, either in what might actually happen after death, or at least in the incessant emphasis placed on this by the church. In *Don Giovanni* Mozart gave one option of how this judgment could be meted out, in that case met with defiance; in the Requiem he presents another side of it, one that will not offend the church, while at the same time speaking to those who thought of the church's obsession with fire and brimstone as hell on earth. Knowing what we know about Mozart from the operas, we should not expect that he would write a run-of-the-mill requiem strictly for religious edification.

Mozart wastes no time in getting right to the drama, in the first instance with his choice of key, D minor, the key of the dark Piano Concerto, K466, and more strikingly of crucial parts of *Don Giovanni*, such as the beginning of the overture and the death associations with the entry of the statue near the end. Just as the beginning and ending of that opera had been framed by D minor, the same holds true of the Requiem, which has an almost palindromic key scheme with beginning, middle, and ending in D minor. The Introit starts gently, although it has a bit of an edge with offbeats in violins and violas, seeming at least partially to underlay the sense of peace; just before the entry of the chorus on the words "Requiem aeternam," we hear loud and jarring blasts from the trombones, demolishing any sense of repose. The voices enter imitatively, starting with the lowest, also loud as though prodded by the trombones, immediately giving the sense that we should ponder the terror that death evokes, instead of any sense of comfort. Certain instruments could take on symbolic significance in the eighteenth century, and the trombone proved to be one of these, often used in association with death, and usually in a fairly menacing way. Even the words "et lux perpetua" (eternal light) near the end of the Introit still have a strident, abrasive edge in the music, softened only in the last repetition, although still with tension as the descending chromatic bass line does not lead to a cadence but instead an *attacca* (attack) which propels into the start of the highly contrapuntal Kyrie.

Mozart used another method to underline the notion of death in the Introit, although it's hard to say how many would have recognized this: he derived much of the material from Georg Frideric Handel's "The Ways of Zion do Mourn," a funeral anthem Handel had written in 1737 for Queen Caroline. Mozart knew Handel's vocal music well, having prepared his own arrangements of the *Messiah* and *Alexander's Feast*, and it provided an excellent model for his own contrapuntal vocal writing. Thanks to his friend Baron van Swieten, whose musical salons included performances of works by Handel and Bach, Mozart's awareness of this otherwise almost forgotten music reached a deep level, and some of his instrumental counterpoint, in keyboard works, quartets, and quintets, also owed much to his discovery of these masters of the past. In the Kyrie, Mozart's counterpoint reaches a high degree of complexity, giving an intense urgency to the words "Lord have mercy on us." The next section, the Dies irae, mostly follows a homophonic pattern for the voices and trombones, and the loud dynamics and syncopations in the strings rivet the listener with the terror of the consequences of the day of wrath. When the text speaks of the quaking that will come from the judge weighing our evil deeds, the music imitates this with its own tremors, using tremolos in the strings.

To this point almost all of the text has been carried by the chorus, but that changes in the Tuba mirum as the soloists now take over, and a drama unfolds here filled with foreboding and terror. In one of the most extraordinary sections of the entire work, the trombone now emerges in its full glory, since instead of being a doubler of voices, a solo tenor trombone opens the section by itself, not only emphasizing the death association, but taking its rightful place in the drama. Its solo call represents the awesome celestial blast of the trumpet that summons all throughout the regions of the dead to come before the throne of God. After two bars the bass sings these words starting with the identical phrase given by the trombone, providing a text almost unnecessary since the trombone had made it so explicit. As the bass sings a long lower held note on "sonum" (sound), the trombone takes over as the melodic voice, and continues that function even when the bass proceeds with the rest of the text, vaulting the trombone into a highly unusual but extremely effective role. Trombone and bass work in tandem until the tenor enters, whereupon both of them drop out, although only temporarily the trombone, whose death call continues for a while yet. The tenor advances the narrative further, starting on a variant of the trombone's theme to tell us of the ghastly sight of people rising from their graves to answer the call to face the judge, and that the book of life will be opened, exposing everything. The alto gives a short extension of this, no longer backed by the trombone, proclaiming that no sinful act will go unpunished.

As she finishes, one of the most glorious moments of the entire work occurs, with the entry of the soprano who now steps apart from this grim narrative and responds in deeply human terms how impossible it is for a poor wretch to reply to this onslaught, which will likely ensnare even the just. At this moment Mozart may be voicing his opposition to this brutally construed notion of the day of judgment, since the music he gives her sets her plaintive plea apart in the extreme from the horrific events just described. Now with no trace of the trombone theme, she starts on a high note leading to a descending line that in some ways may remind us of the extraordinary aria he had recently written for Pamina in Act 2 of *The Magic Flute*, "Ach, ich fühl's." The circumstance of the person facing harsh and unforgiving judgment which may condemn her to eternal torment certainly bears resemblance to the plight faced by Pamina, who imagines herself deprived of her last hope and that only death awaits her. On this level Mozart can make a work such as the Requiem highly operatic, infusing it with the same moving intensity given to an exceptional character in an opera, especially one as freshly minted as Pamina, with a musical similarity that evokes the deepest possible feelings.

Moments as moving and dramatic as this abound in the Requiem, and another one that hits us with even more force happens in the Confutatis maledictis. The text suggests an element of contrast, as it starts off with a continuation of raging hellfire: the sentence on the damned is passed, and all are sent to searing flames. It ends, though, with a supplication to call my name among the blessed, as if to imply something unjust about the damnation—that apparently many will be damned who should not be, and if they cannot be saved, at least they should be remembered as fundamentally good. Mozart takes the dichotomy to the extreme here, not unlike the Tuba mirum, although even more so, using music for the opening Confutatis that borders on violence, both in the angular, choppy lines for the basses and tenors of the chorus, doubled in the winds and trombones, and the frenetic and relentless string accompaniment, never letting up for a moment. Half a bar before sopranos and altos ask to be remembered among the blessed, a gentle segue prepares their plea, now contrasted in the extreme with the hellishness just heard as they sing almost chant-like at sotto voce, sweetly accompanied by violins only. The returning violence of the Confutatis quickly cuts off the plea, and when the plea next returns, it settles in for a longer time; the tone does not change much as the full chorus offers a prayer in hopeless abasement. Again like the Tuba mirum, Mozart gives his most moving music to the lost soul struggling to deal with the hideousness of the final judgment, leaving nothing but resignation. The Lacrymosa that follows, after the tears that flowed for the judgment of guilt, ends with a cry to spare this soul and grant it rest, as hopeless as that may seem. The remainder of the Requiem continues the plea for deliverance, with the intervention of the archangel Michael, extolling the holiness of the Lord, singing Hosannas, and a call for the Lamb of God to take away the sins of the world. Drama gives way to praise and supplication, disengaging man's power from the equation; the work ends in joyful resignation to this possibility.

When Mozart started the Requiem he could not have known that it would be his last work, but in the last weeks of November and beginning of December 1791, that possibility became starkly apparent. Whether or not he ultimately regarded it as his personal requiem, no one can say for certain, but the possibility certainly exists, which may in part account for why he turned it into such a moving work with drama, defiance, and resignation. Despite the issues of authorship, it stands as one of the most extraordinary achievements of one of the greatest geniuses who ever lived.

10

CODA

From Then to Now

Mozart died shortly after midnight on Monday, 5 December 1791, a mere two months before his thirty-sixth birthday, and controversy has swirled around why he died so young ever since. One eyewitness account of his expiration exists, by Constanze's sister Sophie Haibel (née Weber), but since it came a third of a century later (in a letter to Constanze's second husband, Georg Nikolaus Nissen, who wrote the first full biography of Mozart), some have doubted that she got all the facts straight. Perhaps so, but her detailed description is all we have, and aside from questioning if he had the strength to sing passages of the Requiem to Süssmayr just before he lost consciousness for the last time, we have no good reason to doubt most of her words. He had been fairly upbeat about his prognosis even a few days before the end, fully expecting to recover and carry on as he had been, but death came quickly, with only the last day and a half seeming to be dire. On the final day Mozart thanked Sophie for coming, with this request: "You must stay here tonight, you must see me die." She tried to assure him, but he claimed to "have the taste of death on my tongue already." She had to let her mother know she would be away for the night, and while out she tried to find a priest to come, "though the priests hesitated a long time and I had great difficulty in persuading one of these inhuman priests to do it." Finally, "there was a long search for Closset, the doctor, who was found in the theatre; but he had to wait until the play was over—then he came and prescribed *cold* compresses on his burning head, and these gave him such shock that he did not regain consciousness before he passed away. The last thing he did was to try and mouth the sound of the timpani in his Requiem; I can still hear it now." (MLL 569–70)

Her descriptions raise a number of red flags, not only about Süssmayr, but also why priests were reluctant to come (were they put off by his secularism?), and why Dr. Closset would not leave the theater before the end of play. Medical practice then bore no resemblance to our time, and often the cure proved worse than the disease, with excessive bleeding that drained the patient of essential blood, drugs—of which Mozart took many—that often had mercury in them, and Dr. Closset's use of cold compresses, which may have dealt the final blow. Closset recorded the cause of death as "Hitziges Fieselfieber" (a severe fever with a rash), and since modern medicine would regard these as symptoms instead of a cause, many medical people have speculated on what the actual cause may have been. A number of possibilities have been put forward, including rheumatic inflammatory fever, kidney failure, and most recently the possibility that Mozart had a bad habit of indulging in raw pork, but none of the descriptions and diagnoses offer enough precision to know for certain, leaving a mystery that will persist and draw ever more medical Mozart lovers into the fray.

Solving the medical puzzle turns out to be a trifle compared to sorting through some of the conspiracy theories that abound—that instead of natural causes he in fact may have been murdered. The most persistent of these turns Salieri into the villain, claiming that he poisoned Mozart for reasons that prove difficult to explain. Rumors of this possibility started to circulate shortly after Mozart's death, not from especially good sources, and there is also the claim that Salieri himself confessed to it on his deathbed (in an insane asylum), also not from a reliable source. Finding a motive turns out to be elusive, since Salieri wielded all the power in the Viennese musical world that Mozart would have liked to have, and from most reliable accounts the two of them had a cordial relationship. The poisoning theory has proved to be much more useful to fictional writing, where authors can construct motives that suit their literary purposes, as Alexander Pushkin did early in the nineteenth century and Peter Shaffer did much more recently; these will be described below. In both of these, Salieri, the ordinary talented composer, could not for one reason or another cope with the presence of genius, and felt compelled to eliminate Mozart to avoid being completely eclipsed.

Much more fantastically nefarious plots have also seen the light of day, some having to do with the possibility that Mozart, an active Freemason, was poisoned by them because of his betrayal of the order through exposure in *The Magic Flute*. This theory has been fueled by a fair amount of ignorance about Freemasonry in the Habsburg Empire in the late eighteenth century, and like most conspiracy theories it also proves to get its best realizations in fiction. Various of these have surfaced over the years, with one coming as recently as 2008, in the appropriately titled novel *The Mozart Conspiracy* by Scott Mariani. In this case the McGuffin, as Alfred Hitchcock would call it (the elusive evidence), emerges from an initially lost and then conveniently destroyed letter that Mozart allegedly wrote just before he died, the possession of which could be fatal. The "taste of death on my tongue" that Mozart described to Sophie Haibel encourages those who buy into the poisoning theories, suggesting that he knew he had been poisoned and therefore could predict when he would die. Speculation can be fun, and even profitable, but also grotesquely misleading.

MOZART LIVES ON

Mozart did not suffer from neglect during his lifetime, although he may have hoped occasionally that the Viennese would be more responsive. After he died it took some time for audiences to care about his music, since he lived during a century in which new music ruled, but individuals both in the musical world and outside it quickly lionized him, realizing how extraordinary his achievements had been. Composers were the first to do this, starting with his friend Joseph Haydn, who proclaimed him to be the greatest composer known to him as early as 1785; some of Haydn's later works show definite Mozart influences, and Beethoven soon followed suit. Throughout the nineteenth and well into the twentieth century composers sang his praises and modeled some of their works on his—not only the expected ones such as Franz Schubert and Felix Mendelssohn, but others who seemed much less probable, including Franz Liszt with his transcriptions (e.g., on *Don Giovanni*), and Charles Gounod even writing a book about *Don Giovanni*. When asked what he intended to achieve with his own music, Maurice Ravel enigmatically replied that his highest goal was to emulate Mozart's craft, while Richard Strauss found Mozart's operas to be useful models for his *Rosenkavalier* and *Ariadne auf Naxos*. Composers who explored neoclassicism in the twentieth century, such as Sergei Prokofiev and Igor Stravinsky, could hope for no better prototype than Mozart's chamber music and symphonies.

We should not be surprised that composers would recognize his genius and do something about it, but perhaps the most important signs of recognition come from practitioners of entirely different fields, who not only state their admiration in ways that have helped to keep Mozart in focus, but in many cases incorporate his thinking and music into their own works. Those most likely to follow the latter course have come from the literary world, especially playwrights, but also novelists and poets. A group somewhat less predictable but every bit as inclined includes some of the leading philosophers of the nineteenth and twentieth centuries. During the twentieth century a new field has come into being where enthusiasm for Mozart has been almost limitless, that of filmmaking, and this has taken some very interesting turns. A staggering number of films have incorporated the music of Mozart into their soundtracks; online listings of these, such as "Films with Mozart Music" (http://musictimeline.museeks.com), do not even come close to enumerating all the films in which Mozart's music can be heard. In some of these films the music may simply be used for atmospheric purposes, but in others the specific music used has significance for the scene with which it appears, suggesting a special recognition by the directors of the ways that Mozart can permeate their films. Also, some of the finest directors over the past century have made films of Mozart's operas, while others have made films about Mozart himself, sometimes, but not always, presented as biographies.

The category of written biographies turns out to be a distinctive one for Mozart, with literally hundreds of them in existence, especially since the bicentennial in 1956, and they continue to flow at an exponential rate. Some of these are little more than coffee-table books, targeting the Christmas market, all too often written by people who do not know how to assess sources for biography or how to come to terms with the music. Aside from biography, hundreds of books and articles have been written about Mozart and his music, most often by musicologists, and while very important ones sit on library shelves, some of which I have included in the bibliography, I will limit my comments to a single professional writer on music: Edward Dent. Most of us who write about music take a fairly passive approach, hoping those who read our books will gain some new understanding of the music. Dent did this too, with his groundbreaking, if at times exasperating, *Mozart's Operas*, first published in 1913 and revised as a second edition in 1946, but he also did much more, actually playing a role in reviving Mozart's operas in the English-speaking world, both as a stage director and as a translator of librettos. In Great Britain little respect for Mozart's operas could be found at the beginning of the twentieth century, after the deluge of Wagner, Puccini, Strauss, Giordano, Massenet, and others, but resisting this flow, Dent staged a performance in 1911 of *The Magic Flute* in Cambridge, where he spent much of his life, something unheard of at that time in the U.K. It proved to be a great success, after which he established a close working relationship with the Sadler's Wells opera company in London (now the English National Opera), giving advice on productions and providing translations of the operas into English (Dent was completely fluent in five languages). We owe Dent a great debt for showing us a century ago that Mozart's operas belong in the repertoire of major opera companies, and we have never looked back: for its 2012–2013 season, the Metropolitan Opera is performing three Mozart operas, not quite as many as those of Verdi and Wagner (2013 being the 200th anniversary of theirs births and also because of the recent Robert Lepage production of the *Ring Cycle*), but more than those of any other composer.

For the remainder of this chapter I will look at the ways that some outstanding writers, thinkers, and filmmakers have embraced Mozart, taking a fairly small sampling of the numerous ones available. Needless to say I see these as especially important endorsements of Mozart's greatness, and in most cases they have made major contributions toward keeping the composer who lived two and a half centuries ago in sharp public focus. Praise from musicians is one thing, but it is entirely different when it comes from non-musicians who themselves are extraordinary achievers and genuinely understand him, or represent him in entirely unique ways that speak directly to the people of their time. I can find no better way to emphasize my goal in this book, which is to make Mozart relevant to us in the twenty-first century.

❃ ❃ ❃

Alexander Pushkin appears to have been the first major writer to engage directly with Mozart in his works, doing this twice in 1830 with his drama in verse, *The Stone Guest*, which clearly invokes *Don Giovanni*, and even more directly in his short play *Mozart and Salieri*, occasionally performed now by dramatic societies of Russian departments in universities. Salieri poisons Mozart in this play, initiating that as a literary trend, but the motive proves to be of greater importance, spelled out by the lesser composer as envy. Peter Shaffer certainly read this play before writing his own *Amadeus*, although as the discussion below makes clear, Shaffer gives Salieri a somewhat different and more sophisticated motive. Pushkin uses the voice of Salieri in soliloquy to lavish the ultimate praise on Mozart, framing the motive to poison him as a service to art: "To stop him—otherwise, all of us die! . . . What use is there in Mozart living on and reaching yet to new and greater heights? Will he thus lift up art? Not really: art will fall again as soon as he will vanish." He brings celestial tunes "to rouse within us, creatures of the dust, wingless desire and fly away thereafter. So fly away! The sooner now, the better. Here's poison . . ."

Thirteen years later one of the leading philosophers of the nineteenth century, the Dane Søren Kierkegaard, published his *Either/Or*, in which the essay "The immediate stages of the erotic or the musical erotic" appeared in volume one. In this essay about Mozart and *Don Giovanni* he gushes with praise, in ways that may seem embarrassing to us now: "I am like a young girl in love with Mozart"; "Immortal Mozart! Thou, to whom I owe everything; to whom I owe the loss of my reason, the wonder that caused my soul to tremble, the fear that griped my inmost being; thou, to whom I owe it that I did not pass through life without having been stirred by something"; "In Mozart's case it also happens that there is one work, and only one, which makes him a classical composer, and absolutely immortal. That work is *Don Juan*"; "But in what medium is this idea expressible? Solely in music." On and on he continues with this effusion, to the point that the untutored reader might assume that he has no other purpose than to strip his soul bare, as though demeaning himself in the long shadow cast by Mozart. Those who have read his philosophical works more broadly have seen through the ruse, recognizing that this may not be Kierkegaard himself speaking, but a voice he gives himself to set up a philosophical tenet.

This has been described at length by writers such as Daniel Herwitz (in *The Don Giovanni Moment*), so I will give only the bare bones of the argument here. Kierkegaard divides "life's way" into three stages, and each one goes beyond the previous stage: the Aesthetic, the Ethical, and the Religious, and these can best be understood by looking at *Don Giovanni*. The Aesthetic, a premoral stage, involves the incessant pursuit of pleasure, necessary to avoid emptiness, each conquest to be discarded as soon as the next opportunity arises. The second stage, the Ethical, lurks in the background even for the Don, defined by the other characters who follow the rules, get married, have families, work hard, but lose the sense of the erotic from the first stage. The third stage, the Religious, transcends both of the earlier ones, but they must be present for it to be achieved. Going beyond the first two requires a leap of faith, suspending anything rational to find God, including morality. Of course he describes it in infinitely more complex ways than this, raising issues of how to bring the conclusion of the opera into the equation, and he provokes some peculiar notions about gender as well; suffice it to say that one of the great philosophers has in fact been able to build his philosophical principles on Mozart and one of his works. When Gounod writes about this opera we hear the voice of the consummate music dramatist who can find no better guiding principle than in Mozart, but with Kierkegaard this moves to an unexpected plane, providing the basis for the way a philosopher looks at himself and all of humanity. One could argue that this essay does not stand as an effusive aberration, but in fact gives the backbone for a philosopher's life's work.

Just after the turn of the century George Bernard Shaw brought a new perspective to the same subject, now mixing drama, social discourse, and philosophy in his play *Man and Superman* (1903). The middle section of Act 3 turns out to be a play within a play, a dream in fact which picks up the story of *Don Giovanni* after all the leading characters have died and now find themselves in heaven or hell. After a couple of fragments of music from the overture, an old woman arrives, soon to identify herself as Donna Anna (now Ana), who gasps in horror when she discovers she has been sent to hell instead of heaven. Her father, the Commendatore (now the statue, who retained that form instead of his human appearance, since it brought him much more respect), finds heaven to be "the most angelically dull place in all creation," and so he frequently visits Don Juan in hell, which has a much more stimulating environment. The statue, a countertenor instead of a bass, asks Juan if he has repented yet, and Juan reminds him that "I have too much consideration for you to repent, Don Gonzalo. If I did, you would have no excuse for coming from Heaven to argue with me." The statue agrees, but most of the debating goes on between Juan and the Devil, who first emerges to music from the overture distorted by strains of Gounod's *Faust*. Their discussions take direct aim at the Britain of Shaw's time, and the characters in the dream bear strong resemblances to the ones from the play, traveling by car through Spain, where they have been captured by bandits.

Unlike Kierkegaard, who uses *Don Giovanni* as his way of constructing a philosophical principle, Shaw begins where Mozart leaves off, getting at a world that can no longer be as it was, since the battle of the sexes has now left women in control, under the guise of "the life force." Women can wield this force as they like, since the survival of humanity depends on it, and men, despite their bluster, arguing, and imagined sense of superiority, can in the end do nothing but submit to the force, melting into insignificance as women get their way. Shaw plays this out with the triangle of characters Ann Whitefield (Donna Anna), Tanner (Giovanni), and Octavius (Don Ottavio, dubbed Ricky Ticky Tavy by Ann); Octavius assumes Ann will marry him, the solid conventional man, but she chooses the iconoclastic Tanner, who tries to resist but cannot. As the title of the play suggests, Shaw invokes Nietzsche's Übermensch, and Ann/Ana responds to this with "I believe in the life to come. . . . A father—a father for the Superman!" Kierkegaard may have thought Don Giovanni embodied the Superman, but Shaw allows no such possibility; if there ever will be one, the best a man of the present can do is serve as a potential progenitor. Along the way numerous other jabs are taken, at conventional society, politics, religion, and even music itself ("Hell is full of musical amateurs"). Shaw reels in one of his wittiest and most pervasive critiques of his own world by way of the bait cast by Mozart.

Undoubtedly the biggest Mozart splash during the twentieth century came with the making of *Amadeus* by Milos Forman in 1984, an extraordinarily successful film that millions of people around the world have seen. Already an accomplished filmmaker before he left Czechoslovakia in 1968, with works such as *Loves of a Blonde* (*Lasky jedné plavovlásky*, 1965) and *The Firemen's Ball* (1967) under his belt, he soon established himself in the United States with *One Flew over the Cuckoo's Nest* (1975), *Hair* (1979), and *Ragtime* (1981). While in London around 1980 he saw Peter Shaffer's play *Amadeus*, met Shaffer during the intermission, and said if he liked the second act as much as the first, he would make a film of it. The play too achieved international fame, but a film has the potential for a vastly larger audience, and Shaffer agreed to revise the play as a screenplay, which took about half a year of excruciating work with the director to complete. Forman warned Shaffer it would not look the same as a script, and he predicted correctly; original authors often do not make good scriptwriters ("why can't I keep my favorite lines? . . ."), but in this case, after much cursing and conflict, Shaffer came up with words that would not be an obstacle to cinematography.

The resulting film, with F. Murray Abraham playing Salieri and Tom Hulce as Mozart, which swept at the Academy Awards, proved to be the greatest cinematic achievement not only of 1984 but perhaps the decade as well. Mozart scholars immediately got their backs up, carping endlessly about all the biographical inaccuracies, but not knowing much about Shaffer or Forman, they failed to grasp that neither one intended this as a biopic. Forman hated that type of film from the endless stream of them he knew from his youth behind the iron curtain (composers proved to be good subjects because music usually did not offend the state), and Shaffer, as in other plays such as *Equus*, had an agenda which in this case necessitated biographical distortions. Shaffer's primary interest, like Pushkin's, lay in the relationship between a good journeyman creative artist and a genius, and since the genius must be seen through the eyes of the journeyman, his real focus fell on Salieri. Forman insisted that the film would need to change that balance somewhat, shifting more toward Mozart, partly because viewers would all recognize the name Mozart, not Salieri, but still that would not turn it into a biopic.

The other great change that the medium of film allowed was that there could be much more music, and not simply as background or for atmosphere; music in fact could gain the prominence of a leading-role character, not only heard but also seen, especially in the staged opera scenes. To help this prominence along, Forman engaged some of the best people in the business, such as the choreographer Twyla Tharp and the Czech scenographer Josef Svaboda, both of whom played important parts in making opera accessible to filmgoers who would never have seen an opera. No fewer than twenty works by Mozart can be heard (or sometimes seen) in the film, spanning the full range of Mozart's output (with the exception of quartets), including of course the Serenade for 13 Wind Instruments noted in chapter 3, and occasionally, as with that serenade, allowing Salieri to give descriptions of the music that help to make it even more accessible. For anyone who knows a great deal about Mozart there will be annoyances about the biographical distortions, often based on myths that arose after Mozart's death and lack substantiation—most notably the Salieri as murderer of Mozart theory—but at the same time, it's a pleasure to see how much Shaffer and Forman got right, including, for example, Mozart's use of scatological language. In the end the veracity or incorrectness of the details matters little, compared to the fact that an extraordinarily engaging film introduced the music of Mozart to a generation that may otherwise not have discovered it, fostering a love for this music in a most appealing way.

The colossal list of films in recent years including the music of Mozart covers not only art films such as *Elvira Madigan*, *Babette's Feast*, or *Venus Rising*, but many of the most commercially popular films as well, including the likes of the *Ace Ventura* movies, *The Big Lebowski*, or *The Truman Show*. In films such as *Out of Africa*, *Philadelphia*, and *The Shawshank Redemption*, Mozart's music becomes part of the diegesis, not simply heard by the audience but played typically as recordings which the characters in the film hear as well, and may even comment on, as Morgan Freeman does in *The Shawshank Redemption*. In that case Tim Robbins's character marvels at the beauty of the duet between the Countess and Susanna in Act 3 of *Figaro*, which he plays without authorization for all prisoners and guards to hear on the prison PA system, but he has no idea what these women are singing or what it may mean. Aside from atmosphere or the interjection of beauty into a situating needing it, the specific music can serve an actual dramatic purpose, as happens in the fairly recent *The Last Station* (2009), a biopic about the last years of Tolstoy's life. In an outdoor scene with Tolstoy (Christopher Plummer), his wife (Helen Mirren), and other associates, someone produces a gramophone with a disk of Tolstoy himself speaking, and he shows noticeable embarrassment, gesturing to get rid of it. His wife removes the disk and puts on Act 4 of *Figaro*, specifically the scene of the Count asking for forgiveness and the Countess granting it. Much of the film focuses on the strained relationship between Tolstoy and his wife—specifically the manipulation of him away from his family toward being a public cult figure advocating the abandonment of wealth and property. Tolstoy has offended her and urgently needs her forgiveness; when he hears this music, he responds with fervor.

The list of how Mozart has saturated popular culture, or how great minds have embraced him, could go on and on. Other writers who have written at length about Mozart include Eduard Mörike during the nineteenth century (*Mozart on the Way to Prague*), more recently Stephanie Cowell (*Marrying Mozart*), Anthony Burgess (*Mozart and the Wolfgang*), and the philosopher Bernard Williams (with essays collected in *On Opera*; I had the privilege of discussing Mozart with him when I was a graduate student). One of the greatest film directors, the Swede Ingmar Bergman, for whom music played a crucial role in his cinematography, made his television version of *The Magic Flute* (1975) right in the middle of his long career, emphasizing the fun side of it and aiming it very much at children. The scientist Albert Einstein, himself an excellent violinist, praised Mozart above all other composers, and quipped that the purity of his music made it ever-present in the universe, waiting to be discovered by Mozart. He even ventured to say that one of the most unfortunate consequences of atomic destruction would be that we could no longer hear Mozart's music. One of the strangest appropriations of Mozart has been the phenomenon known as the "Mozart Effect," introduced by the French researcher Alfred A. Tomatis as a means of healing certain mental disorders, and popularized by Don Campbell and others as a way of increasing the intelligence of children along with offering spiritual cures that cannot otherwise be explained. As much as Mozart lovers would like to believe these claims, they have been largely debunked, although that has not deterred the sales of recordings of Mozart's music aimed at parents of newborns. Even if these recordings do not have the desired effect, perhaps we should be grateful that Mozart's music has been given another strong push, subliminally prompting future generations of concert-goers. Einstein could relate to Mozart as one genius to another, but for the rest of us who lack those powers, we can still get some inkling and appreciation of the extraordinary achievements of Mozart, and recognize that these are as telling today as they were when he lived.

GLOSSARY

absolute music. Music that has no programmatic or topical meaning beyond the music itself, and can also be referred to as pure music.

alla breve. The symbol for 4/4 (or common) time, C, has a vertical stroke through it, which divides the time in half, yielding two beats instead of four, and moves at double the pace.

appoggiatura. In a progression from one chord to the next a note will be held from the first chord, which creates a dissonance in the next chord until that tone resolves stepwise to the new chord tone.

aria form. A vocal form typically in three parts (ABA) in which the B section contrasts the first section, and the return of A is similar but not necessarily identical to the first section. Earlier in the eighteenth century this was known as da capo form, in which the third section would not be written out, and the singer would be expected to add embellishments to the vocal line in that section.

arioso. A short aria, not in aria form, for singer and orchestra, with potential for great emotional depth despite the short length.

basset clarinet. Differs from the modern clarinet with its extension that adds additional bass notes. The term is useful to distinguish it from the larger bass clarinet.

basset horn. Similar to the basset clarinet, but it is an earlier invention, usually in F instead of the B flat of the modern clarinet, and with the capacity to play a fourth lower.

cadence. A melodic or harmonic conclusion to a phrase or an entire piece, leaving a sense of having arrived.

cadenza. A section typically late in a concerto movement in which the solo instrument, playing by itself, can improvise its own material, prompted by the music from that movement, and often with virtuosic flourishes. Some cadenzas have been written out by the composer of the work, or added by another composer.

castrato. A male soprano whose high voice resulted from castration before reaching the age of puberty. During the eighteenth century these were the most popular singers in Europe, especially for opera, but the practice ended early in the nineteenth century, and the last known castrato died early in the twentieth century.

chromatic. Derived from the chromatic or stepwise scale. Chord progressions can be described as chromatic if they deviate from the usual diatonic progressions by moving in a stepwise manner.

coloratura. Usually virtuosic passages in arias that can be long or short and often exploit unusually high notes. These are usually in soprano arias but can be given to tenors or other voices.

concerto grosso. A musical form from the first half of the eighteenth century in which contrasting sections alternated between the full orchestra and a group of solo players.

continuo. Also referred to as basso continuo, in which a distinctive bass line has numbers to indicate the inversions of the chords to be supplied by the keyboard player (usually harpsichord or organ) above that line. The bass line itself can also be played by a cello or some other bass instrument.

contredanse. A popular fast dance in duple meter related to the English country dance. It did not appear to be exclusive to one social class or another, and involves physical contact of the dancing pairs, something unusual in eighteenth-century dances. For this and other reasons, some moralist dance masters held a negative view of it, believing it to be lascivious.

counterpoint. The interaction of two or more independent lines. The emphasis is on their horizontal motion, but the lines also align harmonically, although not always. J. S. Bach was the great master of counterpoint, with such pieces as two- or three-part inventions and highly complex fugues, typically with four lines.

deutscher. A rustic dance in a fast triple meter such as 3/8, sometimes with leaps or other ungraceful steps.

diatonic. Based on major or minor scales; it can also refer to harmonic progressions which do not deviate from steps between chords that can be found in these scales.

dominant. Next to the tonic (home chord or key), the most important and strongest point of departure in a harmonic progression. In major or minor scales this is a fifth above the tonic, and its importance as a destination applies to both harmonic progressions and the modulation of keys. As a key destination it needs to be prepared by its own dominant, allowing it to be felt as *in* the dominant key and not simply *on* it.

dynamics. The level of loudness or softness of the volume.

fermata. A symbol with a period and curved line above it, placed over a note or a rest, indicating that it should be held longer than the usual duration.

fugue, fugato. A highly developed procedure of imitative counterpoint, in which the theme is stated successively in all voices and undergoes an elaborate expansion or development. It may have more than one theme, and may comprise an entire composition. Fugato refers to a passage or section within a larger composition that behaves in a fuguelike manner.

group. The term I use in discussions of sonata form to distinguish the two sections of the exposition that encompass the two primary key areas. The first group will be in the tonic key, and the second group in the dominant (or relative major if the work is in a minor key). Some older definitions use the word theme instead of group, but this adds confusion since the group may have more than one theme.

Hanswurst. Literally, Jack Sausage. A character in crude comedies from Austria and southern Germany during the eighteenth century who over-indulges in food, drink, and sex (he may have a sausage attached to his belt as a phallic symbol). These comedies were especially popular during carnival time, and some authorities hoped to rid the stage of this unenlightened character.

harmonic rhythm. The rate at which the harmony or the chords change within a progression. Composers can use this strategically, for example to build toward a climax by speeding up the rate of change within a progression.

hemiola. Creating a duple pulse within a triple meter with the use of accents off the beat or by tying notes across the bar.

homophonic. All parts cooperate together in unison or in harmony.

ländler. A moderately paced folk dance in 3/4 time which originated in southern Germany and Austria. It may have large leaps and lines that reflect its folk character.

major, minor. The two most commonly used scales, or musical building blocks, during the eighteenth century. The major scale (do, re, mi, fa, sol, la, ti; also with the names tonic, supertonic, mediant, subdominant, dominant, submediant, leading tone) has seven notes moving upward by these intervals: whole step, whole step, half step, whole step, whole step, whole step (followed by a half step back to the tonic). The minor scale has different harmonic and melodic forms, but the constants are the fact that the mediant (3rd) and submediant (6th) are a half step lower than in the major scale.

meter. With the use of bar lines the number of pulses within the bar defines the meter. During the eighteenth century this will likely be two (2/4), three (3/4), four (4/4 or C for common time), or six (6/8). In each case there will be an alternation of strong and weak beats, with the strongest coming on the first beat, in 4/4 a lesser strong pulse on the third beat, and in 6/8 a lesser strong pulse on the fourth beat. During the eighteenth century pieces or movements were in a single meter, but composers can complicate this by putting accents on normally weak beats to change the meter temporarily.

minuet. A graceful dance in 3/4 time, usually at a moderate pace, which would have been part of courtly entertainments or for courtly dancing.

motif (motivic). A recognizable musical passage shorter than a theme, usually only a few notes, which can be used to generate development.

Neapolitan chord. A chord built on the lowered second degree of the scale, usually in first inversion, which resolves to the dominant. It has a distinctive sound since it is non-diatonic.

obbligato. A passage that features a solo instrument in an orchestral texture.

orchestration. The ways of combining instruments in orchestral writing in order to generate different sound textures in the orchestral palette. Unlike instrumentation, which simply refers to the instruments used, orchestration concerns the nature and quality of sounds that varying combinations produce.

overtone series. A series of frequencies or harmonics which are multiples over a fundamental tone. Only after the eighth partial do chromatic tones occur, and horns or trumpets without values can play these notes by the skillful manipulation of the embouchure.

patronage. The employment available to composers in the eighteenth century in aristocratic courts or the church. The patron was likely to be a wealthy landowner, either in a large city or country estate, who could also afford to keep an orchestra and singers on staff. Contracts with composers often stipulated that the works composed belonged to the patron, and specified the frequency and function of compositions. In the general hierarchy the composer stood above a cook but below a lackey.

pedal tone. A tone held usually for a number of bars while other voices carry on the melodic and harmonic activity above at. Composers sometime reverse this, giving a singer a pedal tone on a high note, while the orchestra plays the interesting material below it.

phrase. A unit of musical syntax, comparable to a sentence in spoken language, which acts as a unit in the construction of larger musical periods or paragraphs.

recitative. In any large vocal work there can be various kinds of recitative, ranging from secco (dry) to get through dialogue quickly (accompanied by continuo only), to accompanied recitative, with musical content that allows it to convey deep emotions (with full orchestral accompaniment). Both are typical of Italian opera, but German opera usually replaces secco recitative with spoken dialogue.

relative major. For works in minor keys the relative major key has the same number of sharps or flats as the home minor key, and is a major third below. For sonata-form movements in minor keys, the second group of the exposition will usually be in the relative major.

rest. A period of time in which there is complete silence, represented in the musical score by a symbol that specifies the duration.

rhythm. The pattern of movement in time. Calibrations of this in eighteenth-century music involve whole notes, half notes, quarter notes, eighth notes, sixteenth notes, and thirty-second notes, each of these being half the length of the previous one, and they can be extended by half the length again by adding a dot after the note. Other patterns can be added, for example by groupings of three to make triplets. In the nineteenth century Chopin sometimes grouped as many as forty notes together, but that does not happen in Mozart's time. Rhythmic patterns can have topical associations, such as with life-affirming dances or even dirge-like evocations.

rondo form. A form often used in symphonic finales, but other movements as well, which involves alternation of a main-theme section followed by a contrasting episode, return to the material of the first section, another episode similar to or different from the previous one, and return to the first section (ABABA or ABACA). This can be longer, or it can be made into a hybrid with sonata form. Typically rondos have a lighter atmosphere than sonata-form movements.

salon. An intellectual or artistic gathering in the home of a wealthy presiding patron which may focus on the ideas or works of a particular writer or artist. These were cultivated most actively in France during the eighteenth century and were emulated in other locations such as Vienna.

Scotch snap. A two-note rhythmic figure consisting of a short note followed by a longer note.

semitone. A melodic interval of a half step. Most scales involve combinations of both semitones and whole steps, although the chromatic scale consists of semitones only.

sinfonia concertante. A type of hybrid between a symphony and a concerto, in which there will always be more than one solo instrument, and often combinations of three or four soloists.

sonata form. See the first section in chapter 2.

sotto voce. Under or below; a subdued voice.

staccato. Detached. Marked with a dot or stroke over a note, indicating its duration should be shortened and detached from the notes beside it.

suspension. The delaying of a note that may result in a dissonance in the next chord before that note resolves.

syncopation. Instead of writing notes on the beats of the bars, composers create syncopation by placing notes in a continuous pattern on the offbeats, thereby generating an element of instability. This became fundamental to jazz in the twentieth century, but composers such as Mozart and Haydn often used syncopation for contrast with more stable material.

theme. A passage usually at least a phrase in length with definable melodic material that gives the movement or piece its distinctive character. Since form in music depends on the engagement of the memory, themes help to define the strong points in a formal structure, such as the return of the opening theme corresponding with the return of the home key to mark the beginning of the recapitulation in sonata form.

timbre. Tone color, texture, or quality.

tonic. In both harmonic and tonal progressions the tonic gives the home harmony or tonality. In the eighteenth century things always start on the tonic and end there as well.

triad. The combination of the three notes that make up a chord in its most basic form, these tones being the first, third, and fifth degrees of the scale. Triads form the building blocks of harmony, and can be in root position (the first degree as the lowest note), first inversion (built on the third), and second inversion (with the fifth as bass). More complex chords, such as sevenths and ninths, still have triads as their base, and then build up in increments of thirds. A triad can be major (major third + minor third, from bottom to top), minor (minor + major), or diminished (minor + minor).

tutti. All: in a concerto or sinfonia concertante this indicates the ensemble as opposed to the solo(s).

SELECTED READING

Allanbrook, Wye Jamison. *Rhythmic Gesture in Mozart:* Le nozze di Figaro *and* Don Giovanni. Chicago: University of Chicago Press, 1983. An excellent study of dance in the various numbers of these two operas.

———. "Two Threads through the Labyrinth: Topic and Process in the First Movements of K. 332 and K. 333." In *Convention in Eighteenth- and Nineteenth-Century Music: Essays in Honor of Leonard G. Ratner,* edited by Wye J. Allanbrook, Janet M. Levy, and William P. Mahrt, 125–71. Stuyvesant, NY: Pendragon Press, 1992.

Anderson, Emily, ed. and trans. *The Letters of Mozart and His Family.* 3rd ed. London: Macmillan, 1985. First published in 1938, this has stood up well, but some translations, especially of Mozart's scatological or other ribald language, now seem dated.

Bauer, Wilhelm A., and Otto Erich Deutsch, eds. *Mozart: Briefe und Aufzeichnungen.* 7 vols. Kassel: Bärenreiter, 1962–1975. The complete letters in German, accessible on the Mozarteum website.

Bauman, Thomas. *W. A. Mozart: Die Entführung aus dem Serail.* Cambridge: Cambridge University Press, 1987.

Berger, Karol. "Toward a History of Hearing: The Classic Concerto, A Sample Case." In *Convention in Eighteenth- and Nineteenth-Century Music: Essays in Honor of Leonard Ratner,* edited by Wye J. Allanbrook, Janet M. Levy, and William P. Mahrt, 405–29. Stuyvesant, NY: Pendragon Press, 1992.

Blume, Friedrich. "Requiem but No Peace." In *The Creative World of Mozart,* edited by Paul Henry Lang, 103–26. New York: Norton, 1963.

Branscombe, Peter. *W. A. Mozart: Die Zauberflöte.* Cambridge: Cambridge University Press, 1991. All of the books in the Cambridge Opera Handbooks series (including Bauman, Brown, Carter, and Rushton) offer fine studies of sources, background, the librettos, the music, other useful information on such matters as performance history, reception, and directors' approaches, as well as synopses.

Broder, Nathan. *The Great Operas of Mozart.* New York: Norton, 1962. A good translation of the librettos, with more emphasis on poetic sense than accuracy. The translators include poets such as W. H. Auden and Chester Kallman.

Brophy, Brigid. *Mozart the Dramatist.* London: Faber and Faber, 1964.

Brown, Bruce Alan. *W. A. Mozart:* Così fan tutte. Cambridge: Cambridge University Press, 1995.

Bucky, Peter A. *The Private Albert Einstein.* Kansas City, MO: Andrews and McMeel, 1992. Contains a brief discussion of Einstein's admiration of Mozart.

Campbell, Don. *The Mozart Effect*. New York: Avon Books, 1997. A New Age approach to how Mozart can be used to heal the mind. It has a sequel, *The Mozart Effect for Children*, on how Mozart's music can aid the development of a child's mind.

Carter, Tim. *W. A. Mozart:* Le nozze di Figaro. Cambridge: Cambridge University Press, 1987.

Clive, Peter. *Mozart and His Circle: A Biographical Dictionary*. New Haven, CT: Yale University Press, 1993. Useful descriptions of almost everyone who crossed paths with Mozart.

Da Ponte, Lorenzo. *Memoirs*. Translated by Elisabeth Abbott. New York: Dover, 1959. Important because Da Ponte was Mozart's main librettist, but the author tends to interpret issues and events as he would like posterity to see them.

Dean, Winton. "Edward J. Dent: A Centenary Tribute." *Music and Letters* 57, no. 4 (1976): 353–61.

Dent, Edward J. *Mozart's Operas*. 2nd ed. London: Oxford University Press, 1947. First published in 1913, Dent's study of the operas has stood the test of time, and it gives a sense of why Dent became involved in the revival of these operas in the English-speaking world.

Deutsch, Otto Erich. *Mozart: A Documentary Biography*. Translated by Eric Blom, Peter Branscombe, and Jeremy Noble. Stanford, CA: Stanford University Press, 1965. An excellent compilation of documents, with commentary, supplemented in 1991 by Cliff Eisen's *New Mozart Documents*.

Einstein, Alfred. *Mozart: His Character, His Work*. New York: Oxford University Press, 1945. The most thorough study of Mozart from the mid-twentieth century. In trying to cover everything, many discussions of the music tend to be superficial.

Eisen, Cliff, ed. *Mozart: A Life in Letters*. Translated by Stewart Spencer. London: Penguin Books, 2006. One of the best, although by no means complete, translations of the letters.

Eisen, Cliff, and Stanley Sadie. *Mozart* [*The New Grove*]. New York: Palgrave, 2002. A useful short biography, with a complete listing of works.

Eisen, Cliff, and Simon P. Keefe. *The Cambridge Mozart Encyclopedia*. Cambridge: Cambridge University Press, 2006. A collection of articles arranged alphabetically on topics related to Mozart (of which I happen to be a contributor).

Goehr, Lydia, and Daniel Herwitz, eds. *The Don Giovanni Moment: Essays on the Legacy of an Opera*. New York: Columbia University Press, 2006. A fascinating collection of essays, mainly by people from fields other than music.

Goethe, Johann Wolfgang von. *Italian Journey*. Translated by W. H. Auden and Elizabeth Mayer. London: Penguin Books, 1962. Contains Goethe's descriptions of carnival time in Italy, which have a bearing on *Don Giovanni*.

———. *The Sorrows of Young Werther*. Translated by Catherine Hutter. New York: The New American Library, 1962. For the purposes of my book Goethe's treatment of the piano as a gendered instrument is of interest.

Gounod, Charles. *Mozart's Don Giovanni: A Commentary*. Translated by Windeyer Clark and J. T. Hutchinson. London: Robert Cocks & Co., 1895. An interesting insight into how another major composer of opera, from the nineteenth century, admired Mozart.

Grayson, David. *Mozart: Piano Concertos Nos. 20 and 21*. Cambridge: Cambridge University Press, 1998. The Cambridge Music Handbooks (including Irving, Lawson, and Sisman) are detailed studies of individual works, with additional background information and discussion of performance issues.

Halliwell, Ruth. *The Mozart Family*. Oxford: Clarendon Press, 1998. A thorough biographical study of the whole family—not just Mozart himself.

Heartz, Daniel. *Mozart's Operas*. Edited, with contributing essays, by Thomas Bauman. Berkeley: University of California Press, 1990. One of the most insightful studies of Mozart's operas, by a leading expert on eighteenth-century music.

Hunter, Mary. *Mozart's Operas: A Companion*. New Haven, CT: Yale University Press, 2008.

Irving, John. *Mozart: The "Haydn" Quartets*. Cambridge: Cambridge University Press, 1998.

———. *Mozart's Piano Concertos*. Aldershot, UK: Ashgate, 2003.

————. *Mozart's Piano Sonatas: Contexts, Sources, Style*. Cambridge: Cambridge University Press, 1997.

Keefe, Simon P. *Mozart's Piano Concertos: Dramatic Dialogue in the Age of Enlightenment*. London: Boydell and Brewer, 2002. Emphasizes the dramatic nature of the concertos, going beyond purely musical considerations.

————, ed. *The Cambridge Companion to Mozart*. Cambridge: Cambridge University Press, 2003. Contains detailed articles on Mozart's genres, background, reception of his works, and performance issues. My own article in this study deals with Mozart in relation to eighteenth-century aesthetics.

Kerman, Joseph. "Mozart's Piano Concertos and Their Audience." In *On Mozart*, edited by James M. Morris, 151–68. Cambridge: Cambridge University Press, 1994.

Kierkegaard, Søren. *Either/Or*, vol. 1. Translated by David F. Swenson and Lilian Marvin Swenson. Princeton, NJ: Princeton University Press, 1959. Contains the provocative essay "The Immediate Stages of the Erotic, or The Musical Erotic," on *Don Giovanni*.

Lawson, Colin. *Mozart: Clarinet Concerto*. Cambridge: Cambridge University Press, 1996.

Maunder, Richard. *Mozart's Requiem: On Preparing a New Edition*. Oxford: Oxford University Press, 1988. Questionable if his edition improves on the one in the *Neue Mozart Ausgabe*.

McClatchy, J. D. *Seven Mozart Librettos*. New York: Norton, 2011. The most recent translation of the librettos, with a focus on the accuracy of the translation.

Miller, Jonathan, ed. *Don Giovanni: Myths of Seduction and Betrayal*. New York: Schocken Books, 1990. Engaging articles mainly by literary critics and historians.

Nagel, Ivan. *Autonomy and Mercy: Reflections on Mozart's Operas*. Translated by Marion Faber and Ivan Nagel. Cambridge, MA: Harvard University Press, 1991.

Pushkin, Alexander S. *Mozart and Salieri*. Translated by Genia Gurarie. En.wikisource.org/wiki/Mozart_and_Salieri. A very short play which explores the possibility of Salieri poisoning Mozart, not out of malice, but as a favor to other creative artists (like himself) who cannot hope to measure up to Mozart.

Radcliffe, Philip. *E. J. Dent: A Centenary Memoir*. London: Triad Press, 1976. Both spent their careers at King's College, Cambridge (Radcliffe was my PhD supervisor).

Rosen, Charles. *The Classical Style: Haydn, Mozart, Beethoven*. New York: Norton, 1972. A ground-breaking work when it appeared, by someone who combined scholarship and musicianship at the highest possible level.

Rushton, Julian. *W. A. Mozart: Don Giovanni*. Cambridge: Cambridge University Press, 1981.

Sadie, Stanley. *Mozart: The Early Years, 1756–1781*. New York: Norton, 2006. The most thorough biography of the young Mozart.

Schroeder, David. *Cinema's Illusions, Opera's Allure: The Operatic Impulse in Film*. New York: Continuum, 2002. Mainly of use to this book for my sections on film versions of *Don Giovanni* and *Così fan tutte*.

————. *Haydn and the Enlightenment: The Late Symphonies and Their Audience*. Oxford: Clarendon Press, 1990. In breaking with traditional ways of writing about composers, I emphasized Haydn's associations with non-musicians, and the bearing of that on his works.

————. *Mozart in Revolt: Strategies of Resistance, Mischief and Deception*. New Haven, CT: Yale University Press, 1999. Here I focus on the letters, and the perils of not reading them in the light of letter-writing during the eighteenth century.

Shaffer, Peter. *Amadeus*. New York: Harper and Row, 1980. A major play, adapted for Milos Forman's film of the same name.

Shaw, Bernard. *Man and Superman: A Comedy and a Philosophy*. Harmondsworth, UK: Penguin, 1946. In Act 3 Shaw sets up a dream sequence in which the characters of *Don Giovanni* relate to each other beyond the grave, getting, of course, at aspects of British society early in the twentieth century.

Sisman, Elaine. *Mozart: The "Jupiter" Symphony*. Cambridge: Cambridge University Press, 1993.

Stafford, William. *The Mozart Myths: A Critical Reassessment.* Stanford, CA: Stanford University Press, 1991. Takes pleasure in punching holes in many of the lingering myths surrounding Mozart's life and works.

———. *Mozart's Death: A Corrective Survey of the Legends.* London: Macmillan, 1991. Much nonsense has emerged about Mozart's death, and Stafford sorts out fact from fiction.

Wates, Roye E. *Mozart: An Introduction to the Music, the Man, and the Myths.* Milwaukee, WI: Amadeus Press, 2010. A type of listener's guide, covering his life as well as works. She finds Forman's *Amadeus* especially objectionable, treating it as a biopic, which it is not.

Williams, Bernard. *On Opera.* New Haven, CT: Yale University Press, 2006. Four essays and other comments on Mozart by one of the leading moral philosophers of the past half-century, who was also highly astute musically.

Wolff, Christoph. *Mozart at the Gateway to His Fortune: Serving the Emperor, 1788–1791.* New York: Norton, 2012. A reassessment of Mozart's last few years, emphasizing new beginnings instead of the usual terminal approach, by a leading scholar of eighteenth-century music.

———. *Mozart's Requiem: Historical and Analytical Studies, Documents, Score.* Translated by Mary Whittall. Berkeley: University of California Press, 1994. A very thorough study of the Requiem, backed up with documents.

Zaslaw, Neal. *Mozart's Symphonies: Context, Performance Practice, Reception.* Oxford: Clarendon Press, 1989. A piece of meticulous scholarship, especially strong on the treatment of archival issues.

———, ed. *Mozart's Piano Concertos.* Ann Arbor: University of Michigan Press, 1996.

———, with William Cowdery, eds. *The Compleat Mozart.* New York: Norton, 1990. Brief but useful descriptions of all Mozart's works.

SELECTED LISTENING

DVDS

Amadeus. Directed by Milos Forman. Burbank, CA: Warner Home Video, 1997.

Amadeus: Director's Cut. Directed by Milos Forman. With special feature documentary: "The Making of *Amadeus.*" Burbank, CA: Warner Home Video, 2002.

Così fan tutte. Directed by Patrice Chéreau. France: Love Streams Productions, 2005.

Così fan tutte. Directed by Peter Sellars. London: Decca Music Group, 1991.

Don Giovanni. Directed by Joseph Losey. Culver City, CA: Columbia Tristar Home Entertainment, 2002.

Don Giovanni. Directed by Jürgen Flimm. Conducted by Nikolaus Harnoncourt. Leipzig: Kinowelt Home Entertainment, 2001.

Don Giovanni Tenorio. Music by Giuseppe Gazzaniga. Directed by Louis Lentin. Burbank, CA: Warner Music Group, 2009.

Die Entführung aus dem Serail. Directed by August Everding. Hamburg: Unitel/Deutsche Grammophon, 2005.

The Magic Flute. Directed by Ingmar Bergman. New York: The Criterion Collection, 2000.

Le nozze di Figaro. Directed by Jean-Pierre Ponnelle. Hamburg: Unitel/Deutsche Grammophon, 2005.

Die Zauberflöte. Directed by Pierre Audi. Hamburg: Unitel, 2006.

CDS

Clarinet Concerto, Clarinet Quintet. Richard Stolzman, Tokyo String Quartet, English Chamber Orchestra. RCA Red Seal Classic Library, 2004. 82876-60866-2. Excellent playing and interpretations by Stolzman.

The Complete "Haydn" Quartets and String Quintets. The Juilliard String Quartet. Sony, 2011. 8 86978 84152 0. With six CDs, this box combines the best-known quartets and all the string quintets, with the clarinet quintet and Haydn's Op. 103 quartet, in lively performances.

The Complete Mozart Edition: Serenades, Dances, Marches. The Academy of St. Martin-in-the-Fields. Conducted by Neville Marriner. Philips, 2006. 00289 464 7802. From the comprehensive recording of all Mozart's works, of which many others are also very fine.

Complete Sacred Music. Concentus musicus Wien. Conducted by Nikolaus Harnoncourt. Teldec Classics, 2011. 2564 67611-1. Excellent performances by players on period instruments, conducted by a musician who puts musicality before all else; also with superb choral and solo singing.

Horn Concertos Nos. 1–4; Quintet in E flat, K452. Dennis Brain, Philharmonia Orchestra. Conducted by Herbert von Karajan. EMI, 1997. 7243 5 56231 2 6. Available at an affordable price, with one of the finest horn players of the twentieth century.

Mozart: Complete Piano Sonatas and Variations. Daniel Barenboim. EMI, 2012. 7 04454 2 8. One of the great pianists of our time.

Mozart String Quartets, Vol. 2: Milan Quartets K155–160. The Coull Quartet. Somm Recordings, 2006. SOMMCD 049. An inexpensive CD of the not readily available recordings of early quartets.

The Piano Concertos. Vladimir Ashkenazy, pianist and conductor. Philharmonia Orchestra. Decca, 2006. 4768904. As both pianist and conductor Ashkenazy takes full control, and finds a highly engaging exuberance in his performances.

Salzburg Symphonies [nos. 16–30]. The English Concert. Conducted by Trevor Pinnock. Deutsche Grammophon, 1994. 439 915-2. On period instruments.

Symphonien Nos. 35–41. Berliner Philharmoniker. Conducted by Karl Böhm. Deutsche Grammophon, 1960, 1966. 447 416-2. Appealing performances on modern instruments.

Symphonies No. 10–12, 31–33, 44–47. Mainzer Kammerorchester. Conducted by Günter Kehr. Adora, Bella Musica, 2001. 206257-360. Inexpensive CD of works from different phases of Mozart career.

Three Wind Serenades [K361, 375, 388]; Sinfonia Concertanta [K297b]. Chamber Orchestra of Europe. Conducted by Alexander Schneider. Musical Heritage Society, 2003. 5270442. The musicians are members of the Chamber Orchestra of Europe, known for its energetic interpretations.

Wind Serenades K375 and 388. Orpheus Chamber Orchestra. Deutsche Grammophon, 1991. D 115273. An excellent American ensemble.

INDEX

ABOUT THE AUTHOR

David Schroeder is professor emeritus at Dalhousie University in Halifax, Canada, and he holds a PhD from Cambridge University. This is his second book on Mozart, the first being *Mozart in Revolt* (1999). He has given frequent pre-concert talks, including for the Mostly Mozart series at Lincoln Center in New York, and has been interviewed by CBC, BBC, NPR, and numerous newspapers. His other books include *Haydn and the Enlightenment* (1990), *Cinema's Illusions, Opera's Allure* (2002), *Our Schubert* (2009, Scarecrow Press), and *Hitchcock's Ear: Music and the Director's Art* (2012). He is currently writing a biography of Hilda Klestadt Jonas, the noted pianist and harpsichordist who fled Germany in 1938.